Financial inclusion of small rural producers

Francisco G. Villarreal
Editor

ECLAC

Economic Commission for Latin America and the Caribbean (ECLAC)
Santiago, November 2017

ECLAC Books

This book was edited by Francisco G. Villarreal, Economic Affair Officer of the Economic Development Unit of the Economic Commission for Latin America and the Caribbean (ECLAC) subregional headquarters in Mexico. The following staff members of the ECLAC subregional headquarters in Mexico worked on the various chapters: Cameron Daneshvar, Stefanie Garry, Jesús López, Jesús Santamaría and Francisco G. Villarreal. The consultants Pedro Argumedo, Melvin Bermúdez, Pilar Campos, Pablo Cotler, Daniela Cruz, Rolando Reyes, Ronald Rojas, César Valenzuela, José Antonio Vásquez C. and José Antonio Vásquez R. also worked on the book.

ECLAC acknowledges the financial support provided by the International Fund for Agricultural Development (IFAD) for the case studies conducted on the financial inclusion of small rural producers and for the publication of this book.

Cover design: Marcela Veas

United Nations publication
ISBN: 978-92-1-121973-9 (print)
ISBN: 978-92-1-058611-5 (pdf)
ISBN: 978-92-1-358072-1 (ePub)
Sales No: E.17.II.G.16
LC/PUB.2017/15-P
Distr.: General

Printed at United Nations, Santiago
S.17-00575

This publication should be cited as: Francisco G. Villarreal (ed.), *Financial inclusion of small rural producers*, ECLAC Books, No. 147 (LC/PUB.2017/15-P), Santiago, Economic Commission for Latin America and the Caribbean (ECLAC), 2017.

Contents

Tables

Figures

Diagrams

Map

Foreword

Despite recent progress, the countries of Latin America and the Caribbean continue to be characterized by high levels of poverty. There are also glaring inequalities between different segments of the population; and these are particularly accentuated in rural areas, where the latest estimates show poverty running at twice the rate in urban zones. Inequalities between urban and rural areas are also clearly visible in other dimensions of well-being, such as health, education, labour market integration and access to social security.

The 2030 Agenda for Sustainable Development represents a paradigm shift because it is a universal agenda that combines the economic, social and environmental dimensions as central pillars of sustainable development. It is transformative because it involves profound changes in modes of production and consumption, and in contemporary lifestyles and coexistence generally. It sets a clear time horizon and traces a path to gender and generational equality, while recognizing the importance of eradicating poverty in the years to come.

In its most recent studies, the Economic Commission for Latin America and the Caribbean (ECLAC) has established equality as the goal to be pursued, advocating the transformation of the production structure into activities and processes that are knowledge-intensive, connected to dynamic markets in a way that stimulates economic activity and job creation, and which favour environmental sustainability as a means and public policy as the instrument.

A cornerstone of this progressive structural change is the inclusive transformation of the rural environment, which enhances the productivity of primary activities, increasing the capacities of small-scale rural producers to generate marketable surpluses and access markets. This transformation calls for strategies to harness innovation and diversify productive activities and livelihoods.

The transformation of the rural environment is subject to three global forces that generate new opportunities and pose new challenges: (i) the economic growth process, which has reduced the share of primary activities in the countries' product basket; (ii) globalization, which has transformed not only the organization of markets, but also the configuration and participation of rural producers in agrifood value chains; and (iii) increasing urbanization, which has resulted in a reorganization of territories, not only at the national level, but also in rural areas, underscoring their complementarity with urban centres.

The commitment to a form of sustainable rural development centred on equality, coupled with the coordination between productive and social policies, can ease the adaptation needed to mitigate the threats posed by climate change and environmental degradation. These include rising temperatures, more intensive drought episodes and heavy rains, compounded by reduced water availability. Progressive structural change in rural areas requires innovative strategies and tools for their implementation, together with greater capacity for coordination among multiple actors and instruments, where the public sector is strategically placed to serve as a catalyst.

Historical evidence shows that no country has managed to overcome poverty without achieving large increases in the productivity of primary activities, which make it possible to produce the surpluses in food, labour and even financial resources that are needed to underpin a country's industrialization and urbanization. Although this transformation implies the long-term convergence of productivity among the different sectors of production, in the short and medium terms the process can have an adverse impact on rural populations. For this reason, it is essential to design and implement public policies that give small rural producers the tools to overcome the barriers they face in accessing productive resources, knowledge, financing and markets. The expected result is a broad spectrum of opportunities arising from progressive structural change, and renewed capacities among small rural producers to take advantage of them.

Financial inclusion, defined as access by the currently excluded population (including poor rural inhabitants) to a broad range of financial services tailored to its needs and supplied by a variety of regulated financial service providers, is a tool that fosters opportunities that enhance the capacity to achieve the Sustainable Development Goals.

By providing a way to make and receive payments; accumulate assets securely; leverage available assets to invest in education, health and physical capital; and mitigate risks, financial inclusion has the potential to help households attain higher levels of economic and social well-being, and to foster a higher level of enterprise productivity and growth. In addition, at the regional and national levels, through better resource allocation, financial inclusion mobilizes funds for innovation, diversification of productive activities and job creation, which contributes to stronger growth and a fairer income distribution.

Achieving the potential of financial inclusion, however, implies the existence of a wide variety of financial services, service providers and distribution channels that suit the needs of the currently excluded populations. Its development requires determined public policy action targeted on implementing and strengthening these inclusive financial ecosystems.

This volume aims to enrich the analysis and formulation of public policies that foster a diverse ecosystem of commercially viable financial- service providers, thereby sustainably increasing access to a wide range of financial services for small-scale rural producers in Latin America. To that end, best public-policy practices are identified by comparing the experience of five countries that are in different phases of the process of formulating and implementing comprehensive financial inclusion strategies.

Alicia Bárcena
Executive Secretary
Economic Commission for
Latin America and the Caribbean (ECLAC)

Chapter I

Financial inclusion of small-scale rural producers: trends and challenges

Cameron Daneshvar[1]
Stefanie Garry[2]
Jesús López[3]
Jesús Santamaría[4]
Francisco G. Villarreal[5]

Introduction

Between 1980 and 2002, the number of poor in Latin America grew by almost 90 million to 225 million people, equivalent to 43.9% of the region's population (ECLAC, 2015). Thanks to a favourable economic environment, improvements in the labour market and the effect of prioritizing social policy on combating poverty and inequality, between 2002 and 2012 poverty fell by 15.7 percentage points to a level of 28.1% (ECLAC, 2015). During the same period, most countries in the region also managed to reduce income inequality. Nonetheless, since 2012 poverty and inequality levels have both remained broadly constant (ECLAC, 2016b).

1 Associate Economic Affairs Officer, Economic Development Unit, Subregional Headquarters of the Economic Commission for Latin America and the Caribbean (ECLAC) in Mexico
2 Associate Economic Affairs Officer, Economic Development Unit, ECLAC Subregional Headquarters in Mexico.
3 Economic Development Unit, ECLAC Subregional Headquarters in Mexico.
4 Economic Development Unit, ECLAC Subregional Headquarters in Mexico.
5 Economic Affairs Officer, Economic Development Unit, ECLAC Subregional Headquarters in Mexico.

Despite the progress achieved, at the end of 2015 there were still 175 million poor people in Latin America, 75 million of whom were living in extreme poverty (ECLAC, 2016b). There are also clear inequalities between broad segments of the population, which are accentuated in rural areas, where the most recent data reveal poverty and indigence rates that are practically double those observed in urban areas (ECLAC, 2016b). This means that, despite encompassing less than 20% of the total population, the rural sector accounts for a third of the region's poor and almost half of its extremely poor. Disparities between urban and rural areas also manifest themselves in other dimensions of well-being, such as health, education and social protection (ECLAC/FAO/IICA, 2015).

With the aim of structuring the design of public policy instruments aimed at closing these gaps and attaining the Sustainable Development Goals (United Nations, 2015), the Economic Commission for Latin America and the Caribbean (ECLAC) has proposed the concept of progressive structural change, as a process whereby the production structure is transformed into productive activities and processes that are knowledge-intensive, connected to dynamic markets in a way that stimulates economic activity and job creation, and favour environmental sustainability (Bárcena and Prado, 2016, ECLAC, 2016a).

The conceptualization of progressive structural change as a roadmap towards equality calls for an inclusive rural transformation that enhances the productivity of primary activities and increases capacity to generate marketable surpluses and access to markets while diversifying production activities and livelihoods (IFAD, 2016a).

There is increasing evidence that fostering financial inclusion has positive effects at both the household and macroeconomic levels (World Bank, 2014; Cull, Ehrbeck and Holle, 2014; Barajas and others, 2015). In view of this, financial inclusion is a tool with the potential to contribute to the inclusive transformation of the rural environment (IFC, 2011 and 2012; IFAD, 2009, 2016a, 2016b and 2016c; Kloeppinger-Todd and Sharma, 2010; Timmer, 2009; Vargas Hill and Torero, 2009). Financial inclusion implies the existence of a varied ecosystem of services, providers and distribution channels (IFAD, 2009). Nonetheless, the development of an ecosystem with such characteristics, targeted on meeting the needs of excluded populations in general, and small rural producers in particular, does not occur automatically (Doran, McFadyen and Vogel, 2009; Höllinger, 2011). This requires public policies that promote the development of inclusive financial ecosystems (Ehrbeck, Pickens and Tarazi, 2012).

Given the cross-cutting nature of financial inclusion, the public policies needed to promote it go beyond those directly linked to the financial sector. The policies in question can be classified into three levels according to their scope of incidence (IFAD, 2009). At the macro level, there are policies that define the scope of action of public and private entities involved in the development and operation of the financial system. At the intermediate level are policies that determine the availability and mechanisms of access to various components of the financial infrastructure and to productive development tools, along with components of the infrastructure and distribution networks that enable small-scale rural producers to increase their productivity, sales and profit margins. Lastly, at the micro level, the relevant policies are aimed at strengthening the capacities of both the users and the providers of financial services, and of the authorities responsible for regulation and supervision of the system.

This volume seeks to strengthen the analysis and formulation of public policies so as to foster a diverse ecosystem of commercially viable financial service providers and improve the access of small rural producers in Latin America to a wide range of financial services. To that end, best public-policy practices are identified by contrasting the experience of five countries in different phases of the process of formulating and implementing comprehensive financial-inclusion strategies.

This first chapter sets out the reasons for the study and highlights the importance of the rural transformation process within the context of the progressive structural change promoted by ECLAC (Bárcena and Prado, 2016; ECLAC, 2016a). It then analyses the potential of financial inclusion as a development tool, along with the mechanisms through which the capacities of small-scale rural producers can be enhanced to attain the Sustainable Development Goals. The chapter concludes with a summary of the main findings and an analysis of the best practices identified from them.

In chapter II, Pablo Cotler contextualizes the need to promote financial inclusion, identifies the general characteristics of a public-policy strategy to achieve this objective, and sets out its foreseeable effects. The remaining chapters summarize the key findings of case studies on the institutional architecture available to foster financial inclusion in Costa Rica (Vásquez Rivera and others, 2017), El Salvador (Argumedo, 2017), Honduras (Valenzuela and Cruz, 2017), the Dominican Republic (Reyes Luna, 2017) and Mexico (Campos, 2017).

A. Rural transformation in the context of progressive structural change

Starting in the second half of the twentieth century, the rural environment underwent a far-reaching transformation driven by various factors. These included: economic growth, which has caused the share of primary activities in the economy to steadily decline; globalization, which has transformed the configuration of agrifood value chains; and growing urbanization, which has involved a reorganization of the territory, not only nationally but also at the local level (Berdegué, Rosada and Bebbington, 2014, Timmer, 2009).

Despite the increasing diversification of activities and livelihoods, small-scale producers continue to dominate the rural productive space (OECD, 2007). This is why the 2030 Agenda for Sustainable Development (United Nations, 2015) stresses the urgent need to provide small-scale rural producers with the means to overcome the barriers that restrict their access to productive resources, specialized inputs, knowledge, financing and markets (IFAD, 2016a). These barriers compound the challenge of meeting the growing demand for food, feed and fibre in a sustainable way (IFAD, 2015).

The historical evidence shows that no country has achieved poverty reduction without increasing the productivity of the agricultural sector (Timmer, 2009). This process is the outcome of a structural change driven by increased agricultural productivity where there is sufficient food, and surpluses of labour and even financial resources to support the country's urbanization and industrialization process.

Although this structural change process implies the convergence of productivity between sectors in the long term (Timmer and Akkus, 2008), in the short and medium terms the transformation can have adverse effects for the rural population (Timmer, 2009). So, promoting an inclusive rural transformation process requires formulating and implementing public policies that expand both the spectrum of opportunities offered to small-scale rural producers, as a result of the structural change process, and their capacity to take advantage of these opportunities (IFAD, 2016a).

B. Financial inclusion as a tool of sustainable development

According to the Organization for Economic Cooperation and Development and the International Network on Financial Education (OECD/INFE, 2012), financial inclusion entails the promotion of affordable, timely and appropriate access to a range of regulated financial products and services, and the expansion of their use by all segments of society through the implementation of personalized and innovative actions that include education and financial knowledge aimed at promoting well-being and economic and social inclusion.

Four key dimensions emerge from this definition. The first, related to access, concerns the availability of financial services in specific localities (Claessens and Perotti, 2007), so lack of access is linked to the absence of financial intermediaries in certain territories (Beck, Demirgüç-Kunt and Martínez Peria, 2008). The second, corresponding to use, refers to the consumption of financial services, which is the outcome of both supply and demand (Claessens, 2006). The lack of use of financial services by individuals does not necessarily reflect a lack of access, because some people may have access to financial services at affordable prices, but choose not to use them for a variety of reasons.

The third dimension relates to the capabilities needed to meet the demand for and supply of financial services. There is widespread recognition of the importance of empowering users to take advantage of the potential benefits of financial inclusion (Garcia and others, 2013; Roa and others, 2014). Equally important, however, are the capabilities of financial sector regulators and supervisors to promote an enabling environment for financial inclusion, and the capacities of financial service providers to identify market needs and design appropriate products (Arnold and Rhyne, 2016).

Lastly, the fourth dimension is related to the purpose of financial inclusion. There is a broad theoretical and empirical literature that sees financial inclusion as a tool with the potential to expand individuals' capacity to increase their well-being (Barajas and others., 2015; Beck, Demirgüç-Kunt and Levine, 2007; Claessens and Perotti, 2007; Cull, Ehrbeck and Holle, 2014; Galor and Moav, 2004; King and Levine, 1993a and 1993b; Schumpeter, 1976). By making it possible to safely accumulate assets, leverage the available assets to invest in both human and physical capital, and manage risks, the financial inclusion of small rural producers contributes to the attainment of at least the following Sustainable Development Goals (IFAD, 2016b):

- Goal 1: End poverty in all its forms everywhere, through a consumption profile that is less vulnerable to contingencies;
- Goal 2: End hunger, achieve food security and improved nutrition and promote sustainable agriculture, by increasing the productivity of small producers;
- Goal 3: Ensure healthy lives and promote well-being for all at all ages, by increasing resources for education and health;
- Goal 5: Achieve gender equality and empower all women and girls, by improving women's access to financial services;
- Goal 8: Promote inclusive and sustainable economic growth, employment and decent work for all, by improving the allocation of available resources so that increased investment generates greater economic growth and results in job creation;
- Goal 9: Build resilient infrastructure, promote sustainable industrialization and foster innovation, by encouraging small-scale producers to join value chains and adopt best practices, and by providing access to specialized inputs; and
- Goal 10: Reduce inequality within and between countries, by increasing access for disadvantaged groups and reducing the costs of public transfers.

The challenges that limit the financial inclusion of excluded population groups at the national level are accentuated in rural areas (De Olloqui, Andrade and Herrera, 2015). Firstly, sparse population density, compounded by low income levels, offer very low margins to compensate for the high operating costs of incorporating excluded populations, especially through traditional business schemes. Secondly, the users' limited financial capacities restrict demand, while those of the financial service providers constrain effective supply in the absence of products suited to the needs and conditions of small rural producers. This is compounded by the persistence of perverse incentives for non-payment, associated with clientelism in public-policy actions (Campos, 2017); the vulnerability of the rural environment to risks of various kinds (Argumedo, 2017, ECLAC/FAO/ IICA 2015); low rates of formal property ownership which reduce the range of collateral-eligible assets (Valenzuela and Cruz, 2017); and limitations in terms of both the coverage and the quality of the available infrastructure (Reyes Luna, 2017).

C. Key findings

As discussed in Chapter II, in Latin America and the Caribbean indicators of access to financial services show significant progress, which is also confirmed for usage indicators, albeit to a lesser extent. At the regional level, commercial banks serve as the key financial intermediary, the main destination for savings and the principal source of financing for the private sector. Nonetheless, commercial bank penetration rates are very low in rural areas. Notwithstanding recent developments, Latin America and the Caribbean as a whole is still lagging behind other developing regions.

An additional challenge to financial inclusion is that there is no clear correspondence between the holding of an account and the use of other saving, credit, or insurance products. This suggests that the financial services offered are mainly used as a transactional means of receiving and withdrawing money. While such a transactional medium may benefit from better transmission vehicles (cell phones and correspondent banks), accounts do not appear to be a product linked to savings or loan decisions. The limited use of financial products and services is more acute among citizens who belong to the poorest 40% and those who live in rural areas.

According to Pablo Cotler (see chapter II), a financial inclusion strategy needs to be built around the following four axes:

(i) financial products appropriate to the characteristics of the poorest population;

(ii) financial institutions characterized by a solid governance structure, that are financially viable and interested in participating in underserved markets;

(iii) design and dissemination of relevant and understandable information to combat mistrust, improve decision-making and develop products that are consistent with the needs and constraints of the potential users, and

(iv) the construction of a legal framework conducive to adequate development of the financial infrastructure, so that the financial-inclusion strategy does not undermine the stability of the financial system.

As noted above, the five countries analysed are at different stages of the process of formulating and implementing a comprehensive public financial-inclusion strategy. In Costa Rica —which José Antonio Vásquez Rivera, Melvin Bermúdez, Ronald Rojas, and José Antonio Vásquez Castro consider in chapter III— despite relatively high levels of access to financial services and the existence of various initiatives to promote inclusion, it was not until 2016 that the intention to adopt a comprehensive strategy was announced, under the leadership of the Central Bank of Costa Rica, with technical support from the Alliance for Financial Inclusion.

In chapter IV, Pedro Argumedo analyses the experience of El Salvador, where since 2011 the Central Reserve Bank, with support from the Alliance for Financial Inclusion and the United States Department of the Treasury, has led the development of a financial-inclusion agenda, in which public and private institutions have collaborated. As a result, the Financial Inclusion Facilitation Act came into force in 2015, and specialized financial inclusion units were created both within the Central Reserve Bank and the Superintendency of the Financial System. Since 2016, the Central Reserve Bank has been conducting a series of household and business surveys to empirically diagnose the status and challenges of financial inclusion.

In Honduras, whose experience is discussed by Daniela Cruz, Jesús López and César Valenzuela in chapter V, the process of formulating the National Strategy for Financial Inclusion was completed in 2015. This strategy is based on an evidence-based diagnosis that identifies the main causes of exclusion, proposes specific components to address the different causes, identifies the relevant actors within the framework of an institutional coordination structure led by a Presidential Commissioner for Financial Inclusion, and defines verifiable short- and medium-term goals. Nonetheless, the strategy was still awaiting implementation in early 2017.

As Rolando Reyes argues in chapter VI, in the Dominican Republic, the authorities of the Central Bank of the Dominican Republic have focused on the formulation of a National Strategy for Economic and Financial Education, which draws on the findings of the Survey of Economic and Financial Culture, details of which were released in early 2017.

Lastly, the case of Mexico is studied by Pilar Campos in chapter VII. Since 2009, efforts have been made to diagnose the status of financial inclusion in the country and to formulate evidence-based government actions, based on a robust institutional framework coordinated by the National Council for Financial Inclusion, led by the National Banking and Securities Commission as of 2011. These efforts culminated in the adoption of the National Financial Inclusion Policy in mid-2016.

An initial finding of the five experiences analysed is the existence of marked differences between recent financial inclusion strategies and earlier initiatives. Among them, the focus is placed on a broad basket of financial services aimed at meeting the needs of small-scale rural producers, and not just the provision of credit for primary activities. Secondly, it seeks to develop an environment that encourages the private provision of services with sustainability criteria, both in relation to the users and providers of financial services at the individual level, and for the financial system as a whole. Lastly, a key element of the new strategies is the development and strengthening of the capacities of all the actors involved.

A second finding is that there are several common factors in the diagnosis of the determinants of financial exclusion generally and of small-scale rural producers in particular. These can be classified in two groups: factors that restrict the supply of financial services and those that hinder demand. The first group identifies the high operational cost of supplying financial services to people located in areas of sparse population and relatively low income levels, as well as the high risk of financing poorly diversified activities that face productive and market risks. This is compounded by the moral hazard that cannot be mitigated through traditional guarantees owing to low rates of formal property ownership. Factors that affect demand include the difficulties in accessing financial services through traditional rural channels, the scarce and inadequate supply of available products, and the users' limited entrepreneurial and financial skills.

Third, several common components are identified in the strategies that seek to address the exclusion factors, as detailed below.

To reduce the operating cost of serving excluded populations, simplified accounts have been introduced, requiring less costly documentation in exchange for more limited functionality, as well as banking correspondents, through which some financial services are supplied.

Also, to guarantee systemic stability, there is recognition of the need to broaden the regulatory universe and adapt its application to encompass entities that have traditionally provided financial services on an unregulated basis. Examples are cooperatives and new players providing financial services through digital platforms—such as telecommunication firms providing mobile money and payment services, or financial technology (fintech) enterprises providing online financial services.

Of particular importance for the inclusion of small-scale rural producers and for risk reduction is the fact that legislation has been strengthened in all of the countries analysed. This opens up the possibility of offering non-real-estate collateral, although progress in the creation of centralized registers is uneven.

A major effort is also being made to strengthen the role of development banks in promoting financial inclusion. In addition, most countries are taking steps to digitize public transfers and payments, which reduces administrative costs and encourages the use of financial instruments.

Lastly, although the importance of strengthening the financial capacities of the users of financial services is widely recognized, efforts thus far have been poorly focused and their impact remains uncertain.

D. Best practices

As discussed above, public policies and best practices in this domain can be classified by their field of incidence. At the macro level, the five countries recognize that a comprehensive financial inclusion strategy requires the coordination of public policies that go beyond the regulation and supervision of the financial system, including monetary, financial, productive development, and rural and territorial development policies. This requires detailed, evidence-based diagnoses that identify the determinants of financial exclusion and its consequences. The cases of El Salvador, Mexico and the Dominican Republic are key in this regard, since they have conducted various specialized surveys to ascertain the financial-inclusion status of households and firms.

A second key element is the need for strong political leadership at the highest level, together with the relevant institutional framework to ensure coordination between the different entities involved. As noted, all five countries have received clear leadership —Costa Rica, the Dominican Republic and El Salvador from their central banks, and Honduras and Mexico from their financial system supervision authorities. Nonetheless, the relevant coordination mechanisms are only explicitly provided for in Honduras, through the executing agency of the Presidential Commissioner for Financial Inclusion, and in Mexico, through the National Council for Financial Inclusion, which is the only such mechanism actually operating.

One of the key challenges is to ensure continuity of the initial effort to diagnose, formulate, and implement policies by monitoring achievements and adjusting policies accordingly. In this respect, the clear definition responsibilities and goals of the National Strategy for Financial Inclusion in Honduras is noteworthy. In Mexico, a second round of the National Survey of Financial Inclusion has already been implemented, which reports on the progress achieved between 2011 and 2015 and, in principle, should represent a key input for the adjustments needed to implement the National Financial Inclusion Policy.

One of the main challenges in financial regulation and supervision is to strike the right balance between the objectives of promoting financial inclusion and of ensuring the stability of the system as a whole. This is complicated by the risks and opportunities arising from the use of technological platforms to offer innovative financial services through new distribution channels. In this connection, El Salvador has made major efforts to regulate the domestic use of electronic money; and Mexico has endeavoured to extend the use of correspondent banks by popular saving and loan institutions.

Despite the heterogeneity observed in the experience of the five countries studied, three key areas can be identified at the intermediate level. The first is the need to improve access for financial service providers serving small rural producers to essential components of the financial infrastructure, such as information from credit rating agencies, payment systems, mobile centralized collateral registries, deposit insurance and consumer protection mechanisms. Costa Rica has developed the SINPE Móvil retail payment system in this regard. In the case of consumer protection mechanisms, the regional benchmark is undoubtedly Mexico's National Commission for the Protection and Defence of Users of Financial Services (CONDUSEF).

The second key area involves the creation and strengthening of business development services that complement efforts to promote financial inclusion, fostering greater productivity among small-scale rural producers. These services include the extension and supply of specialized inputs, the telecommunications network, along with infrastructure associated with product distribution and storage, and information systems. In this field, the rural areas of the countries analysed display pronounced gaps, despite the wide coverage of telecommunications in Costa Rica, the Dominican Republic and El Salvador.

The third critical area of public policies at the intermediate level relates to the public-sector support instruments, where there are ample opportunities for improvement, especially in terms of the targeting and coverage of the instruments, and coordination among the different public-sector entities. In this context, given the weak penetration of commercial banks in rural areas and the multiple challenges faced by the cooperative and microfinance sectors in meeting the needs of small-scale rural producers, development banks have played a key role in fostering financial inclusion in the five countries studied. This has been achieved through a combination of instruments, both first and second tier, and the operation of guarantee fund arrangements and various specialized trusts.

At the micro level, the main public-policy challenge is to strengthen the capacities of both the users and the providers of financial services, particularly those that primarily serve rural areas. As noted above, although there are a variety of financial education initiatives, these are often disjointed and are limited to transmitting a few basic concepts, and not necessarily to strengthening the capacities of the users in a comprehensive way (García and others, 2013). The Dominican Republic's National Strategy for Economic and Financial Education stresses the development of financial capacities based on the incorporation of issues that are relevant to the national education system, and the formulation of an institutional governance framework for its implementation.

Capacity-building among financial service providers includes the Technical Assistance Programme for Rural Microfinance implemented in Mexico. This programme, operated by the National Savings Bank and Financial Services (BANSEFI), provides technical assistance to popular saving and loan institutions to achieve the financial inclusion of rural clients in highly marginalized areas.

An unresolved issue in capacity development is the regulatory and supervisory authorities' awareness of the business environment faced by most financial institutions that serve small rural producers. It is costly to comply with a regulatory framework that does not always reflect the risk represented by institutions of this type.

Bibliography

Argumedo, P. (2017), "Inclusión financiera de pequeños productores rurales: estudio de caso en El Salvador" (LC/MEX/W.21), *Project Documents*, Mexico City, Economic Commission for Latin America and the Caribbean (ECLAC)/International Fund for Agricultural Development (IFAD), January.

Arnold, J. and E. Rhyne (2016), *A Change in Behavior: Innovations in Financial Capability*, Centre for Financial Inclusion.

Barajas, A. and others (2015), "Financial inclusion: can it meet multiple macroeconomic goals?", *Staff Discussion Notes*, No. 15/17, Washington, D.C., International Monetary Fund (IMF), September.

Bárcena, A. and A. Prado (2016), *El imperativo de la igualdad: por un desarrollo sostenible en América Latina y el Caribe*, Buenos Aires, Economic Commission for Latin America and the Caribbean (ECLAC)/Siglo XXI, May.

Beck, T., A. Demirgüç-Kunt and R. Levine (2007), "Finance, inequality and the poor", *Journal of Economic Growth*, vol. 12, No. 1, Berlin, Springer.

Beck, T., A. Demirgüç-Kunt and M. S. Martinez Peria (2008), "Banking services for everyone? Barriers to bank access and use around the world", *The World Bank Economic Review*, vol. 22, No. 3, Oxford, Oxford University Press.

Berdegué, J., T. Rosada and A. Bebbington (2014), "The rural transformation", *International Development: Ideas, Experience, and Prospects*, B. Currie-Adler and others (eds.), Oxford, Oxford University Press.

Campos, P. (2017), "Inclusión financiera de pequeños productores rurales: estudio de caso en México" (LC/MEX/W.21), *Project Documents*, Mexico City, Economic Commission for Latin America and the Caribbean (ECLAC)/International Fund for Agricultural Development (IFAD).

Claessens, S. (2006), "Access to financial services: a review of the issues and public policy objectives", *The World Bank Research Observer*, vol. 21, No. 2, Oxford, Oxford University Press, August.

Claessens, S. and E. Perotti, (2007), "Finance and inequality: channels and evidence", *Journal of Comparative Economics*, vol. 35, No. 4, Amsterdam, Elsevier.

Cotler, P. (2017), "La inclusión financiera en América Latina", *La inclusión financiera de pequeños productores rurales*, F. Villarreal (ed.), Santiago, Economic Commission for Latin America and the Caribbean (ECLAC).

Cull, R., T. Ehrbeck and N. Holle (2014), "La inclusión financiera y el desarrollo: pruebas recientes de su impacto", *Enfoques*, No. 92, Washington, D.C., Consultative Group to Assist the Poorest (CGAP), April.

De Olloqui, F., G. Andrade and D. Herrera (2015), "Inclusión financiera en América Latina y el Caribe: coyuntura actual y desafíos para los próximos años", *IDB Discussion Paper*, No. 385, Washington, D.C., Inter-American Development Bank (IDB).

Doran, A., N. McFadyen and R. Vogel (2009), "The missing middle in agricultural finance: relieving the capital constraint on smallholder groups and other agricultural SMEs", *Oxfam Research Report*, Oxford, Oxfam International, December.

ECLAC (Economic Commission for Latin America and the Caribbean) (2016a), *Horizons 2030: Equality at the Centre of Sustainable Development* (LC/G.2660/Rev.1), Santiago, July.

___(2016b), *Social Panorama of Latin America 2015* (LC/G.2691-P), Santiago.

___(2015), *Inclusive Social Development. A New Generation of Policies for Overcoming Poverty and Reducing Inequality in Latin America and the Caribbean* (LC.L/4056/Rev.1), Santiago.

ECLAC/FAO/IICA (Economic Commission for Latin America and the Caribbean/Food and Agriculture Organization of the United Nations/Inter-American Institute for Cooperation on Agriculture) (2015), *The Outlook for Agriculture and Rural Development in the Americas: A Perspective on Latin America and the Caribbean 2015-2016*, San José.

Ehrbeck, T., M. Pickens and M. Tarazi (2012), "Ecosistemas financieros inclusivos: la función de los gobiernos en la actualidad", *Enfoques*, No. 76, Washington, D.C., Consultative Group to Assist the Poorest (CGAP), February.

Galor, O. and O. Moav (2004), "From physical to human capital accumulation: inequality and the process of development", *Review of Economic Studies*, vol. 71, No. 4, Oxford, Oxford University Press.

García, N. and others (2013), "La educación financiera en América Latina y el Caribe: situación actual y perspectivas", *Políticas Públicas y Transformación Productiva series*, No. 12, Andean Development Corporation (CAF).

Höllinger, F. (2011), *Agricultural Finance. Trends, Issues and Challenges*, German Agency for International Cooperation (GIZ), Eschborn, July.

IFAD (International Fund for Agricultural Development) (2016a), *Rural Development Report 2016: Fostering Inclusive Rural Transformation*, Rome, September.

___(2016b), "Rural finance: sustainable and inclusive financing for rural transformation", Rome, June [online] https://www.ifad.org/documents/10180/4fd6dee5-71fe-45fa-bd7e-3c2ded5a918b.

___(2016c), "Servicios financieros inclusivos en las zonas rurales: nota sobre la ampliación de escala", Rome, August.

___(2015), "Getting to work: financing a new agenda for rural transformation", Rome, June [online] https://www.ifad.org/documents/10180/7762419/Getting+to+work+financing+a+new+agenda+for+rural+transformation/35c9e07b-abf0-48f4-8dc5-d50d263da881.

___(2009), *Financiación rural: política*, Rome, August.

IFC (International Finance Corporation) (2012), *Innovative Agricultural SME Finance Models*, Washington, D.C., Global Partnership for Financial Inclusion (GPFI)/International Finance Corporation (IFC), November.

___(2011), *Scaling Up Access to Finance for Agricultural SMEs: Policy Review and Recommendations*, Washington, D.C., Global Partnership for Financial Inclusion (GPFI)/International Finance Corporation (IFC), October.

King, R. and R. Levine (1993a), "Finance, entrepreneurship and growth: theory and evidence", *Journal of Monetary Economics*, vol. 32, No. 3, Amsterdam, Elsevier, December.

___(1993b), "Finance and growth: Schumpeter might be right", *The Quarterly Journal of Economics*, vol. 108, No. 3, Cambridge, MIT Press, August.

Kloeppinger-Todd, R. and M. Sharma (eds.) (2010), "Innovations in rural and agriculture finance", *2020 Focus*, No. 18, Washington, D.C., International Food Policy Research Institute (IFPRI)/World Bank, July.

OECD (Organization for Economic Cooperation and Development) (2007), "Promoting pro-poor growth: policy guidance for donors", *DAC Guidelines and Reference Series*, Paris.

OECD/INFE (Organization for Economic Cooperation and Developoment/International Network on Financial Education) (2012), "Principios de alto nivel de la OCDE/INFE sobre estrategias nacionales de educación financiera", August.

Reyes Luna, R. (2017), "Inclusión financiera de pequeños productores rurales: estudio de caso en la República Dominicana" (LC/MEX/W.24), *Project Documents*, Mexico City, Economic Commission for Latin America and the Caribbean (ECLAC)/International Fund for Agricultural Development (IFAD), January.

Roa, M. J. and others (2014), *Educación e inclusión financieras en América Latina y el Caribe: programas de los bancos centrales y las superintendencias financieras*, Mexico City, Centre for Latin American Monetary Studies (CEMLA)/Bank of the Republic of Colombia.

Schumpeter, J. (1976), *La teoría del desenvolvimiento económico: una investigación sobre ganancias, capital, crédito, interés y ciclo económico*, Mexico City, Fondo de Cultura Económica (FCE).

Timmer, C. (2009), *A World without Agriculture: The Structural Transformation in Historical Perspective*, Washington, D. C., AEI Press, February.

Timmer, C. and S. Akkus (2008), "The structural transformation as a pathway out of poverty: analytics, empirics and politics", *Working Paper*, No. 150, Washington, D.C., Centre for Global Development (CGD), July.

United Nations (2015), "Transforming our world: the 2030 Agenda for Sustainable development" (A/RES/70/1), New York.

Valenzuela, C. and D. Cruz (2017), "Estudio de caso sobre estrategias para promover la inclusión financiera de pequeños productores rurales en Honduras" (LC/MEX/W.22), *Project Documents*, Mexico City, Economic Commission for Latin America and the Caribbean (ECLAC)/International Fund for Agricultural Development (IFAD), January.

Vargas Hill, R. and M. Torero (eds.) (2009), "Innovations in insuring the poor", *2020 Focus*, No. 17, Washington, D.C., International Food Policy Research Institute (IFPRI), December.

Vásquez Rivera, J. A. and others (2017), "Evolución reciente, situación actual y perspectivas de inclusión financiera de pequeños productores rurales en Costa Rica" (LC/MEX/W.23), *Project Documents*, Mexico City, Economic Commission for Latin America and the Caribbean (ECLAC)/International Fund for Agricultural Development (IFAD), January.

World Bank (2014), *Global Financial Development Report 2014: Financial Inclusion*, Washington, D.C.

___(2013), *Global Financial Development Report 2013: Rethinking the Role of the State in Finance*, Washington, D.C.

Chapter II

Financial inclusion in Latin America

Pablo Cotler[1]

The financial capacity of the poor is constrained not just by low incomes but also by the characteristics of the instruments available to them.[2]

Introduction

One of the hallmarks of Latin America is its sharp income inequality, partly resulting from the concentrated ownership of productive assets, the uneven quality of education services, and the inequitable penetration of financial products suitable for accumulation and insurance. These factors generate an economic concentration with political ramifications that restrict social mobility and make inequality a structural feature of the economy.

Unequal access to the products offered by the financial system has several causes. These include the difficulties in achieving economies of scope in communities of low population density; differences in average operating costs (resulting from the unequal income distribution); the existence of financial products that are not suited to the needs and budget constraints of the low-income population; lack of and asymmetries in information, and mistrust of financial institutions, owing both to bad experiences and to lack of adequate information.

1 Full time academic at the Department of Economics of the Universidad Iberoamericana, Mexico City. Email: pablo.cotler@ibero.mx. The author gratefully acknowledges support provided by Rodrigo Carrillo.

2 See Collins and others, 2009.

As a result, strategies are being developed in many Latin American countries, both by the State and by the private sector, to enable a larger percentage of the population to make use of the products and services supplied by formal financial institutions. According to Soto (2015, p.4), financial inclusion seeks to provide services to people who are traditionally excluded from formal financial services, using products and services that suit their requirements and are not necessarily provided by banks, but also by other institutions such as cooperatives, and saving and loan associations —all to enable people to improve their quality of life.

There are five major differences between the current financial inclusion strategies and those pursued by Latin American governments in the past. First, the emphasis is not only on increasing the availability of financing, but rather on promoting the supply of a basket of financial products that include saving, insurance and loan instruments. Second, it is not a question of constructing a State financial entity to take the place of private sector institutions, but of fostering an institutional framework that encourages the presence of bank and non-bank entities from the private and social sectors that can supply products that meet the needs of the low-income population. Third, it seeks to design and implement financial education strategies that have an impact on the supply of and demand for financial products and services. On the supply side, such initiatives should help to generate financial products suited to the needs and constraints of low-income populations and to produce adequate information on those products. On the demand side, the financial education strategy should target the dissemination of knowledge to enable potential users to make wiser decisions. Fourth, the supply of financial products needs to be profitable and permanent, which requires building a framework that fosters competition and technological innovation. Both the third and fourth strategies are also needed to reduce the mistrust that large sectors of the population feel towards many of the existing financial institutions, which constitutes a barrier to further inclusion. As a fifth point, the financial inclusion strategy should not pose a threat to financial stability. It is therefore a strategy that, with limited risk, aims to be a tool to reduce the vulnerabilities of the poorest sectors of the population and to build a more inclusive economy.

This chapter contextualizes the need to achieve greater inclusion and describes both the general characteristics of a strategy to achieve that goal and its foreseeable effects. To that end, the rest of the chapter is divided into four sections. Given the existence of a large supply of informally contracted products, section A argues that an inclusion strategy is, first and foremost, a formalization strategy. Section B describes the current state of access and use of formal financial services in Latin America. With the current situation as a backdrop, section C then reviews the economic literature to contextualize the expected benefits of expanding financial inclusion among the poorest people. Lastly, section D discusses the government strategy most frequently implemented to expand financial inclusion, describing its objectives, strengths and potential areas for design improvement.

A. Inclusion as a formalization strategy

One of the most salient features of life is economic uncertainty. No one knows when they will face a drop in their income, when there will be an opportunity to increase it, or when unforeseen expenses will be incurred. If such contingencies cannot be dealt with, the person in question and his/her family environment very likely suffer a loss of well-being. The role of financial services offered by institutions and individuals is to minimize this loss, (Collins and others, 2009; Banerjee and Duflo, 2007; and Rutherford, 2000).

Both formal and informal contractual arrangements are available for this purpose. Mechanisms offered by individuals to safeguard savings, participation in reciprocity mechanisms such as rotating savings and credit agreements between individuals are examples of transactions made under informal arrangements, since they are not governed by a regulatory framework that protects their counterparties from financial abuse. In the case of institutional suppliers both formal and informal contractual arrangements are used. Some financial institutions are authorized to offer savings, credit or insurance products; and others which, despite being only authorized to supply financing, also offer saving products; and others that operate outside the corresponding regulatory framework. There are also non-financial institutions which, while legally constituted, supply financial products without a regulatory framework issued by a financial authority. Examples of this could be the acceptance of savings by civil society organizations or credit granted by suppliers. On the latter, see Cotler (2015).

In the case of Latin America, the World Bank (2015a) reports that, while 40% of the population saved, only 13% did so in a formal financial institution. In terms of credit, 32% of the population borrowed, but only 11% sought a loan from a regulated institution. In the case of transfers between private entities (which include remittances), López-Moctezuma (2013) estimates that in Mexico only 40% of the transfers were made through formal intermediaries. Under the implicit assumption that the use of financial products acquired informally generates a lower level of welfare, the financial inclusion strategy can firstly be seen as a welfare-enhancing strategy.[3]

Nonetheless for formally supplied saving products to be attractive, particularly to users of informal financial services, they firstly need the trust of the savers; and, secondly, the products in question must be sufficiently liquid and profitable. As savings are a valued asset, trust is a key determinant of where to place them. Thus, in areas where the local inhabitants have interacted very little with formal financial institutions, the existence of a government body that supervises these institutions does little to facilitate financial inclusion. This means that the formality of the institutions does not mitigate risk perception, especially when based on ignorance of their

[3] This is consistent with the assumption that the use of informal financial transactions must reflect access problems, lack of adequate information or inadequate financial education.

operating rules. Thus, institutional complexity implies the challenge of disseminating information that is relevant and relatively easy to understand. Moreover, mistrust is further reduced when these institutions make a positive contribution to the communities with which they coexist.[4]

With respect to liquidity, it is worth noting that, in many countries, automatic teller machines (ATMs) have two characteristics that reduce the liquidity of deposits: the existence of a minimum withdrawal amount and multiples thereof. In Mexico, for example, this means that people who earn the minimum wage cannot withdraw all their money through this channel or obtain fractions of it if they have saved.

In terms of financing, low-income populations may have access to loans that informal lenders and pawn shops offer for small amounts and for short periods (Bazán Levy and Saraví, 2012). They can also borrow from friends and family members who, while they may not charge an explicit interest rate, may demand conditions that impose a cost on the borrower. Something similar often happens with supplier financing: no explicit interest is charged, but there may be a requirement to accept anti-competitive practices (for example, pressure on the credit beneficiary not to use or market competing products).

To favour formal over informal financing, some of the following conditions need to be met: (i) the documentation required needs to be appropriate to the characteristics of the socioeconomic environment in question; (ii) decision-making processes need to be agile; (iii) the conditions of the financing —in particular, amount, rate, period and periodicity of payment— need to be convenient; and (iv) there must be certainty that the supply of financing from the formal sector will be durable (that there are welfare gains from a good credit reputation). These conditions are undoubtedly easier to meet when the suppliers of financing are institutionally developed, since they will have a greater capacity to offer products that are suited to the characteristics of the population, exploit economies of scale and organization, and further diversify credit risk.

Given the advantages and disadvantages of informal financial services, it should not be surprising that there are people and businesses that use both formal and informal modalities (CAF, 2011; Dabla-Norris and others, 2015a; Fang, Ke and Zhou, 2015). Moreover, some strategies involve the use of financial products from both markets; and there are situations in which users enter and leave one market or another (Cotler and Rodríguez-Oreggia, 2010). In this context, the financial inclusion strategy makes it possible to increase access to broader baskets of financial products. Nonetheless, the type of financial product that will be consumed will depend on the preferences and constraints

---

4 In some respects, this is similar to the process of adopting new technologies in rural areas. Even if a new production process or a new machine has all the official endorsements, its adoption in rural areas will depend on community leaders' experience with the new technology.

of the individuals targeted for inclusion, the characteristics of the products on offer, the information available to potential users, and the financial education they possess to process it.

In view of this, the financial inclusion strategy should focus on developing: (a) financial products adapted to the characteristics of the low-income population; (b) financial institutions characterized by a solid governance structure, which are financially viable and interested in participating in underserved markets; (c) designing and disseminating relevant and understandable information to combat mistrust, improve decision-making and generate products that meet the needs and constraints of potential users; and (d) build a legal framework that fosters adequate development of the financial infrastructure, so that the financial inclusion strategy does not undermine the stability of the financial system.

B. Current situation

In Latin America, commercial banks are the main financial intermediaries, since they absorb a large proportion of voluntary saving and are the main providers of financing to the private sector.[5] Considering that both the level of deposits and loans tend to rise with a country's wealth and level of economic development, both indicators are expressed as a percentage of per capita GDP at purchasing power parity (PPP).[6]

While, in principle, one would expect that the higher the per capita GDP, the greater would be the use of financial products and services, figures II.1 and II.2 show that there is no clear correspondence between the value of deposits or the credit portfolio as a percentage of GDP and the country's economic development level. Given the extremely unequal distribution of income that exists in the vast majority of Latin American countries, a macroeconomic snapshot will not show how much the population participates in the financial market or the characteristics of the participating population, what obstacles can limit access and what determines the use of the different products.[7] Accordingly, indicators of financial inclusion are used to supplement the information provided by measures of financial depth.[8]

---

[5] Consideration of voluntary savings alone disregards the compulsory savings that formal workers make to finance their retirement. Although many countries in Latin America have a stock exchange, citizen participation in it is very sparse —by contrast to the United States, for example— so this is also excluded. Lastly, although there are many non-bank financial institutions that accept savings and make loans, their market share remains very small in nearly all cases.

[6] Although comparing stocks with flows may not be the best practice, it is a standardization widely used in the literature.

[7] According to World Bank figures, the richest 20% in Latin America accounted, on average, for 55% of total consumption. For countries such as Germany, the United States, France and the United Kingdom, the average was 41% (see World Bank [online] http://data.worldbank.org/indicator).

[8] The concept of financial depth seeks to measure the value of financial aggregates relative to some indicator of economic activity, as described in figures II.1 and II.2. Although financial depth in a geographical area may be great, this does not reflect how much the population in that area actually uses the financial products and services in question.

Figure II.1
Latin America and the Caribbean: commercial bank deposits, 2014
(Percentages of per capita GDP)

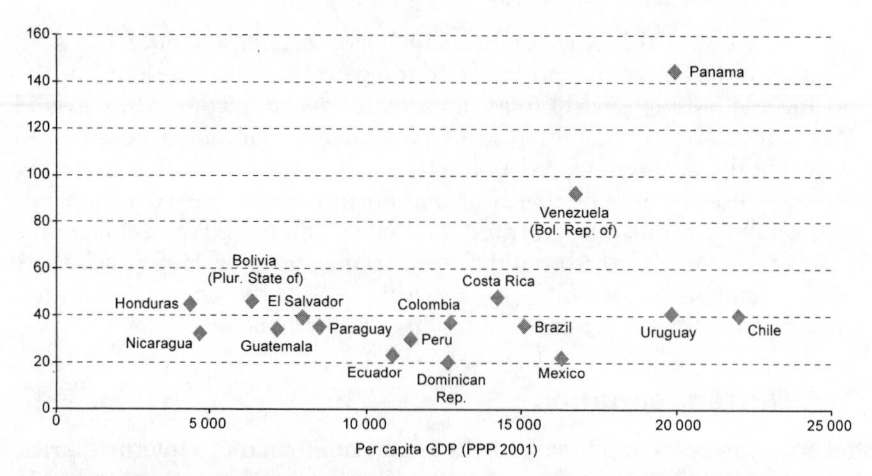

Source: Prepared by the author, on the basis of World Bank, World Development Indicators, 2015 [online] http://data.worldbank.org/data-catalog/world-development-indicators; and International Monetary Fund (IMF), "Financial Access Survey", 2015 [online] http://data.imf.org/?sk=E5DCAB7E-A5CA-4892-A6EA-598B5463A34C.
Note: The data on commercial bank deposits for El Salvador and Paraguay refer to 2013.

Figure II.2
Latin America and the Caribbean: commercial bank loan portfolio, 2014
(Percentages of per capita GDP)

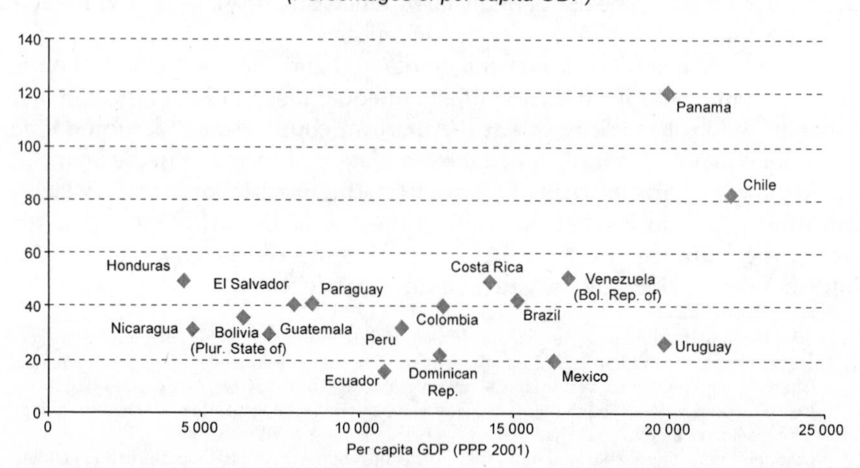

Source: Prepared by the author, on the basis of World Bank, World Development Indicators, 2015 [online] http://data.worldbank.org/data-catalog/world-development-indicators; and International Monetary Fund (IMF), "Financial Access Survey", 2015 [online] http://data.imf.org/?sk=E5DCAB7E-A5CA-4892-A6EA-598B5463A34C.
Note: The loan portfolio data for El Salvador refer to 2013.

To gain an understanding of the population's participation in the formal financial sector, it is first necessary to analyse the degree of access to financial product distribution channels. Table II.1 shows the degree of access to the three main forms of interaction with the providers of formal financial services: bank branches or offices, ATMs and the Internet. A first glance at the data in table II.1 shows the great heterogeneity that exists among Latin American countries, where, for example, the number of branches per 100,000 adults ranges from 253 in Colombia, to just 7 in Nicaragua. A comparison of this variable nationally with its value in each country's largest city is a measure of decentralization, and again reveals considerable heterogeneity. Thus, the aggregate number of branches does not necessarily reflect the degree of access that exists in a country.

Table II.1
Latin America and the Caribbean: indicators of access to financial product distribution channels

	Bank branches, 2014 *(per 100 000 adults)*	ATMs, 2014 *(per 1 000 km²)*	Population in the largest city, 2015 *(percentages of the total population)*	Commercial bank branches in the largest city, 2015 *(percentages of the national total)*	Bank branches, 2015 *(per 100 000 inhabitants in the largest city)*	Internet users, 2014 *(per 100 persons)*
Argentina	13.2	6.9	35.0	n.a.	n.a.	64.7
Bolivia (Plurinational State of)	15.1	2.3	19.6	14.8	7.6	39.0
Brazil	46.3	23.9	10.1	8.3	9.0	57.6
Chile	16.7	10.7	36.3	48.9	16.7	72.4
Colombia	253.2	13.0	20.2	49.3	30.8	52.6
Costa Rica	22.3	57.3	24.3	60.8	10.3	49.4
Dominican Republic	11.6	51.0	28.0	42.1	19.4	49.6
Ecuador	77.2	18.0	16.8	27.4	11.1	43.0
El Salvador	11.8	72.1	17.9	n.a.	n.a.	29.7
Guatemala	34.5	31.8	17.9	34.4	41.1	23.4
Honduras	23.3	11.9	13.9	25.9	72.2	19.1
Mexico	14.8	22.5	16.5	18.4	18.4	44.4
Nicaragua	7.6	4.0	15.7	42.4	16.7	17.6
Panama	23.0	23.2	42.6	69.2	24.7	44.9
Paraguay	10.8	2.8	35.5	37.5	9.0	43.0
Peru	8.0	9.6	31.5	52.4	11.4	40.2
Uruguay	12.2	8.0	49.7	33.3	18.4	61.5
Venezuela (Bolivarian Republic of)	16.6	11.0	9.4	25.8	31.2	57.0

Source: Prepared by the author, on the basis of World Bank, World Development Indicators, 2015 [online] http://data.worldbank.org/data-catalog/world-development-indicators; and International Monetary Fund (IMF), "Financial Access Survey", 2015 [online] http://data.imf.org/?sk=E5DCAB7E-A5CA-4892-A6EA-598B5463A34C, and data from the central banks, superintendencies and banking commissions of the individual countries.

Note: Data for "Commercial bank branches in the largest city, 2015 (Percentages of the national total)" and "Bank branches, 2015 (Per 100,000 inhabitants in the largest city)" refer to September 2015, except in the cases of Chile (August 2015), Ecuador (March 2014), Honduras (2014), Nicaragua (2014), Panama (December 2015) and Venezuela (Bolivarian Republic of) (January 2016). In Honduras, in addition to bank branches the figure includes service windows, correspondents and other service points. The term "Largest city" refers to the size of an agglomeration in population terms. Branch data are for metropolitan areas with the exception of Brazil (not specified), Costa Rica and Panama (provinces) and Honduras (department).

Technological progress and regulatory changes have enabled financial institutions to increasingly rely on ATMs and online channels to provide their services; but, in this respect, all Latin American countries fall far short of their European peers. While France and Italy have over 100 ATMs per km^2, the weighted average for the Latin American countries included in table II.1 is only 20. Such disparity may explain why some Latin American countries have a much larger number of branches per capita than Germany and France, which have 14 and 38 branches for every 100,000 adults, respectively. In this respect, the appropriate indicator for measuring access is not a temporally static variable, since it depends on the economy's development level. In the case of Internet users, the data show a very high correlation (0.87) between Internet use and the country's per capita income. It could therefore be inferred that greater access to online financial products would not necessarily have a major impact in terms of increasing financial inclusion among low-income population sectors.

The use of formal financial services depends on the possibilities for access to such services and the interest they can arouse. To assess how much the products and services supplied by formal financial institutions are used, table II.2 shows that there is no clear correspondence between the holding of an account and the use of saving and credit products. The financial services provided by the bank seem in many cases to be used as a means of transaction: an account is used to receive and withdraw money. While this transactional medium may be enhanced by the availability of better distribution channels (mobile phones and correspondents), the accounts in question do not seem to be a product that is associated with saving and borrowing decisions.

Given the difficulty of using a single variable to measure the degree of inclusion, an index is proposed that reflects the global use of the different types of formal financial products and services. This global inclusion index is constructed from a simple average of the six variables shown in table II.2 (Martínez Pería, 2014; Dabla-Norris and others, 2015a). The results confirm that the poorest countries (Honduras and Nicaragua) report the least global inclusion.

Given the very unequal distribution of income prevailing in Latin America, table II.3 disaggregates the data from table II.2 to assess the situation of the poorest 40% in each country, while table II.4 provides a breakdown for the population living in rural areas. The results show that accounts in financial institutions are less used by the poorest and rural populations. Although accounts in these institutions are important vehicles for capturing income received from work or transfers, the evidence shows that the population does not consider them a useful tool for managing their funds.

Table II.2
Latin America and the Caribbean: household use of financial products, 2014
(Percentages)

	Global inclusion index	ATM as main withdrawal medium	Account in a financial institution	Debit card	Saving in a financial institution	Credit from a financial institution	Credit card
Argentina	35.2	78.0	50.2	44.2	4.1	8.3	26.6
Bolivia (Plurinational State of)	25.6	40.3	40.7	23.1	23.5	19.7	6.2
Brazil	43.2	75.4	68.1	59.2	12.3	11.9	32.0
Chile	42.8	80.8	63.2	54.1	15.0	15.6	28.1
Colombia	31.8	80.9	38.4	30.0	12.3	15.6	13.7
Costa Rica	42.1	83.2	64.6	53.6	24.2	12.7	14.5
Dominican Republic	27.5	39.5	54.0	22.6	26.5	11.8	10.9
Ecuador	25.3	46.5	46.2	25.6	14.3	13.4	5.7
El Salvador	27.2	66.5	34.6	21.8	14.0	18.2	8.0
Guatemala	22.1	36.9	40.8	16.2	15.2	17.2	6.3
Honduras	16.8	23.7	30.0	14.2	14.5	12.3	6.1
Mexico	29.5	69.1	38.7	26.8	14.5	9.7	17.8
Nicaragua	19.0	57.9	18.9	11.3	8.1	14.3	3.5
Panama	28.8	63.5	43.4	25.3	20.4	10.4	9.8
Peru	22.9	51.8	29.0	21.4	12.3	11.2	11.7
Uruguay	40.2	84.9	45.4	37.7	12.5	21.0	39.8
Venezuela (Bolivarian Republic of)	38.6	78.9	56.9	49.6	22.8	2.0	21.5
Latin America and the Caribbean	34.8	71.1	51.1	40.4	13.5	11.3	21.6

Source: Prepared by the author, on the basis of World Bank, Global Findex Database, 2014 [online] http://datatopics.worldbank.org/financialinclusion.

Note: The global inclusion index is calculated as a simple average of the following variables: percentage of the population over 15 years of age who hold an account in a formal financial institution, use the ATM as the main means of withdrawal, has a debit card, had a loan from a financial institution during the previous year, had money saved in a financial institution the previous year and owns a credit card. Paraguay was omitted owing to a lack of data.

Table II.3
Latin America and the Caribbean: use of financial products by the poorest 40% of households, 2014
(Percentages)

	Global inclusion index	Account in a financial institution	Debit card	Saving in a financial institution	Credit from a financial institution	Credit card
Argentina	20.4	44.4	36.6	1.1	4.6	15.4
Bolivia (Plurinational State of)	12.4	25.6	11.7	11.3	10.5	2.7
Brazil	26.8	58.5	42.9	5.7	7.5	19.6
Chile	29.2	56.4	45.2	10.3	13.1	20.9
Colombia	11.1	23.4	14.7	5.7	6.4	5.2
Costa Rica	29.3	61.3	46.8	16.1	9.7	12.8
Dominican Republic	17.7	41.8	11.9	16.0	13.7	5.2
Ecuador	13.7	32.4	13.7	9.1	12.1	1.4
El Salvador	10.5	21.6	11.1	4.1	13.5	2.3
Guatemala	9.7	26.7	4.6	7.0	7.2	3.3
Honduras	7.5	18.4	5.2	6.6	5.9	1.3
Mexico	13.3	28.6	15.3	7.0	6.5	9.1
Nicaragua	5.4	8.3	5.5	2.9	9.3	1.1
Panama	15.1	32.1	15.8	14.8	8.8	4.1
Peru	9.6	18.4	11.2	5.8	7.4	5.3
Uruguay	22.1	35.0	25.8	5.3	19.0	25.4
Venezuela (Bolivarian Republic of)	n.a.	48.0	39.6	18.8	n.a.	13.7
Latin America and the Caribbean	18.9	40.9	27.6	6.9	6.9	12.3

Source: Prepared by the author, on the basis of World Bank, Global Findex Database, 2014 [online] http://datatopics.worldbank.org/financialinclusion.

Note: Paraguay was omitted because data are not available.

Table II.4
Latin America and the Caribbean: use of financial products by the rural population, 2014
(Percentages)

	Global inclusion index	Account in a financial institution	Debit card	Saving in a financial institution	Credit from a financial institution	Credit card
Argentina	21.2	38.1	33.9	3.6	8.5	21.7
Bolivia (Plurinational State of)	11.7	20.8	6.3	14.2	14.6	2.4
Brazil	25.4	54.1	33.0	9.4	10.1	20.3
Chile	18.1	37.1	18.8	13.4	6.8	14.4
Colombia	13.9	26.9	15.3	8.5	12.6	6.3
Costa Rica	27.5	51.4	45.2	18.2	11.6	11.3
Dominican Republic	12.8	29.6	12.2	3.8	13.5	5.0
Ecuador	15.4	35.3	13.0	13.7	9.2	5.8
El Salvador	7.9	12.1	8.8	9.9	3.8	5.1
Guatemala	11.5	20.4	9.2	9.8	13.3	4.9
Honduras	7.6	16.2	7.7	5.9	5.5	2.9
Mexico	8.4	13.6	10.9	4.8	6.2	6.3
Nicaragua	5.5	10.3	4.3	4.9	6.4	1.7
Panama	12.6	22.7	8.2	14.2	9.8	8.2
Paraguay	7.5	13.3	5.1	5.7	10.5	3.0
Peru	9.9	14.3	9.8	7.1	13.2	4.8
Uruguay	16.0	21.0	14.4	5.3	15.4	24.0
Venezuela (Bolivarian Republic of)	18.8	41.4	34.2	10.6	1.6	6.1
Latin America and the Caribbean	17.4	35.0	22.2	8.5	9.2	12.2

Source: Prepared by the author, on the basis of World Bank, Global Findex Database, 2014 [online] http://datatopics.worldbank.org/financialinclusion.

The data in tables II.2, II.3 and II.4 can be used to compare the global inclusion index for each country, along with the indices for the low-income population and for inhabitants of rural areas. As shown in figure II.3, the scant use of financial products and services is most acute among the poorest 40% of citizens and rural inhabitants. Accordingly, the financial inclusion strategy should be targeted on low-income populations and especially on those living in rural areas.

Tables II.2, II.3 and II.4 reveal a certain degree of heterogeneity in the degree of financial inclusion achieved in each country for the different population segments. Of all countries considered, Costa Rica displays the one of the highest degrees of inclusion; while Mexico has a very low rate, despite its high level of economic activity. The data show that the lowest inclusion rates are concentrated in places where the poorest population lives and in rural areas.

Martínez Pería (2014) and Dabla-Norris and others (2015a) propose constructing a potential inclusion index from the forecast resulting from econometric estimations.[9] This estimate can be used to construct a gap by subtracting the potential index from its observed value, such that a positive (negative) gap would indicate an inclusion level that is lower (higher) than expected according to international standards.

Figure II.3
Latin America: financial inclusion index for three different populations, 2014

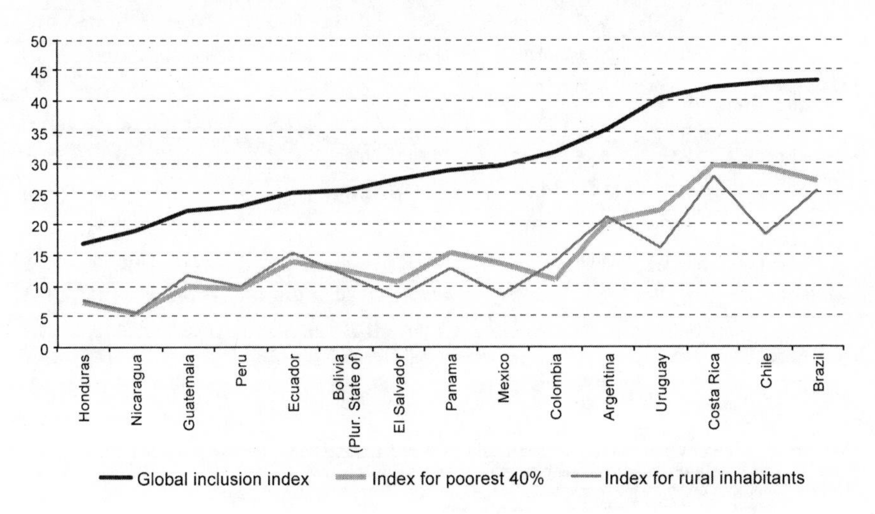

Source: Prepared by the author, on the basis of World Bank, Global Findex Database, 2014 [online] http://datatopics.worldbank.org/financialinclusion.
Note: Paraguay and the Bolivarian Republic of Venezuela were omitted because no data are available.

With data from 146 countries spanning Latin America, Asia and Europe for 2011, estimations were performed for three types of variables associated with the degree of financial inclusion. The first corresponds to the global index that was analysed above; the second is the percentage of people who save in a financial institution; and the last is the percentage of people who are debtors of a financial institution. The explanatory variables of these three approaches include the logarithm of per capita GDP at PPP prices, two variables related to compliance with the law and one referring to access to ATMs.[10] Three different population samples were considered for the estimation: the total population, the poorest 40%, and the population living in rural areas (see table II.5).

---

9 For a detailed discussion of the methodology, see Beck and Feyen (2013).

10 The education level of the adult population, degree of inequality, inflation volatility and bank concentration were also considered as potential explanatory variables, but none of them proved statistically significant. The estimations reported in table II.5 do not include these variables.

Table II.5
Estimations of the use of financial products

	Total population			Poorest 40%			Rural population		
	Global inclusion	Saving	Loan	Global inclusion	Saving	Loan	Global inclusion	Saving	Loan
Latin America and the Caribbean (LAC)	**-11.49**	-1.23	0.90	**-15.08**	-1.74	-1.04	**-11.27**	-0.44	0.48
	(-3.83)	(3.10)	(1.36)	**(4.41)**	(2.94)	(1.30)	**(4.39)**	(3.06)	(1.41)
Legal certainty	**0.30**	**0.37**	0.06	**0.38**	**0.35**	0.06	**0.34**	**0.42**	0.08
	(0.14)	**(0.09)**	(0.06)	**(0.16)**	**(0.08)**	(0.06)	**(0.16)**	**(0.09)**	(0.07)
ATMs per 100 000 adults	**0.14**	0.00	0.00	**0.15**	0.00	0.01	**0.14**	0.00	0.01
	(0.04)	(0.03)	(0.01)	**(0.04)**	(0.03)	(0.02)	**(0.05)**	(0.03)	(0.01)
Log real per capita GDP	**22.61**	**5.45**	1.59	**22.58**	**5.89**	1.40	**22.33**	**5.23**	0.72
	(4.31)	**(2.91)**	(1.63)	**(4.70)**	**(2.75)**	(1.70)	**(4.81)**	**(2.80)**	(1.80)
Informal economy	**-0.30**	**-0.29**	-0.05	**-0.33**	**-0.20**	-0.01	**-0.32**	**-0.21**	-0.05
	(0.17)	**(0.09)**	(0.07)	**(0.17)**	**(0.08)**	(0.07)	**(0.17)**	**(0.09)**	(0.08)
Constant	**-42.38**	-8.12	2.96	**-52.43**	**-17.40**	0.62	**-45.45**	**-14.55**	4.33
	(14.78)	(9.31)	(6.14)	**(15.15)**	**(7.96)**	(6.37)	**(15.26)**	**(8.73)**	(6.92)
Observations	128	126	126	126	126	126	122	122	122
Adjusted R^2	0.80	0.63	0.15	0.81	0.64	0.13	0.78	0.63	0.13

Source: Prepared by the author, on the basis of World Bank, Global Findex Database, 2014 [online] http://datatopics.worldbank.org/financialinclusion.
Note: Method: ordinary least squares. Robust standard errors in parentheses.
Statistically significant parameters high lighted in bold.
Independent variables: (a) LAC. Dichotomous indicator taking the value 1 for countries of Latin America and the Caribbean; (b) Legal certainty. Variable measured on a scale of 0 to 100, where 100 is the highest possible level of confidence in compliance with the law. See World Bank [online] http://databank.worldbank.org/data/reports.aspx?source=global-financial-development [consultation date: October 27, 2015]; (c) Informal economy. Estimate of the percentage of goods and services output (as a proportion of GDP) that was deliberately concealed from the authorities in 1999-2007 for one of the following reasons: (i) avoidance of income tax, value added tax or some other tax; (ii) avoidance of social security contributions; (iii) avoidance of compliance with certain labour standards, such as minimum wages, hours of work and safety standards; and (iv) avoidance of compliance with certain administrative procedures, such as completing statistical questionnaires or other administrative forms. See Schneider, Buehn and Montenegro (2010); (d) Given the heterogeneity that exists between countries, the test was conducted with a more homogeneous sample, by excluding countries whose per capita income exceeded the highest in Latin America and those that were poorer than the poorest in Latin America. The results did not change significantly.

In the case of the dependent variable "Global inclusion index" described above, the results reported in table II.5 for the total population are consistent with conventional theories. Regardless of the type of population sample considered, lower income levels, lower degree of compliance with the law and larger size of the informal economy are all associated with less financial inclusion. Although the estimation also controlled for a variable that measures the banking infrastructure, the binary variable used to identify Latin America and the Caribbean (LAC) has a coefficient which suggests that membership of the Latin American region depresses the potential inclusion index. Thus, if Latin America as a whole increased its number of ATMs to the average in Europe and Asia, if the region's per capita GDP were similar to Colombia's and if its business informality rate were that of Mexico, potential inclusion could rise 8.6 by percentage points.[11] In the case of the poorest 40% of the population and those living in rural areas, a similar exercise would raise the potential inclusion rate by 8.6 and 7.6 percentage points, respectively.

Estimations of the dependent variable that measures how much the savings products are used show that, for the total population, this is positively related to income level and respect for the law.[12] None of the explanatory variables considered to explain participation in formal credit markets proved statistically significant. This may partly be due to the heterogeneity of the credit methodologies used by banks and non-bank financial institutions, the distortions that could be introduced by public bank lending operations, and, in general, the absence of variables related to credit collateral and characteristics of the project and loans.

The results reported in table II.5 can be used to extrapolate the degree of global inclusion and use of savings products that would be expected for each Latin American country, thereby making it possible to construct a gap measuring the difference between the potential and observed values of the index (Martínez Pería, 2014; Dabla-Norris and others, 2015a). A positive gap signifies that the country in question has an inclusion index that is below potential, according to international standards.[13]

Table II.6 shows that of the 17 Latin American countries, inclusion is below potential in seven, using any of the three population samples. Of these, Chile, Mexico and Uruguay stand out because they are among the six countries with the highest per capita income, and Chile is also the country with the highest rate of credit penetration. This means that a country's degree of economic development or credit penetration is not synonymous with the degree of inclusion or how far from the possibilities frontier it is. Moreover, the size of the global inclusion gap does not necessarily reflect what happens in the poorest populations. In Chile, Mexico, Peru and Uruguay, for example, the gaps are smaller at the national level than those found in the lower-income populations, which suggests the need for financial inclusion policies that may have to be targeted.

---

11 Such measures mean that the number of ATMs in the region would have to increase by 64%; the level of business informality would have to fall by 9 percentage points; and per capita GDP would need to increase by 1 point.

12 While this result makes sense, if more information were available, it would be interesting to see whether the degree of legal certainty is associated with the use of informal saving products.

13 This methodology is sensitive to the explanatory variables used, since the gap represent the estimation error. In this connection, consideration of 146 countries involves very different economies and societies; and it assumes, in principle, that all should follow the same path of financial development, which is debatable. Moreover, the use of cross-sectional data prevents correcting for endogeneity problems.

Table II.6
Latin America and the Caribbean: inclusion and saving gaps, 2011

Country	Total population		Poorest 40%		Rural population	
	Inclusion	Saving	Inclusion	Saving	Inclusion	Saving
Bolivia (Plurinational State of)	-10.2	-8.5	-9.5	-6.2	-6.3	-7.5
Brazil	-2.7	**10.1**	**3.7**	**8.1**	-3.7	**9.7**
Chile	**19.5**	**22.5**	**24.4**	**20.4**	**23.2**	**20.8**
Colombia	**3.7**	**6.5**	**9.7**	**7.3**	**4.3**	**6.3**
Costa Rica	-10.9	-4.7	-8.1	1.0	-15.2	-5.6
Dominican Republic	-4.3	-1.8	-16.8	-7.0	-15.5	-9.1
Ecuador	-7.5	-4.7	-6.6	-5.3	-9.7	-6.2
El Salvador	**12.0**	-3.7	**7.6**	-0.5	**10.2**	-1.3
Guatemala	-2.9	-5.4	-5.7	-4.7	-4.8	-5.5
Honduras	-4.3	-3.1	n.d.	n.d.	-3.6	-0.9
Mexico	**15.9**	**10.8**	**20.2**	**8.8**	**26.6**	**10.9**
Nicaragua	**0.4**	**1.0**	-3.0	**0.3**	**1.0**	**2.1**
Panama	**9.3**	-1.3	**3.4**	-3.0	**8.1**	-1.4
Paraguay	-1.5	-0.6	**2.9**	**1.6**	**3.6**	**2.2**
Peru	**3.9**	-1.6	**6.9**	**1.5**	**6.4**	**0.5**
Uruguay	**18.5**	**14.3**	**22.5**	**13.7**	**18.4**	**15.9**
Venezuela (Bolivarian Republic of)	-12.0	-6.1	-11.4	-4.7	-13.3	-5.8

Source: Prepared by the author, on the basis of World Bank, Global Findex Database, 2014 [online] http://datatopics.worldbank.org/financialinclusion.
Note: A positive gap denotes a situation where the country is below its potential (shown in bold).

In general, the different realities of Latin American countries mean there is no unique history of the causes of currently existing financial inclusion gaps. For example, the most prosperous countries do not necessarily display the smallest gap; and the sign and size of the gap seems to depend on the population group being analysed (total, rural or poorest 40%). Nonetheless, despite these heterogeneities, the data show that a stronger rule of law, a more adequate financial infrastructure, and an increase in economic activity are variables that can help raise the global inclusion rate and the percentage of the population that save in the formal financial system.

C. A review of the literature

Theoretical studies show that the presence of frictions in financial markets can hinder the accumulation of human and physical capital, affect occupational decisions and generate poverty traps (Banerjee and Newman 1993; Aghion and Bolton 1997). Moreover, empirical studies indicate that greater access to credit products can have positive effects on income and consumption (Karlan and Zinman, 2010), help reduce poverty (Beck, Demirgüç-Kunt and Levine, 2007), reduce vulnerability to income shocks (Lensink, Servin and Van Den Berg, 2015) and increase the accumulation of productive assets (Cotler and Woodruff, 2008, Cotler and Rodríguez-Oreggia, 2010).

Although, from a macroeconomic standpoint, studies such as Beck, Demirgüç-Kunt and Levine (2007) show the importance of greater financial depth, the impact on growth depends on a number of factors. For example, risk aversion by potential borrowers (Zeller and Sharma, 2002), the use and efficiency of credit bureaus (Beck, Demirgüç-Kunt and Martínez Pería, 2007), the entrepreneurs' human capital (Karlan and Valdivia, 2011) and the intensity of competition between the suppliers of financial products are all factors influencing the impact of the availability and use of formal financial services on economic activity.

Nonetheless, evidence of the impact of financing at the household and individual level is inconclusive. The studies by Pitt and Khandker (1998), Morduch (1998), Banerjee and Duflo (2004), Alexander-Tedeschi and Karlan (2006), Duflo and others (2013), Hermes and Lensink (2011) and Khandker and Samad (2014) represent a sample of the breadth of research analysing the impact of access to formal financing on the wellbeing of the beneficiary individuals. The findings reported in this literature are heterogeneous; and there is no conclusive statement as to whether loans have a positive and lasting effect on the well-being of their clientele.

This heterogeneity in the results should not come as a surprise, as it reflects the use of different methodologies to measure the impact, the various decisions that borrowers can make on how to use the financing, which variables are considered when measuring well-being, and the time horizon of the empirical studies. Nonetheless, the evidence shows that credit products can boost investment and generate new income. They can therefore be perceived as a local lever for the growth of low-income population sectors, which would help alleviate deficits in areas such as housing and food, two key targets of social policy.

This begs the question of why credit products supplied by formal institutions are so little used. The answer draws on the concepts of access and participation. As Beck, Demirgüç-Kunt and Martínez Pería (2007) explain, access tends to be defined under a geographical dimension, so that lack of access is associated with the absence of financial institutions in certain locations. Yet, according to Claessens (2006), the use of credit products is the outcome of both supply and demand. This distinction is important because it recognizes that underuse of financial services may stem from low rates of access or rationing in the credit market. In the latter case, it is also necessary to know whether the rationing is voluntary, either because the individual in question does not need financing or because he/she self-excludes on the presumption of rejection; or else involuntary owing to the borrower's high risk, to incompatibility between the interest rate and the project, the existence of products that are not compatible with needs, or else simple discrimination.

Thus, in a context of full access, the demand for these products will determine the decision to participate in institutional financial services. Following Dabla-Norris and others (2015b), in a context of full access, there are two factors that restrict the demand for formal financing: the quality of credit collateral and the presence of asymmetric information.

The deficient legal framework that characterizes many countries in Latin America leads financial institutions to demand greater collateral, which tends to reduce the demand for financing, with possible regressive effects on the distribution of such funds. Moreover, the seminal work of Stiglitz and Weiss (1981) shows that the frictions caused by asymmetric information between the banking institutions and the potential borrowers force the former to monitor the latter. If people living in poverty and those working informally, as well as less productive companies and those with fewer business links, are considered most likely to be monitored, the intermediation cost is an additional factor that depresses demand, generates regressive effects and can serve as a source of inefficiency and voluntary exclusion.

In view of this situation, Dabla-Norris and others (2015b) argue that there are two channels through which greater financial inclusion can affect economic activity and inequality. First, because the more efficient distribution of credit funds (in other words, a distribution that is oriented more towards entrepreneurial talent than wealth) increases output. Second, because having more efficient contracts reduces friction costs and increases access to the credit products and their use. These two channels lead to loans being directed to the most talented entrepreneurs with the best projects. While this should increase economic activity, its effect on inequality is unclear. Initially inequality may increase because talented entrepreneurs already receive higher incomes; however, increased access can also enable previously rationed individuals and entrepreneurs to make use of these loan funds because, as is well known, many microenterprises have a high marginal return. In this regard, greater financial inclusion not only contributes to poverty reduction (through growth), but can also help reduce the inequality of opportunities and income (Beck, Demirgüç-Kunt and Levine, 2007).

The low rate of use of formal saving products by the low-income population can be similarly characterized. For example, Karlan, Lakshmi and Zinman (2014) describe the access barrier of high transaction costs. Given the small and erratic amounts of savings that these populations maintain, financial institutions face high entry and operating costs, which discourages their presence in some localities (Dupas and Robinson, 2013). It is therefore no coincidence that legislative measures have been introduced in some countries to oblige commercial banks to provide basic accounts, which make no charge for account opening or for the number of transactions, but have a ceiling on the balance that can be maintained.

Weak supply incentives are compounded by other factors that reduce the demand for formal saving products. The lack of products that seek to capture low and erratic income flows, in conjunction with social norms that reward the construction of social capital and, hence, encourage the use of informal arrangements, and the presence of intertemporal preferences that are heavily biased towards the present are factors that reduce the level of saving sought and the use of formal products (Xu and Zia, 2012; Karlan, Lakshmi and Zinman, 2014).

The characteristics of formal saving and credit instruments, their potential as complements or substitutes for informal financial products, the fungibility of financing and individual preferences and constraints are some of the factors that explain the mechanisms through which the use of formal financial services can influence well-being.

Identifying which variables will impact the potential for greater access to financial products and services is not easy. Nonetheless, if the products are adequate and accessible, have a low transaction cost, are supplied by supervised financial institutions and have appropriate methodologies, the most likely impact would be to increase the use of formal financial services. Insofar as this makes it possible to cope with income fluctuations more securely, and provided this participation is voluntary, then it will be welfare-enhancing.

Combating low levels of financial inclusion and showing results is important from a socioeconomic and political point of view. In this respect, the unit of measurement of the success of the strategy should be, for example, the number of people who wanted to have an account at a financial institution and opened it thanks to the presence of more outlets. However, the metrics used are those in which the use of a given product is measured (the number of accounts per 100,000 people). A measure of this type does not indicate whether an increase in its value corresponds to persons who were excluded or self-excluded and who —as a result of the financial inclusion strategy— freely decide to change their relationship with the financial system. While taking into account the short-term political benefits of increased financial inclusion, traditional metrics may induce the authorities to force particular population groups to open a bank account even if it is not attractive to them. An example is the opening of accounts to receive public transfers. While there may be a valid justification for such a measure, it would offer a distorted picture of financial inclusion. Cases such as this make it necessary to introduce a new term —effective financial inclusion— which would exclude inactive accounts from the calculation along with those that are only used as a means to receive a public transfer.

D. Financial inclusion strategies

In general, the statistics show that in Latin America the services offered by the formal financial system are underused —especially among the poorest population groups and rural inhabitants. When considering the potential advantages of using the products and services offered by formal financial institutions versus informal alternatives, it is concluded that the poorest populations and rural inhabitants are more vulnerable to income shocks and more likely to face borrowing constraints. The problems of asymmetric information, the externalities generated by a very unequal income distribution and the difficulty in achieving economies of scope in sparsely populated communities are some of the causes of this situation, which therefore calls for a public policy to address these issues.

A successful financial inclusion strategy entails enhancing the accessibility of the services in question and, at the same time, making them attractive enough to elicit demand. This means improving financial infrastructure, especially in rural areas, and promoting the development of financial products that are compatible with the seasonality that still affects rural activity, with small and erratic amounts saved by low-income groups and prices that are compatible with income levels of the target population. Seeking to ensure that this goal is achieved on a sustainable basis, requires the strategies for achieving this to carry limited risk, so as to guarantee the stability of the financial system. To that end, five strategies are presented below.

1. Financial products

A first strategy involves the design of financial products that are better aligned with the needs of the poor and rural population. This strategy reflects the basic characteristics of these population segments: low, erratic or seasonal incomes, which are unpredictable and difficult to prove, and assets that are not easily tradable.

A population with such characteristics needs financial products that match the liquidity changes of the target population (Labie, Laureti and Szafarz, 2013). Yet, this is not a typical feature of traditional banking products or of those offered by institutions that use microfinance techniques. The former offer saving products requiring a minimum balance and limits on the number of transactions. They also offer credit products requiring prior documentation, which conflicts with the informality in which the population lives and with the time frames required to meet urgent needs. On the other hand, the vast majority of non-bank entities that use microfinance techniques, the most common being short-term loans, with periodic payments (weekly after receiving the loan) of constant amount, with phased loans and zero tolerance of missed payments. These characteristics discourage the implementation of projects of longer maturity, making it necessary to take out several loans while ignoring the high vulnerability to income shocks.

This lack of flexibility among institutions that use microfinance techniques to some extent reflects the pursuit of discipline in the client and a mechanism aimed at reducing operating costs. However, given the characteristics of the population that it is intended to include, a degree of flexibility in financial products can benefit potential customers and the financial institutions that serve them. Adequate flexibility can increase the likelihood of repayment, encourage the channelling of funds into high-yielding projects, and diminish the attractiveness of informal lenders (Mallick, 2012). Pearlman (2012), for example, shows that one of the reasons for the low penetration of microfinance institutions is the difficulty of mitigating the risk associated with the potential users. Hence, the implementation of credit products containing risk protection clauses should be considered, among other things.

2. Financial institutions

To help make financial products more attractive among the poor, a second strategy involves the development of financial institutions that are better attuned towards greater inclusion. While there are banks and non-bank financial institutions that can help achieve this goal, public policy has tended to focus on finding mechanisms to achieve greater bank penetration. Focusing on banks largely reflects two factors: the first based on the levels of assets held by banks with respect to those of non-bank institutions (such as cooperative saving and loan associations, and those operating with microfinance techniques); and a second factor related to the lack of knowledge among the financial authorities in many countries regarding the way these non-banks operate. Nonetheless, because this inclusion movement began just as the international financial crisis was erupting, the authority sought greater inclusion, while regulating banks with a view to averting financial instability.

The potential conflict between inclusion and financial stability and the lack of interest shown by bank managers —with certain exceptions— in making institutional changes have resulted in a dominant strategy of expansion through the use of correspondents and mobile branches. Yet, as explained above, the main constraint on including an important sector of the rural and low-income population resides in its credit methodology and in the characteristics of its main products. This requires consideration of whether public policy to promote financial inclusion should be articulated around banks.

The vast majority of non-bank financial entities use microfinance techniques or operate under cooperative rules, and they serve a niche market consisting of people who are excluded from the financial system for various reasons. Accordingly, they should be key instruments of greater inclusiveness. In many countries, however, the microfinance industry is highly concentrated, and many of its constituent institutions are too small to achieve economies of scale and also pose risk management problems and lack a strong governance structure. In such situations, mechanisms are needed to promote greater competition, as this may boost demand for formal financial services. To that end, public policy should focus on seeking mechanisms to encourage mergers to consolidate a more competitive and less concentrated industry. An example of this may be the use of financial support to enable the best organized and financially sound non-bank financial institutions to access central bank funding and participate in ATM networks. While this type of measure may cause greater concentration, it could also serve as an incentive for the development of partnerships between medium-sized entities.

Another common form of non-bank financial institution that exists in several countries of the region consists of saving and loan cooperatives. In some countries, these entities have succeeded in building a governance structure that has enabled them to circumvent systemic financial crises. By making credit services conditional on saving capacity, institutions of this type offer advantages and disadvantages compared with banks and microfinance institutions. Their advantages include the supply of basic saving and credit services, the charging of lower interest rates on loans and the payment of generally higher deposit rates for savings. They have two disadvantages: individuals with low saving capacity can find it hard to obtain financing; and institutional capacity to achieve sustained growth in the loan portfolio is restricted by the ability to capture savings. Thus, the rules of operation of these cooperative institutions may become incompatible with financial inclusion policies.

As can be seen, all of the financial institutions that could be vehicles of greater inclusion have both advantages and disadvantages; so the best strategy would not be to target a single type of financial institution but to forge alliances between different entities and, at the same time, generate a competitive environment.[14]

3. Distribution channels

Increasing the efficiency of the supply of financial products requires an institutional framework that fosters the development of new financial technologies that make the provision of financial services cheaper. Thus, a third strategy is to promote the role of correspondents (also referred to banking agents) as a way to reduce the operating cost of maintaining branches of financial institutions and lower the transaction costs incurred by both suppliers and users.[15] A correspondent, or agent, is a third party that sets up

---

[14] This is supported by Vanroose and D'Espallier (2013), who use global data to show that the interest rates charged by microfinance institutions tend to be lower, the greater the presence of banks in the relevant markets.

[15] In several countries, initially only banks could have correspondents; but this rule was later relaxed to include other legally established non-bank entities.

a business relationship with a financial institution, to represent it and thus be able to supply the institution's products and services.[16] As the operation becomes cheaper, an increase in access and use is expected, so the degree of inclusion should increase. To achieve this, the expansion strategy needs to target rural areas —where population density is lower— and mainly supply financial products that are used for saving and credit.

4. Financial education

The emergence of new institutions and new products always arouses fear and uncertainty among populations with recent access to them. So, a fourth strategy involves the provision of financial education services. For this strategy to serve as a mechanism for increasing inclusion, it may be necessary to divide it into two parts. A first substrategy should aim to show the advantages of using the financial products offered by formal financial entities. In other words the focus should be on highlighting their advantages over what is supplied informally. This is a task mainly for the public institutions that regulate and supervise financial institutions. So, in addition to designing adequate regulation and good supervision, these agencies should fund a permanent media campaign showing the benefits of participating in the formal financial system, placing special emphasis on the financial products offered by financial institutions serving low-income populations as niche markets.

A second substrategy should provide elements for the best financial decision-making. While this strategy, in which both regulators and financial institutions tend to participate actively, can also help display the benefits of formal products, it has generally been geared more towards providing educational services to people who often were already included. Although this substrategy has its benefits, several studies have noted that, to increase inclusion, a strategy that reduces the cost of entry and participation is superior to the provision of financial education. For example, Cole, Sampson and Zia (2010) find that financial education has no discernible effect on the opening of a savings account; but a programme based on financial subsidies that can raise the interest rate on deposits does have a significant effect.

5. Regulatory framework

Lastly, to ensure that the proposed strategies do not jeopardize the financial system, a fifth strategy is needed to implement a set of measures to reduce the problems of asymmetric information that may have an impact on credit risk and the financial solvency of credit institutions. These include strengthening

[16] Alongside the creation of this instrument, the strategy also involves the creation of mobile branches that enable financial operations to be carried out by mobile phone.

the credit information industry (also known as credit bureaus) to provide positive and negative information to clients and extend their scope of action to financial operations in the rural sector. Secondly, the government plays a major role in the supply of financing in many countries. So it is essential to rationalize this supply in order to prevent over-borrowing and holding back financial development. To this end, the public institutions and programmes that offer financing need to share their credit information with credit bureaus. The latter measure aims to reduce the cost of asymmetric information that disproportionately affects population sectors that do not participate in formal labour or goods markets and which are usually low-income groups or rural inhabitants.[17]

A second type of measure entails re-examining those sections of the regulatory framework governing the operations of financial institutions that may impair access to financial products and services. For example, the relevance of a regulation that restricts lending to businesses that have been in existence for less than two years needs to be reviewed. It is also necessary to analyse the reasons underlying a regulation that unnecessarily increases the provisions that a banking institution must create in respect of group loans. On the savings side, the regulation restricts incentives to capture private savings through the regulatory cost generated by certain anti-money-laundering measures. Here, it is necessary to analyse whether this regulation manages to reduce illicit activities or if its main cost is to reduce incentives to attract deposits.

A third and last measure involves the strengthening of consumer protection regulations. This is very important because evidence shows that —even when the information is transparent— potential customers who are capital-poor and of lower education level are more vulnerable to abuse.

Even if adaptations are made in the supply of financial products and demand is increased, it needs to be remembered that the direction of causality runs from economic growth towards financial development (Levine, 2005). Thus, changes of a financial nature on their own are not enough to increase potential inclusion and close the gap. It is also necessary to make changes that afford social validity to the rule of law and enhance the productivity of economic activities.[18]

---

17 There are other measures that seek to enhance the profitability of projects in the rural sector while mitigating the impact of climate risks; but these are beyond the scope of this study. For information on this type of measure, see IFC (2011) for example.

18 In the case of small-scale rural producers, it is necessary to analyse the proposals made by the IFC (2011) to set up producer associations as a way of increasing productivity. Although Latin America does not have a successful history of such partnerships, it is important to consider why the opposite is true in many developed countries. On this point, the reader is recommended to review the vast literature available in the *Annals of Public and Cooperative Economics*.

Bibliography

Aghion, P. and P. Bolton (1997), "A theory of trickle-down growth and development", The Review of *Economic Studies*, vol. 64, No. 2, Stockholm, Stockholm University, April.

Alexander-Tedeschi, G. and D. Karlan (2006), "Microfinance Impact: Bias from Dropouts", Financial Access Initiative/Innovations for Poverty Action [online] http://aida.econ.yale.edu/karlan/papers/MicrofinanceDropouts.pdf.

Allen, F. and others (2012), "The foundations of financial inclusion: understanding ownership and use of formal accounts", *Policy Research Working Paper*, No. 6290, Washington, D.C., World Bank.

Ayyagari, M., A. Demirgüç-Kunt and V. Maksimovic (2010), "Formal versus informal finance: evidence from China", *Review of Financial Studies*, vol. 23, No. 8, Oxford, Oxford University Press.

Banerjee, A. and A. Newman (1993), "Occupational choice and the process of development", *Journal of Political Economy*, vol. 101, No. 2, Chicago, University of Chicago Press.

Banerjee, A. and E. Duflo (2007), "The economic lives of the poor", *Journal of Economic Perspectives*, vol. 21, No. 1, Nashville, American Economic Association.

___(2004), "Do firms want to borrow more? Testing credit constraints using a directed lending programme", *CEPR Discussion Paper*, No. 4681, London, Centre for Economic Policy Research.

Bazán Levy, L. and G. A. Saraví (2012), *La monetarización de la pobreza: estrategias financieras de los hogares mexicanos*, Mexico City, Centre for Research and Higher Learning in Social Anthropology.

Beck, T. and E. Feyen (2013), "Benchmarking financial systems. Introducing the financial possibility frontier", *Policy Research Working Paper*, No. 6615, Washington, D.C., World Bank.

Beck, T., A. Demirgüç-Kunt and M. Martínez Pería (2007), "Reaching out: access to and use of banking services across countries", *Journal of Financial Economics*, vol. 85, No. 1, Amsterdam, Elsevier.

Beck, T., A. Demirgüç-Kunt and R. Levine (2007), "Finance, inequality and the poor", *Journal of Economic Growth*, vol. 12, No. 1, Berlin, Springer.

CAF (Development Bank of Latin America) (2011), *Servicios financieros para el desarrollo: promoviendo el acceso en América Latina*, Caracas [online] http://www.caf.com/media/3895/RED2011.pdf.

Claessens, S. (2006), "Access to financial services: a review of the issues and public policy objectives", *The World Bank Research Observer*, vol. 21, No. 2, Oxford, World Bank/Oxford University Press.

Cole, S., T. Sampson and B. Zia (2010), "Prices or knowledge? What drives demand for financial services in emerging markets?", *Harvard Business School Working Paper*, No. 09-117, Cambridge, Harvard University.

Collins, D. and others (2009), *Portfolios of the Poor: How the World's Poor live on $2 a Day*, Princeton, Princeton University Press.

Cotler, P. (2015) "Crédito de proveedores, tamaño de empresa e informalidad", *El Trimestre Económico*, vol. 82-3, No. 327, Mexico City, Fondo de Cultura Económica, July-September.

Cotler, P. and C. Woodruff (2008), "The impact of short-term credit on microenterprises: evidence from the *Fincomun-Bimbo* Programme in Mexico", *Economic Development and Cultural Change*, vol. 56, No. 4, Chicago, University of Chicago Press, July.

Cotler, P. and E. Rodríguez-Oreggia (2010), "Microfinanzas y la tenencia de activos no financieros en México", *Investigación Económica*, vol. 69, No. 274, Mexico City, National Autonomous University of Mexico (UNAM), October-December.

Dabla-Norris, E. and others (2015a), "Financial inclusion: zooming in on Latin America", *IMF Working Paper*, No. 15/206, Washington, D.C., International Monetary Fund (IMF).

___(2015b), "Identifying constraints to financial inclusion and their impact on GDP and inequality: a structural framework for policy", *IMF Working Paper*, No. 15/22, Washington, D.C., International Monetary Fund (IMF).

Duflo, E. and others (2013), "The miracle of microfinance? Evidence from a randomized evaluation", *NBER Working Paper*, No. 18950, Cambridge, Massachusetts, National Bureau of Economic Research (NBER).

Dupas, P. and J. Robinson (2013), "Savings constraints and microenterprise development: evidence from a field experiment in Kenya", *American Economic Journal: Applied Economics*, vol. 5, No. 1, Nashville, American Economic Association.

Fang, H., R. Ke and L. Zhou (2015), "Rosca meets formal credit market", *NBER Working Paper*, No. 21683, Cambridge, Massachusetts, National Bureau of Economic Research (NBER).

Hermes, N. and R. Lensink (2011), "Microfinance: its impact, outreach, and sustainability", *World Development*, vol. 39, No. 6, Amsterdam, Elsevier.

IFC (International Finance Corporation) (2011), "Scaling Up Access to Finance for Agricultural SMEs. Policy Review and Recommendations", Washington, D.C. [online] https://www.gpfi.org/sites/default/files/documents/G20_Agrifinance_Report%20%28FINAL%20ONLINE%29.pdf.

IMF (International Monetary Fund) (2015), "Financial Access Survey" [online] http://data.imf.org/?sk=E5DCAB7E-A5CA-4892-A6EA-598B5463A34C.

Karlan, D., A. Lakshmi and J. Zinman (2014), "Savings by and for the poor: a research review and agenda", *Review of Income and Wealth*, vol. 60, No. 1, Ottawa, International Association for Research in Income and Wealth (IARIW), March.

Karlan, D. and M. Valdivia (2011), "Teaching entrepreneurship: impact of business training on microfinance clients and institutions", *Review of Economics and Statistics*, vol. 93, No. 2, Cambridge, Massachusetts, MIT Press, May.

Karlan, D. and J. Zinman (2010), "Expanding credit access: using randomized supply decisions to estimate the impacts", *The Review of Financial Studies*, vol. 23, No. 1, Oxford, Oxford University Press, January.

Khandker, S. and H. Samad (2014), "Dynamic effects of microcredit in Bangladesh", *Policy Research Working Paper*, No. 6821, Washington, D.C., World Bank.

Labie, M, C. Laureti and A. Szafarz (2013), "Flexible products in microfinance: overcoming the demand–supply mismatch", *CEB Working Paper*, No. 13/044, Brussels, Free University of Brussels.

Lensink, R., R. Servin and M. Van Den Berg (2017), "Do savings and credit institutions reduce vulnerability? New evidence from Mexico", *Review of Income and Wealth*, vol. 63, No. 2, Wiley.

Levine, R. (2005), "Finance and growth: theory and evidence", *Handbook of Economic Growth*, vol. 1, part A, P. Aghion and S. N. Durlauf (eds.), Amsterdam, Elsevier.

López-Moctezuma, C. (2013), "Implementación de canales alternativos para la oferta de servicios financieros en México", *Las microfinanzas en México: instrumento de desarrollo e inclusión financiera*, P. Cotler and P. López (coords.), Mexico City, Mexican Institute of Finance Executives.

Mallick, D. (2012), "Microfinance and moneylender interest rate: evidence from Bangladesh", *World Development*, vol. 40, No. 6, Amsterdam, Elsevier.

Martínez Pería, M. (2014), "Financial inclusion in Latin America and the Caribbean", *Emerging Issues in Financial Development: Lessons from Latin America*, T. Didier and S. Schmukler (eds.), Washington, D.C., World Bank.

Morduch, J. (1998), "Does microfinance really help the poor? New evidence from flagship programmes in Bangladesh", Stanford, Stanford University, unpublished.

Pearlman, S. (2012), "Too vulnerable for microfinance? Risk and vulnerability as determinants of microfinance selection in Lima", *Journal of Development Studies*, vol. 48, No. 9, Abingdon, Routledge.

Petersen, M. and R. Rajan (1997), "Trade credit: theories and evidence", *Review of Financial Studies*, vol. 10, No. 3, Oxford, Oxford University Press.

Pitt, M. and S. Khandker (1998), "The impact of group-based credit programmes on poor households in Bangladesh: does the gender of participants matter?", *Journal of Political Economy*, vol. 106, No. 5, Chicago, University of Chicago Press.

Roa, M. (2015), "Financial inclusion in Latin America and the Caribbean: access, usage and quality", *Research Papers*, No. 19, Mexico City, Centre for Latin American Monetary Studies (CEMLA).

Rutherford, S. (2000), *The Poor and Their Money*, Oxford, Oxford University Press.

Schneider, F., A. Buehn and C. Montenegro (2010), "Shadow economies all over the world. New estimates for 162 countries from 1999 to 2007", *Policy Research Working Paper*, No. 5356, Washington, D.C., World Bank.

Soto, I. (2015), "Avances en la inclusión financiera en la región centroamericana, Panamá y República Dominicana", *Notas Económicas Regionales*, No. 84, San Jose, Executive Secretariat of the Central American Monetary Council.

Stiglitz, J. and A. Weiss (1981), "Credit rationing in markets with imperfect information", *American Economic Review*, vol. 71, No. 3, Nashville, American Economic Association.

Uchida, H., G. Udell and W. Watanabe (2006) "Are trade creditors relationship lenders?", *RIETI Discussion Paper Series*, No. 06-E-026, Tokyo, Research Institute of Economy, Trade and Industry.

Vanroose, A. and B. D'Espallier (2013), "Do microfinance institutions accomplish their mission? Evidence from the relationship between traditional financial sector development and microfinance institutions' outreach and performance", *Applied Economics*, vol. 45, No. 15, Abingdon, Routledge.

World Bank (2015a), *The Little Data Book on Financial Inclusion 2015*, Washington, D.C. [online] http://data.worldbank.org/products/data-books/little-data-book-on-financial-inclusion.

___(2015b), World Development Indicators [online] http://data.worldbank.org/data-catalog/world-development-indicators.

___(2014), Global Findex Database [online] http://datatopics.worldbank.org/financialinclusion.

___(undated), Global Financial Development [online] http://databank.worldbank.org/data/reports.aspx?source=global-financial-development

Xu, L. and B. Zia (2012), "Financial literacy around the world: an overview of the evidence with practical suggestions for the way forward", *Policy Research Working Paper*, No. 6107, Washington, D.C., World Bank.

Zeller, M. and M. Sharma, (2002), "Access to and demand for financial services by the rural poor: a multicountry synthesis", *The Triangle of Microfinance: Financial Sustainability, Outreach and Impact*, M. Zeller and R. Meyer (eds.), Baltimore, John Hopkins University Press/International Food Policy Research Institute (IFPRI).

Chapter III

Recent developments, current situation and prospects for financial inclusion among small-scale rural producers in Costa Rica

José Antonio Vásquez R.[1]
Melvin Bermúdez[2]
Ronald Rojas[3]
José Antonio Vásquez C.[4]

Introduction

In Costa Rica, efforts to increase the supply of credit to small-scale producers in rural areas have historically gone hand in hand with the development of public banks. Rural credit boards, sponsored by the National Bank of Costa Rica since their inception, and the nationalization of banks since 1948, laid the foundations for financial inclusion. This was achieved through credit targeted on agricultural production and the opening of bank branches virtually throughout the country. The transition from an agro-export development model to a model based on exports of services and manufacturing resulted

---

1 Holds a master's degree in Business Administration from INCAE Business School, and has experience in areas of strategy, finance and technology.

2 Holds a master's degree in Development Project Management and a master's degree in Business Administration from the Technological Institute of Costa Rica; Economics graduate from the National University of Costa Rica, with experience in rural development projects in Costa Rica.

3 Former National Credit Director at the National Bank of Costa Rica.

4 Former Deputy General Manager at the National Bank of Costa Rica.

in a steady decline in lending to small-scale rural producers and thus undermined the process of financial inclusion from which they had benefited for many years with these instruments.

Trust funds, which emerged in the 1990s as a vehicle for providing support to farmers, have been a constant feature of governments' strategies to assist small-scale rural producers. The National Development Trust (FINADE), created following the passing of the Development Banking System Law in 2008, is the most explicit instrumentation of a public policy targeted on agricultural production and, hence on small-scale rural producers in Costa Rica.

In terms of the tools available to promote financial inclusion, Costa Rica has a broad legal and regulatory framework for financial entities regulated by the General Superintendency of Financial Entities (SUGEF). Nonetheless, institutional coordination in applying the relevant rules is weak. The absence of a comprehensive public policy to promote financial inclusion hampers the effective inclusion of diverse segments of the population, particularly small-scale rural producers. The liberalization of the telecommunications sector since 2009 has encouraged the use of information and communication technology (ICT) platforms by the financial sector. Online transactions and mobile payments are clear examples of the positive effects of the sector's liberalization.

The specific programmes of the Superintendency of Telecommunications (SUTEL), implemented through the programmes of the National Telecommunications Fund (FONATEL), aim to reduce the digital divide in rural areas, promoting financial inclusion in services complementary to the supply of credit. Lastly, the presence of publicly-owned banks, with 531 branches and over 1,400 automatic teller machines (ATMs) across all regions of the country, offers a broad platform for financial inclusion among rural producers. Nonetheless, this population segment still lacks a specific financial education programme.

This chapter analyses the strategies implemented in Costa Rica to promote the financial inclusion of small-scale rural producers through formal financial institutions. Section A describes the evolution and current situation of financial inclusion in Costa Rica, focusing on the provision of financial services in rural areas; and section B outlines initiatives that have fostered financial inclusion in the country. Section C reviews the current institutional architecture, while section D identifies the available public policy instruments. Lastly, section E concludes with a discussion of the key challenges facing the financial inclusion of small-scale rural producers in Costa Rica.

A. Recent trends in financial service access and use

As illustrated by the figures reported in table III.1, Costa Rica is a small country with a per capita income slightly above the Latin American average, whose adult population is relatively young and still lives mainly in rural areas.

Table III.1
Costa Rica, Latin America and the Caribbean, and the rest of the world: selected indicators of financial inclusion, 2011-2014

Population category	World	Latin America and the Caribbean	Costa Rica
Population over 15 years of age *(millions)*	5 231.2	428.2	3.7
Per capital GDP *(US$)*	10 683.0	9 542.0	9 550.0
General data *(percentages of the population over 15 years of age)*			
Total adults	61.5	51.4	64.6
Women	58.1	48.6	60.2
Adults belonging to the poorest 40%	54.0	41.2	61.3
Young adults (15-24 years of age)	46.3	37.4	61.6
Adults living in rural zones	56.7	46.0	67.3
Account in a financial institution *(percentages of the population over 15 years of age)*			
Total adults, 2014	60.7	51.1	64.6
Total adults, 2011	50.6	39.3	50.4
Access to an account in financial institutions *(percentages of the population over 15 years of age)*			
Account with debit card, 2014	40.1	40.4	53.6
Account with credit card, 2011	30.5	28.9	43.8
ATM as main withdrawal mode *(percentages of those with an account)*, 2014		71.1	83.2
ATM as main withdrawal mode *(percentages of those with an account)*, 2011	48.3	57.0	72.2
Digital payments in last year *(percentages of the population over 15 years of age)*			
Uses a debit card to make payments	23.2	27.7	35.3
Uses a credit card to make payments	15.1	18.0	10.8
Uses Internet to pay bills or make purchases	16.6	6.9	10.4
Savings in the last year *(percentages of the population over 15 years of age)*			
Savings in a financial institution, 2014	27.4	13.5	24.2
Savings in a financial institution, 2011	22.6	9.6	19.9
Credit in the last year *(percentages of the population over 15 years of age)*			
Loans from a financial institution, 2014	10.7	11.3	12.7
Loans from a financial institution, 2011	9.1	7.9	10.0

Source: Prepared by the authors, on the basis of figures from World Bank, Global Findex Database, 2014 [online] http://datatopics.worldbank.org/financialinclusion.

In general terms, indicators of access to, and use of, formal financial services show Costa Rica in a favourable light compared with both Latin America and the rest of the world. The proportion of adults who hold an account in a formal financial institution rose from 50.4% in 2011 to 64.6% in 2014. This rate surpasses not only the regional, but also the world average, and is reflected in the percentage of the population that uses debit cards and ATMs. On the use of financial services, however, the evidence is more varied. While Costa Rica's position relative to the region and the world remains positive in terms of credit use, its use of savings instruments is below the world average.

The figures on transfers, savings and credit show Costa Rica to be lagging in the use of mobile services as a means of payment. This can be explained by the relatively late liberalization of the telecommunications sector in Costa Rica. Until 2008, the sector's economic model featured the monopolistic provision of telecommunications services by the Costa Rican Electricity Institute (ICE), a situation that generated major gaps that still persist with respect to the rest of Latin America.[5] Nonetheless, the implementation of mobile payment systems, notably SINPE Móvil, launched in 2015, should have a positive impact on the distribution of financial services through mobile platforms.

According to figures published by the Costa Rican Banking Association (Camacho and Jiménez, 2010), the population with access to financial services grew from 46.3% in 2010 to 58.2% in 2015, mainly owing to the expansion of bank coverage. This expansion compensated for reductions in the coverage of non-bank financial entities, which retreated from 5.3% to 3.5%, and in the use of informal financial services, which fell from 4.8% to 2.1% over the same period.

The most widely used financial product is a current account denominated in the national currency (the *colón*), used mainly by men between 35 and 44 years of age, belonging to the upper socioeconomic level. While 61% of those surveyed in the Greater San José metropolitan area have a savings account, the proportion rises to 66% in the rest of the country. The main reasons mentioned for not having a savings account include insufficient income and a preference for using cash.

When account-holders were questioned about the reasons for holding a savings account, 70.7% of respondents indicated that they had opened it voluntarily, while 23.1% and 8.8%, respectively, said they held the account as a requirement or decision, either by their employer, presumably for paying wages, or by an institution, in particular to receive deposits from non-contributory schemes administered by the Costa Rican Social Security Fund.

[5] ICE holds the State monopoly on electricity generation and distribution and telecommunications.

A mapping exercise performed by the national newspaper *El Financiero* found that Costa Rica has 764 bank branches and 2,334 ATMs. While nearly half of the branches and ATMs are located in the San José area, most of the country's cantons have at least one bank branch. Although the entity with the largest number of branches is the Bank of Costa Rica (Banco de Costa Rica), the bank with the broadest cantonal coverage is the National Bank of Costa Rica (Banco Nacional de Costa Rica).

B. Financial inclusion initiatives

This section describes the main financial inclusion initiatives that the Government has implemented over the last 30 years, highlighting the motivations and the objectives pursued, along with the institutional framework through which they have operated. In the recent past, ICT access has played a key role in expanding financial inclusion to rural areas. These technologies have, among other things, succeeded in fostering access to telephony and mobile connectivity through telecommunication providers, a situation considered as one of the key turning points in terms of financial inclusion processes in rural areas.

The section starts with a general presentation of the composition of production in rural areas in Costa Rica and ends with an analysis of perceptions of the scope of financial inclusion that has been achieved, especially targeting rural areas.

1. Composition of production in the rural area

Like most Latin American countries, Costa Rica's productive development has been essentially agricultural since colonial times, based, since the second half of the nineteenth century, on the production and export of coffee, and on products obtained from industrial-scale sugarcane processing and bananas. As the population grew and migrated to urban centres, agricultural production moved increasingly into outlying areas. Three socio-productive milestones have marked development in the peripheral and rural regions of the country.

The first milestone occurred in the 1830s, when coffee-growing began and paved the way for Costa Rica's entry into the international market. The second stemmed from the development of railways in the 1880s and the introduction of bananas, which were mainly grown by foreign firms on an enclave basis, thereby restricting the development of the country's peripheral and rural areas. The most recent milestone event occurred in the 1980s, when, due to the crisis of the agro-export model, Costa Rica's production structure underwent a major shift. The adoption of structural adjustment programmes meant the abandonment of subsidies for agricultural activities such as the cultivation of basic grains, coffee and bananas, which were giving way to non-traditional products such as pineapple, but above all to an economy oriented more towards trade and services.

Since production activities have a direct relationship with financing sources, the availability of credit to rural producers suffered from the reduction in agriculture's contribution to the Costa Rican economy; and it was only possible to sustain them through time thanks to the expansion strategy implemented by public banks.

Figure III.1 shows how the number of farms grew steadily from 1950 to 1984, but thereafter started to decline as a result of a change in the socio-productive activity undertaken in the country, which, in recent years, has focused on microprocessor production, tourism, and commerce in general.

Figure III.1
Costa Rica: number of farms per census, 1950-2014[a]

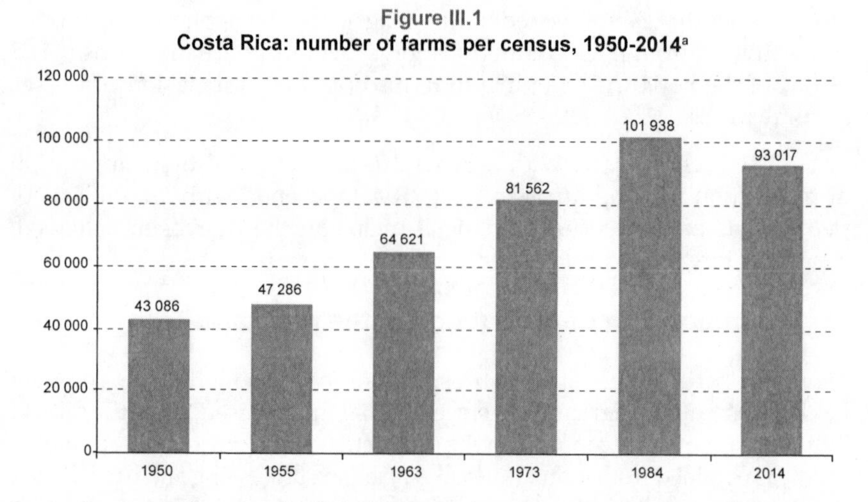

Source: Prepared by the authors, on the basis of National Institute of Statistics and Censuses, "VI Censo Nacional Agropecuario. Características de las fincas y de las personas productoras", San José, 2015.

[a] The censuses of 1950, 1955 and 1963 defined a farm (*finca*) as an area of land the size of one block or more. The censuses of 1973, 1984 and 2014 did not have this restriction.

Census data show that coffee growing and livestock farming are the main activities in more than 52% of Costa Rican farms, and are the most traditional farming activities. By province, the largest number of farms is registered in the province of Alajuela, with 25,176 (27%), since this province contains eminently rural cantons such as those located in the north. The "outlying" provinces jointly account for 37% of the farms registered in the census, distributed as follows: Limón 9.7%, Guanacaste 11.7% and Puntarenas, Costa Rica's largest province, 15.6%.

The reduction in the number of farms has been an outcome of the urbanization process unfolding in the country. This has been accompanied by an increase in average farm size —especially in the province of Guanacaste, where large sugarcane, rice and cattle farms are located, and in the province of Puntarenas, where production is concentrated in oil palm, rice and pineapple.

2. Evolution of the financial system

The Costa Rican financial system has several specific features worth analysing, which have influenced the prevailing degree of financial inclusion, even in the absence of a comprehensive public policy on the subject.

As noted above, the introduction and expansion of coffee growing caused major changes in the Costa Rican economy. One of these was the appearance of the first banks around 1863 with the creation of Banco Anglo Costarricense, constituted with private capital. In 1872 the first project of the rural mortgage lender, Banco Rural de Crédito Hipotecario, was launched with the aim of promoting and assisting agriculture, combined with a reduction in interest rates. In 1914, the Government tasked Banco Internacional with creating and organizing agricultural credit boards, prioritizing the districts that contributed relatively more to supplying the economy.[6] The creation of Banco Internacional had a positive effect on Costa Rican society, especially in the rural area, due to the financial support it gave to agriculture.

Since their creation, public banks have been involved in the process of financing activities in rural areas, such that there is at least one branch of a public bank in 78 of Costa Rica's 81 cantons.

Of the three public banks (Banco Nacional de Costa Rica, Banco de Costa Rica and Banco Crédito Agrícola de Cartago), and also taking into account the Popular Bank (Banco Popular) which was created by a special law, Banco Nacional has operated a financial inclusion policy since its inception. The implementation of the rural credit boards, which will be explained below, represents the clearest example of how this bank managed to reach the most remote parts of Costa Rica.

In the past, the main and most successful institution dedicated to lending to small-scale producers in Costa Rica was the rural credit department of Banco Nacional. Since 1914, with the creation of the rural credit services (*cajas*) in the International Bank of Costa Rica, the authorities have shown interest in improving rural producers' access to credit. Two important institutional innovations were introduced with the *cajas*, which largely explained their success.

---

6 Banco Internacional, which in 1933 changed its name to Banco Nacional de Costa Rica (National Bank of Costa Rica), is publicly owned.

First, the allocation of credit was entrusted to a board of five neighbours who had considerable autonomy to decide who was creditworthy. Second, the members of the boards were responsible for loan recovery (which they guaranteed with a personal mortgage), and for some time the bank paid them a commission for recovered loans.

The situation of the indebted small-scale producer worsened in the First World War, when many were unable to keep up their payments and thus forfeited crops and properties. Banco Internacional proposed that the rural boards should be district-based. Initially, they would be set up in districts known for their contribution to food supply and capable of producing better results, owing both to the resources available and to human capital.

The boards had a minimum of three and a maximum of five members, who had to be over 25 years of age, local residents, farmers and property-owners without liens. Having been chosen by the bank, board members would select the chairperson, secretary and treasurer from among their number. Once organized, the Bank would allocate the money it considered suitable for agricultural development in the chosen district. People seeking a loan had to explain how the money would be used, the period of return and the collateral offered to the bank. Each request was reviewed by the board members, who had to ensure that the collateral was satisfactory, the money would be paid back within a year, and that it would be used in agricultural work.

In 1938, Banco Nacional issued a new regulation bringing the rural boards within the section of Rural Boards of Agricultural Credit, which was tasked with directing and controlling their operations, organizing rural credit under rational rules, and educating the small-scale producer. The boards would appoint an inspector delegate, who had to be an agronomist or someone with thorough knowledge of the region and its agricultural production. Under the new regulation, the rural boards were organized in circuits, the first four of which were Puriscal, Orotina, Santa Cruz de Guanacaste and Turrialba. The activities that the rural boards financed were quite diverse and included traditional export products such as coffee, sugar cane and livestock, along with staple products such as maize, rice and beans.

Since their founding in 1914, the rural boards were not only in charge of providing working capital credit for agricultural supplies, cattle breeding, rebuilding or rural development, but also for providing technical assistance. Assistance was considered vital for farmers to achieve, in the medium and long term, the economic and social progress that the National Bank proposed from the outset. After 1950, the rural boards continued to allocate credit for the development of subsistence farming (basic grains) and commercial agriculture (coffee, bananas, cocoa, sugar cane).

Interest in developing cattle farming also increased, when the country entered the international market with the export of meat and the domestic market was energized, and there was a clear intention to introduce technology into the Costa Rican countryside by mechanizing agriculture. The rural boards worked on this task for several years with the Technical Service for Agricultural Cooperation and the National Production Council.

As all provinces in Costa Rica were served by two or more boards, Banco Nacional contributed to the provision of rural credit services throughout the country. The expansion of the rural boards and their importance for rural finance continued during the 1950s and 1960s, but by the mid-1970s, and especially with the economic crisis of the early 1980s, the importance of the boards declined. This contraction, which is evident in the number of operations and in the amounts provided, occurred both at the geographic level and by activities.

With the change in Costa Rica's production model and with the liberalization of the financial sector in 1998, Banco Nacional's rural boards disappeared. Nonetheless, following the creation of the Banking System for Development (SBD), and with the aim of achieving the regionalization goal, a project has recently been proposed to resuscitate the rural board mechanism, for the purpose of extending SBD funds to rural producers.

The Costa Rican financial system, established by the National Banking System Organic Law (Law No. 1644), promulgated on 26 September 1953, together with the Organic Law of the Central Bank of Costa Rica (Law No. 1552), of 23 April 1953 and its subsequent amendments, defines the constitution, nature, operations and provisions that govern banking activity in the country. These laws were created to put banking activities on an organized footing, and to authorize the operation of private banks. At that time, the only private bank was Banco Lyon, and its functions were limited by the Bank Nationalization Decree (1948), which precluded it from accepting demand deposits from the public. Its main source of funding were time deposits known as investment certificates.

In the first few months of the Carazo administration (1978-1982), a wide-ranging debate was aroused around the national banking system. A campaign was conducted to demonstrate that nationalized banking was subject to political rather than economic criteria and that the institutions in question were unable to respond to the country's needs. The possibility of ending the State's monopoly on deposits was again raised with a view to allowing competition between private banks. During the Carazo administration, a number of measures were approved which, while not implying a break in the monopoly of demand deposits, represented a step towards the decision to leave them to the free play of economic market forces.

These possibilities were supported by the Ministry of Finance and the Board of Directors of the Central Bank. The reform of the Currency Law (Ley de la Moneda), passed on 19 August 1984, afforded greater scope of action to private banks and allowed access to Central Bank credit programmes on the same footing as State banks. In a period of 30 years, and under these conditions, four private banks were constituted: (i) Banco Lyon, S.A. (April 14, 1947); (ii) Bank of Central America, S.A., currently BAC San José (September 19, 1968); (iii) Banco de Santander, later Banco Fincomer, S.A. (December 6, 1977); and (iv) Banco del Comercio, S.A. (February 5, 1979).

In the 1980s there was a surge in the creation of private banks. In 1988, the Central Bank authorized these entities to raise funds through certificates of deposit. In the same year Banco Banex and Banco Internacional de Exportaciones, S.A. started operations, although the latter filed for bankruptcy in the late 1980s.

In 1982, three new banks were created: Banco Cooperativo Costarricense, R.L., Banco Interfin, S.A. And Weeden Bank Internacional, S.A. (declared bankrupt in 1989). In 1984, Banco BCT, S.A. and the Banco de Fomento Agrícola, S.A opened for business. In 1985, three more banks started operating: Banco de la Industria, S.A., Banco Metropolitano, S.A. and the Cooperative Bank of Alajuela, R.L. In 1986 Banco Continental and Banco Cofisa, S.A., were established; and, in 1987, Banco Mercantil de Costa Rica and Banco Germano Centroamericano were created, the latter filing for bankruptcy in 2000.

Over the years, several advantages of private banking were identified, among them the greater flexibility to contract goods and services, and a much more flexible staffing regime. Although prudential regulation and supervision applies to public and private banks alike, the former are subject to closer scrutiny, under constitutional principles governing the public sector, such as the principle of legality, access to administrative procedures, audit by the Comptroller General's Office, and others.

Currently, very few private banks operate in peripheral areas providing finance to rural producers, since these entities serve the niche market of medium-sized and large firms. Recently, only BAC San José has implemented a small-business financing project, but this programme does not target rural producers, but rather full-functioning enterprises in the formal sector.

As is the case in countries such as Argentina and Mexico, the trust fund mechanism targeting rural producers was set up in Costa Rica as a public-policy instrument that has made it possible to solve specific problems. Use of a trust fund, as a legal instrument through which assets, cash flows, business, rights and so forth can be ring-fenced in an independent fund for specific purposes, has been spreading in Costa Rica for some 20 years.

In general, trust funds have been used as the main public policy tool to implement government actions targeting the agriculture sector, especially when international cooperation funds are received or when, due to a particular situation, it is necessary to serve a specific region or activity.

Perhaps the most important trust for rural development is the Farming and Livestock Protection and Development *Trust* for Small and Medium-sized Producers (FIDAGRO), created in 2001 with the purpose of reactivating production units.[7]

3. The liberalization of telecommunications and their role in financial inclusion

The fundamental role of ICTs in everyday activities in the modern world is undisputed. This section highlights the crucial role played by ICT access for expanding financial inclusion to rural areas. Among other things, in recent years, these technologies have managed to broaden access to telephony and mobile connectivity through telecommunications providers, a situation that has been considered one of the key turning points in terms of rural financial inclusion processes.

The Law Creating the Costa Rican Electricity Institute (Law No. 449) of 8 April 1949 authorized ICE to provide telecommunications services, with the consequent assignment of frequencies of the radioelectric spectrum for its use. From the outset, Law No. 449, created a multisectoral institute, specifically linked to the development of electricity production. Accustomed to a monopolistic scenario, ICE and its companies constitute the so-called "historical operator", due to its dominant share of the national market.

Law No. 449 was amended by Law No. 3226 of 28 October 1963, which, more specifically, provided ICE with the powers to operate networks and supply telecommunications services, establishing the conditions for providing the service as a public utility.

The October 1963 reform gives the public enterprise specific responsibilities for developing the activity of the telecommunications sector. At the same time, Law No. 3293 of 18 June 1964, created Radiográfica Costarricense, S.A. (RACSA) by transferring the telecommunication services concession referred to above to ICE; and the latter, in turn, joined RACSA, a joint stock corporation which for a long time had held a large share of the Internet access market.

---

[7] For the purpose of the trust fund, small agricultural producers are defined as all producers who operate economic units in which family participation is 75%; their farm or productive activity and most of the production is for subsistence, with only surpluses being placed on the domestic market; and annual gross income is under US$ 25,000 (or the equivalent thereof in national currency).

Current telecommunication regulations are incomplete and disperse. Both ICE and RACSA have enjoyed special status and, in practice, have operated under a "de facto monopoly." The scope of the legal powers of the multisectoral regulatory authority, the Public Services Regulatory Authority (ARESEP), was quite restricted with respect to the telecommunications sector, with relatively narrow regulatory functions, as is clear from the Law on the Public Utilities Regulatory Authority (Law No. 7593) of 9 August 1996. The telecommunications services provided by ICE were the only services subject to regulation. Public entities, such as RACSA, were not regulated by ARESEP.

Telecommunication services in Costa Rica have historically been supplied under a public monopoly. Nonetheless, due to increasing international commercial activity and various issues related to free trade, in 2008 the country began a process of opening up this market. This allowed the entry of new telecommunications enterprises and brought with it greater technological progress and easier access to these services, which, in turn, caused a break with the natural monopoly paradigms which formed the basis for the maintenance of public-sector monopolies.

In keeping with the trade liberalization processes that have unfolded since the mid-1990s and culminating in the signing of the Dominican Republic - Central America-United States Free Trade Agreement (CAFTA-DR), Costa Rica was forced to join the new reality in the telecommunications sector, a situation that was consolidated following the breakup of the monopoly that until 2008 had been held by the ICE telecommunications area.

In general, Costa Rica has opted for a liberalization model that is regulated and guided by the State, under an approach conceived from the standpoint of competitiveness and human development of the population. The sector's transformative regulatory framework sees liberalization in terms of competition with effective regulation, with clear policies defining the sector's development process. This model aims to guarantee effective competition, fostering market transparency, which generates benefits for the end-user of the services, as well as a continuous flow of investment in the sector for its development.

The model also aims to be inclusive and seeks non-discriminatory access to telecommunications services for all inhabitants, regardless of their geographical or socioeconomic status. In the regional trade context, and beyond the commitment made by Costa Rica under CAFTA-DR, recent legal initiatives reflect this dynamic new world order in telecommunication technologies.

Within this new context of telecommunication operations, where liberalization triggered competition among mobile telephony and Internet providers, it became necessary to create a specialized supervision body in this area.

Although Costa Rica has a multisectoral regulator (ARESEP), which is responsible for developing a regulatory framework on issues such as competition, access and interconnection, the framework of solidarity and universal access, the user protection regime and the price-setting system, a specialized regulatory body was set up as a critical condition for the success of liberalization. The creation of SUTEL, the top-level deconcentration body attached to ARESEP, meets this need.

In general, the liberalization of telecommunications represented a milestone in the expansion of access to mobile telephony and Internet. This has also had a significant impact on the financial inclusion process, because the development of technological and mobile platforms has implied a major qualitative and quantitative leap, enabling financial institutions to develop ever closer relations with the urban and rural population.

With the liberalization of telecommunications and the creation of SUTEL, the National Telecommunications Fund (FONATEL) was also created, which aims to bring telephony and Internet to areas and communities where there is still no service, promoting universal access, universal service and solidarity, as proclaimed in the General Telecommunications Law (Law No. 8642).

With these measures, FONATEL seeks to reduce the digital divide, ensure greater equality of opportunities, and enjoy the benefits of the information and knowledge society through the promotion of connectivity, infrastructure development and the availability of access devices and broadband services.

Thus far, FONATEL has implemented four programmes with potential to directly increase the rural population's access to connectivity, leading in principle to financial institutions offering their products and services to these areas. The following paragraphs give a brief explanation of these programmes.

Connected Communities Programme

This programme seeks to expand the supply of telecommunications services to the population and centres providing public services located in remote rural areas that are classified as socially, economically and culturally vulnerable. The centres in question include public schools and colleges, the headquarters of basic equipment for comprehensive health care, education and nutrition centres, and regional childcare centres and intelligent community centres.

Under this programme, FONATEL finances infrastructure deployment in the target areas, together with connectivity to the public utility delivery centres selected by the competent institutions.

The Connected Communities Programme is managed and executed by SUTEL and forms part of the Digital Solidarity Agenda of the National Telecommunication Development Plan and Costa Rica's Digital Strategy of (*Costa Rica Digital*), with the aim of universalizing telecommunication services throughout the country.

Connected Households Programme

This Programme is an initiative of SUTEL, in its role as administrator and executor of FONATEL programmes and projects. The aim is to provide a fixed Internet connection to prequalified households included in the databases of the Joint Institute for Social Aid (IMAS), together with a laptop computer that generates opportunities for development, education and productivity. FONATEL pays part of the cost of the Internet connection and laptop with funds provided by all of the country's telephone, internet and cable TV companies.

Connected Public Centres Programme

This initiative is being implemented by SUTEL in its role in the management and implementation of FONATEL, to provide broadband Internet access devices to public service delivery centres, including schools run by the Ministry of Public Education, Intelligent Community Centres, Education and Nutrition Centres, Comprehensive Childcare Centres, and the hospitals, health areas and clinics of the Costa Rican Social Security Fund, which have been connected to the Internet under the Connected Communities Programme. The programme plans to deliver a total of 40,000 devices in two stages during the 2016-2018 biennium. The Connected Public Centres Programme is also part of the Costa Rica Digital Programme being implemented by the Government.

Connected Public Areas Programme

This is another SUTEL initiative, through FONATEL, to provide a national broadband network offering free Internet access through wireless connections in public spaces of the main districts of the cantons selected using criteria provided by the State.

Through this Programme, FONATEL finances a high-capacity network for the siting of internet access points in public areas to allow users to access the Internet free of charge, with certain characteristics, such as time of use restrictions, user identification and security appropriate to the type of service, such as content blocking. The Connected Public Areas Programme is also part of the Government's *Costa Rica Digital* Programme.

4. Scope of public initiatives to promote financial inclusion

Although Costa Rica has no comprehensive public policy aimed at encouraging and regulating financial inclusion, in practice the Government has designed programmes and tools that have encouraged general financial inclusion. For rural producers, there are several specific initiatives directly related to the implementation of SBD, which are analysed below.

As noted above, the coverage of publicly owned banks and Banco Popular consists of 531 branches, with 1,402 ATMs located in all the capital towns of the cantons of Costa Rica, which is an important tool for financial inclusion.

Social protection systems, such as non-contributory pension schemes, IMAS assistance programmes or the National Scholarship Fund (FONABE), have required their beneficiaries to open savings accounts in a publicly owned bank, so that transfers can be made from these programmes to those accounts. This has also contributed to financial inclusion in Costa Rica.

The launch of accounts involving simplified formalities in the second half of 2015 is expected to enable 35% of citizens over 15 years of age who currently do not have access to formal financial services (1.4 million people) to open a saving account at a financial institution. This will allow them to start building a track record that qualifies them to access credit, savings and insurance products, and use the various channels available in the national financial system to manage money electronically.

The implementation of this new type of account will also provide financial entities with operational conditions enabling them to reduce the costs of complying with the "Know Your Customer" policy and target their supervision and monitoring activities on customers that pose potential money-laundering and terrorist-financing risks.

The simplified accounts also seek to ensure that low-income sectors have more opportunities to access the services supplied by financial institutions, by eliminating documentary and information requirements that currently disqualify them as customers and impose high costs relative to their economic possibilities.

In principle, the process of expanding the use of banking services through simplified accounts will grow the financial institutions' customer base and make it easier to introduce new services in the industry, thereby helping to make economic agents' saving, consumption and investment decisions more efficient.

The SINPE Móvil service is a new payment mechanism, built with support from the main financial institutions in Costa Rica, and technological support from the National Electronic Payment System (SINPE), which was put into operation in the central bank on 7 May 2015.

Thanks to this service, people who own an account in *colones* in a commercial bank, cooperative savings and loan or credit union, and have an active mobile phone line, have the possibility to execute payments from any online banking channel to a fund account associated with a mobile phone number.

The Development Banking System (SBD) comprises all public financial intermediaries and the National Institute of Cooperative Development (INFOCOOP), along with public institutions providing non-financial and business development services, and both State and non-State institutions or other organizations that channel public funds to finance and promote productive projects. The objective of the system is to fund and nurture viable productive projects, in accordance with Costa Rica's development model as it relates to the social mobility of beneficiary subjects:

- Entrepreneurs: person or group of people who have the motivation and ability to detect business opportunities, organize resources for their use and execute actions to obtain an economic or social benefit for them. This is viewed as a phase prior to the creation of a microenterprise.
- Microenterprises: business units with fewer than 15 employees.
- Small and medium-sized enterprises: business units with between 16 and 30 employees.
- Micro, small and medium-scale agricultural producers: production units that engage in manufacturing, marketing and commercialization processes that add value to agricultural, livestock, aquaculture, forestry, fisheries and other seafood products, in addition to the production and marketing of inputs, goods and services related to these activities.
- Business association models: cooperation mechanisms in which relationships or connections are established between any SBD beneficiaries.

The law prioritizes projects promoted by women, older adults, ethnic minorities, people with disabilities, young entrepreneurs, development associations and cooperatives, microcredits supplied through microfinance institutions, and projects that satisfy the parameters specified in the law. The projects in question must also be implemented in relatively less-developed areas defined by the social development index calculated by the Ministry of National Planning and Economic Policy (MIDEPLAN). These financial and non-financial support policies will afford these groups equitable access for to loans, endorsements, guarantees, conditions and non-financial services and business development. Priority will also be given to projects that incorporate or promote the concept of cleaner production, which is understood as an integrated preventive strategy that applies to processes, products and services to increase efficiency and reduce risks.

C. Institutional architecture

In the early 1980s a set of reforms was introduced to modernize the Costa Rican financial system. These include the liberalization of interest rates and credit, the opening up of the capital account, greater flexibility for private banks to raise funds, and improvements to the regulatory framework.

In the mid-1990s, the new Organic Law of the Central Bank of Costa Rica (Law No. 7558), eliminated the State monopoly over current account deposits, thereby fostering competition for deposits between State and private banks. The law also allowed private banks to access rediscount facilities with the Central Bank and accept deposits and other funding in foreign currency. In terms of supervision, the powers of SUGEF were strengthened and the National Council for the Supervision of the Financial System (CONASSIF) was created. The Superintendency of Pensions (SUPEN), the General Superintendency of Securities (SUGEVAL) and, more recently, the Superintendency of Insurance (SUGESE) were also created.

Regulatory changes transformed the financial environment. The key trends include: greater participation by private and regional banks and, more recently, also by international banks; merger and acquisition processes; strengthening of corporate and retail banking; and the disappearance of institutions that had high operating costs and low technological levels.

1. Financial intermediaries

As of May 2016, the Costa Rican financial system had 53 entities supervised by SUGEF. Table III.2 shows the trend of the number of intermediaries since 2000, which fell by 22 in total, mainly as a result of the mergers and acquisitions carried out by some of these entities and the disappearance of a number of non-bank financial firms.

Since 2000, new participants subject to SUGEF supervision have entered the market, such as specialized housing financiers and foreign exchange bureaus, and, more recently, entities that can participate in derivatives markets and others that can perform hedging operations. As Table III.2 shows, however, the national banking system still represents over 82% of the total assets of the national financial system, with publicly owned banks accounting for a dominant 40% share. According to SUGEF figures, of the total credit portfolio in the national banking system, only 3.4% is used to fund primary activities.

As of January 2016, the Costa Rican Network of Microenterprise Organizations (REDCOM) encompassed 18 development organizations providing microenterprise and small business financing. These served 13,952 customers, 41% of whom are women; and the credit portfolio totalled 30.7 million colones, 85% of which is located in rural areas.

Table III.2
Costa Rica: number of financial entities supervised by SUGEF/national financial system, 2000, 2005, 2009 and 2016[a]

Groups of entities	2000	2005	2009	2016
1. National banking system [b]	26	17	16	17
1.1. Publicly owned commercial banks	3	3	3	3
1.2. Banks created by special laws	2	2	2	2
1.3. Private and cooperative banks	21	12	11	12
2. Non-bank financial firms	13	9	6	5
3. Saving and loan cooperatives	26	28	31	25
4. Entities authorized for housing finance	4	3	3	2
5. Other financial entities	1	1	1	1
6. Foreign exchange market entities	5	2	3	3
Total No. of entities in the national financial system	75	60	60	53
7. Financial conglomerates and groups	21	22	22	19

Source: Prepared by the authors, on the basis of figures from the General Superintendency of Financial Entities (SUGEF).

[a] The figures for 2000, 2005 and 2009 correspond to December, while those for 2016 refer to May.

[b] Two of these entities can operate in the foreign exchange derivatives market, while two can also can hedge transactions with derivatives.

There is also a large network of microfinance institutions mainly serving the rural sector. Its fundamental characteristics include the fact that the entities in question are not regulated by SUGEF, they are governed by their own micro-lending regulations, and they lend to customers that the banking system would not consider creditworthy.

Microfinance is sourced from international cooperation, along with funds obtained through second-tier operations of the national banking system and more recently SBD.

The Central American and Caribbean Microfinance Network (REDCAMIF, 2015) characterizes Costa Rican microfinance institutions as small entities with few incentives to formalize and expand their activities owing to the large market share of publicly owned banks. In general, their portfolio size and number of clients are small compared to the figures of the microfinance sector at the regional level; and in terms of portfolio quality there has been an improvement associated with best practices in the management of the credit process. As most entities are unregulated, accounting quality and the level of transparency varies, with the highest standards seen only in institutions linked to microfinance networks. The same publication concludes that the transparency in prices, the level of customer protection and the information supplied by the credit risk registers are adequate.

The findings reported in a joint study by the Economist Intelligence Unit and the Inter-American Development Bank, titled *Global Microscope 2016. The Enabling Environment for Financial Inclusion* (EIU/IDB, 2016), show Costa Rica to be a laggard in adopting financial inclusion policies, starting with the application of specific regulations and specialized capacity-building and skills development through financial education and literacy programmes. The study notes that banks have not been active in granting loans to low-income customers, even though SBD requires them to allocate resources to specific products for the low-income population.

2. Financial services and distribution channels

The supply of financial services can be grouped into three categories, as shown in table III.3.

Table III.3
Costa Rica: supply of financial services

1. Funding products that comprise deposit services (they form part of the financial institution's liabilities)	2. Assets associated with loan products (they form part of the financial institution's assets)	3. Other types of products and services
(a) Electronic accounts	(a) Personal loan	(a) Transfers
(b) Current accounts	(b) Housing loan	(b) Sale and purchase of foreign currency
(c) Savings accounts	(c) Vehicle loan	(c) Foreign exchange derivatives
(d) Intelligent accounts	(d) Credit cards	(d) Digital signature
(e) Programmed savings	(e) Leasing	(e) Automatic payment of receipts
(f) Short-term investments	(f) Business loans	(f) Trusts
(g) Term deposit certificates	(g) Corporate loans	(g) ATMs
(h) Demand deposits	(h) Loans to micro, small and medium-sized enterprises (MSMEs)	
	(i) Agricultural loans	
	(j) Tourism loans	

Source: Prepared by the authors.

For the first group of services, the distribution channels include bank branches and bank correspondents, along with Internet and mobile banking. The latter channel offers facilities for managing short-term investments, but not for opening accounts. Under the partial reform of the general regulation on legislation against drug trafficking, related activities, money laundering, terrorist financing and organized crime of the Costa Rican Drug Institute, it is intended to streamline the opening of financial accounts and speed up the spread of banking services throughout the country.

For the second group of services, loans granted by financial institutions can be managed and paid through electronic media, such as Internet or mobile banking. Nonetheless, the initial granting of any of these products usually has to be done at a bank or correspondent branch.

For the third group, the products and services listed in (a), (b) and (e) can be accessed through digital media, while the other services need in-person support at a bank or correspondent branch.

The technology component is essential in the provision of financial services and serves as a cornerstone in any financial inclusion programme or strategy. Digital government and digital signature programmes have been central elements in the innovation process embarked upon by the Government several years ago, where public and private financial institutions have taken advantage of this substantive basis to be able to carry out online financial transactions.

3. Payment systems

Costa Rica's main payment system is SINPE. This technology platform, which is developed and managed by the Central Bank of Costa Rica, connects the country's financial entities and public institutions through a private telecommunications network that allows them to transfer funds between client accounts online, and to participate in the trading markets organized by the Central Bank. Entities involved in the national financial system and public institutions can participate in SINPE as associates.

This technological platform was launched on 17 April 1997 and started to operate with the cheque clearing and settlement service. Since then, other government services have been added, such as fund transfers to third parties, along with direct debits and credits.

According to figures from the Central Bank, the total value settled in SINPE as of December 2015 represented 9.5 times current GDP. In terms of individual services, transfers to third parties represent the largest traded value relative to total payments, followed by real-time debits and direct credits.

4. Mechanisms for protecting users of financial services

Law No. 7472 for the Promotion of Competition and Effective Consumer Protection designates the National Consumer Commission as the body that protects the rights of consumers, including users of financial services. In terms of computer security, the different superintendencies have a regulation that provides for the adequate management of information technology by regulated entities. There are no regulations on computer security for unregulated entities.

D. Public-policy instruments to promote the financial inclusion of small-scale rural producers

1. Second-tier banks

One of the objectives of second-tier banking is to facilitate access to financial services, mainly credit, to sectors that are not served by traditional banks. The main providers of second-tier services are publicly owned banks, saving and loan cooperatives, private banks and, more recently, SBD, which has focused on lending for agricultural development. The main entities that access second-tier funding are mutual organizations, cooperative systems, solidarity-based associations, microfinance institutions, foundations, corporations, cantonal agricultural centres and also development associations. They finance any type of productive activity that has technical and financial viability.

The funding used by organizations that engage in second-tier banking operations comes directly from the national financial system, international funders and, in some cases, international cooperation. In recent years, one of the second-tier bank funding sources that has gained strength is SBD, a mechanism designed to fund and expedite viable MSME projects in a timely and effective way.

The development banking system (SBD) aims to finance and promote projects that are productive, viable and technically and economically feasible, in line with the country's development model. This mechanism is based on the Development Banking System Law (Law No. 8634) of 2008 and the comprehensive reform adopted in 2014.

The development banking system provides priority funding to viable projects promoted by women, indigenous development associations, young entrepreneurs, cooperatives, small and medium-scale farmers and MSMEs.

The system operates mainly with funds obtained from three sources: (a) agricultural trusts (under which the National Development Trust (FINADE) has been created); (b) a 5% levy on the profits of public banks; and (c) a banking levy paid by private banks for the right to accept current account deposits.

The development banking system is chaired by a Governing Council that has a Technical Secretariat for the implementation, coordination and implementation of the provisions of the Development Banking System Law. The Governing Council is composed of the Minister of Agriculture and Livestock; the Minister of Economy, Industry and Commerce; a representative of the industrial and services sector appointed by the Chamber of Industries of Costa Rica; a representative of the agricultural sector designated by the National Chamber of Agriculture and Agribusiness of Costa Rica; and an independent member appointed by the Governing Council from a shortlist of three submitted by the College of Professionals in Economic Sciences of Costa Rica.

2. Credit guarantees for rural producers

The chief objective of the Special Fund for the Development of Micro, Small and Medium-sized Enterprises (FODEMIPYME) is to promote and strengthen the development of such firms, and of socially and economically viable job-creating enterprises. Its main functions are to extend guarantees and credit, and to support the development of projects financed by the Popular and Community Development Bank, aimed at strengthening and developing MSMEs in areas such as training, technical assistance, innovation, research and technology transfer.

FINADE, for its part, issues guarantees to financial operators authorized by SBD, to support the financing of up to 75% of the loans requested by MSMEs.

As a way of facilitating access to credit for individuals or businesses that do not have registered real estate, in 2014 the Movable Collateral Law (Law No. 9246) was passed with the aim of increasing access to credit, broadening the categories of goods that can be pledged as collateral and the scope of the rights thereon. Under the aforementioned law, tangible or intangible assets, accounts receivable, crops, inventories, contracts, trademarks, intellectual property, livestock, machinery and equipment and other movable property may be presented as collateral. Complementarily, the Computerized System for the Registration of Movable Collateral entered into force, which will function as a centralized registry of such collateral, operated by the National Registry.

3. Tools for productive development in the rural sector

The Ministry of Economic Affairs, Industry and Commerce (MEIC) has functions that include participation in the formulation of the Government's economic policy and in national planning within its jurisdiction. In addition, it is the governing body of the State's public policies for the promotion of business development and entrepreneurial culture in the industrial, commercial and service sectors, as well as for MSMEs.

Although interagency articulation processes and specific projects, such as the simplification of procedures, are based on government decrees, the degree to which they are implemented in the regions depends very much on the willingness, availability and commitment of the officials present in the regions.

For its part, the Ministry of Agriculture and Livestock (MAG) of Costa Rica is responsible for all public policies targeting the agricultural sector. The Ministry has tools that enable funds to be transferred to initiatives promoted by cooperatives, development associations, producer associations, and associations that exist to obtain infrastructure, equipment, machinery and tools, and even the possibility of donating to rural producers the livestock and animals necessary for their productive development.

In addition, through its regional offices, MAG has a network of agricultural extension agencies located mainly in the cantonal capitals. Although the institutional and regulatory architecture is broad in terms of serving the rural productive sector, the trends of a more service-oriented economy have reduced the impact of agricultural production within the productive structure.

E. Key challenges

Although the adoption of a comprehensive public policy strategy to promote financial inclusion was announced recently, in practice such a strategy is still lacking. Nonetheless, the public institutions have created tools and instruments which have fostered financial inclusion among participants in the national financial system. The presence of publicly owned banks, with 531 branches and over 1,400 ATMs distributed throughout the country, offers a broad platform for the financial inclusion of rural producers.

Based on the findings presented in this chapter, both publicly owned and private banks are considered to have sufficient financial capacity to promote the inclusion of productive projects in rural areas. This could be enhanced through the wide availability of institutional guarantees to facilitate access to funds for new projects. This could be improved if both the MEIC and MAG or the local municipalities allocated part of their funds to support this type of projects, as is done in Mexico through the mechanisms of Nacional Financiera.

The Development Banking System could be used to promote financial inclusion among rural producers, since the spirit of the Development Banking System Law includes financing for agricultural activities.

The development of telecommunications and the establishment of FONATEL have improved connectivity in rural areas, thereby making it possible to expand connectivity and access to ICTs.

From the Government, the requirement for social protection programmes —such as supplementary pensions, student grants, subsidies to poor families and the granting of free housing vouchers— to be made by transferring funds to beneficiaries have contributed to the financial inclusion of a population segment which could not otherwise be included.

The existence of a financial institution framework and legal security generates a consistent basis for financial inclusion programmes and projects, from both a private and a public perspective.

Both MAG and the Rural Development Institute (INDER) have the infrastructure needed to provide technical support to rural producers, and there must be interaction and coordination with the financial inclusion programmes that target the rural sector.

Information is an essential asset of organizations, which must evolve in parallel with the business strategy in an integrated way and pursue long-term business objectives. In this sense, the strategic management of ICT can offer an environment for permanent value creation in the entities; and this is essential for increasing the competitiveness of participants in the financial system, in addition to being necessary to reduce the costs of these services.

Financial institutions are taking advantage of the growing adoption of mobile technologies and the Internet to understand customers better and bring financial services to the base of the pyramid, where, because of their dispersion, customers do not have a banking infrastructure or traditional payment points nearby. This is where technology plays a key role in achieving the authentic spread of banking services.

Following the implementation of simplified accounts, it is estimated that the density of banking and, consequently, the use of financial services will expand significantly in Costa Rica. In addition, the SINPE Móvil service still has a great opportunity for penetration at the base of the pyramid, and in rural areas, so a joint marketing strategy by the two initiatives to exploit its benefits could contribute to both access and the use of financial services and, consequently, inclusion.

Also, through FONATEL, whose main purpose is to bring telephony and the Internet to areas and communities where there is still no service (all of which are rural areas), the goal is to reduce the digital divide and ensure more equal opportunity. Accordingly, success requires giving this initiative the tools needed to adequately follow-up the projects derived from the Fund.

Although technologies are being improved, ensuring a positive impact requires platforms that are more intuitive for the customer, have better interfaces and whose main attribute is understanding the needs of users. The latter is in the hands of the financial system and regulators.

The supply of formal financial services in Costa Rica is very wide-ranging, with enough access to credit for end-users, but subject to cumbersome and slow procedures. The change introduced by the Development Banking System Law increased facilities by granting loans to established microfinance institutions and agribusiness cooperatives, which were already credit subjects of publicly owned banks that preferred the backing of real collateral.

Development banks extended the endorsement of the collateral provided by the financial operator (promissory notes, bills of exchange, guarantees and pledges on crops), thereby hastening the response time for the user. The Non-real Estate Collateral Law is a complementary instrument that can enhance access to credit for rural producers and thereby improve their financial inclusion.

Informal financial services (lenders) will remain in the business, since they are more focused on the value of the real collateral provided than the financial valuation of the project, so the response time is two to three days.

As unregulated operators, microfinance institutions have greater flexibility in providing credit to rural producers; and the higher interest rates charged by these entities are associated with a higher level of risk.

The risk variable among rural producers can only be solved through the emergence of microinsurance services. Until such services become well established, the risk variable will lead some financial operators not to consider lending to rural producers, and microfinance and private lenders will have a market in which to operate.

Lastly, financial inclusion for rural producers should not be confined to access to credit or to the opening of a savings account. Instead, it should be a comprehensive process involving complementary services, such as microinsurance, technical support, financial education and access to ICTs, which enhance the migration of rural producers to more productive systems with less systemic risk.

Bibliography

Camacho, E. and R. Jiménez (2010), *Acceso a servicios financieros en Costa Rica*, San José, Costa Rican Banking Association.

EIU/IDB (Economist Intelligence Unit/Inter-American Development Bank) (2016), *Global Microscope 2016. The Enabling Environment for Financial Inclusion*, New York.

INEC (National Institute of Statistics and Censuses) (2015a), Encuesta Nacional de Hogares 2015, San José.

___(2015b) "VI Censo Nacional Agropecuario. Características de las fincas y de las personas productoras", San José.

___(2014), Encuesta Nacional de Hogares 2014, San José.

___(2010), Encuesta Nacional de Hogares 2010, San José.

PEN (State of the Nation Programme) (2015), *Vigésimo primer Informe Estado de la Nación en Desarrollo Humano Sostenible*, San José.

REDCAMIF (Central American and Caribbean Microfinance Network) (2015), *Boletín Microfinanciero de Centroamérica y del Caribe*, No. 6, Managua, December.World Bank (2014), Global Findex Database, Washington, D.C. [online] http://datatopics.worldbank.org/financialinclusion.

World Bank (2014), Global Findex Database [online] http://datatopics.worldbank.org/financialinclusion.

Chapter IV

Financial inclusion in El Salvador

Pedro Argumedo[1]

Introduction

Financial inclusion provides a new opportunity to foster broader access to the different types of financial services, and promote their use, thereby improving people's well-being. El Salvador faces the challenge of pursuing a national strategy based on an institutional framework that coordinates public and private initiatives, combining innovations in traditional and mobile banking services, which will help lower their costs and expand access to new services in neglected areas.

Some international surveys on financial inclusion, such as those undertaken by the World Bank (Demirgüç-Kunt and others, 2015), show how technological development is spawning innovations that enhance access to financial services and promote their use. This is particularly true in rural areas, where distance to a financial institution is one of the key constraints. Moreover, a comparison of results across countries reveals that an effort to improve access is being pursued through a combination of technologies, regulations and banking and telephone networks.

---

1 Senior Researcher in Economic Studies, Salvadoran Foundation for Economic and Social Development.

The experience of the countries that have progressed furthest in financial inclusion (Villasenor, West and Lewis, 2016; EIU/IDB, 2016) reveals three factors that contribute to the further development of this process. First, there must be an institutional vehicle that can lead and coordinate public and private initiatives, to expand access to financial services and increase their use. Second, a national strategy must be agreed on that identifies the different phases, with their programmes and stakeholders, establishing appropriate measures for attending to underserved segments, such as those in the rural area. Third, it is necessary to support the implementation of reforms and public policies that hasten the process, and to be able to evaluate their effects.

For financial inclusion to have a greater impact in countries like El Salvador, in which informality is widespread, the agenda must be framed in a broader public policy of inclusive development (Alliance for Financial Inclusion, 2012). In El Salvador, just one in every four members of the economically active population (EAP) has a formal job; only 35% have social security, and even fewer do so in rural areas (15.6%). While the national poverty rate is 31.8%, in the rural sector it exceeds 37.9% (DIGESTYC, 2015). This very low-income reality highlights the importance of creating job opportunities, supported by financial inclusion.

According to figures published by the Central Reserve Bank of El Salvador (BCR), 47% of the Salvadoran population had access to financial accounts in 2016 (BCR, 2016), compared to the World Bank's estimate of 36.7% two years earlier.[2] The results of these studies show that the main gateway consists of savings or current accounts offered by financial intermediaries (34.6%), with a growing share of accounts operated through mobile phones (4.6%). A key point to note is that 28.1% of accounts in financial institutions were held in rural zones in 2014, 13 percentage points less than the urban share. This gap reflects both income asymmetry and access problems owing to the relatively low population density in rural zones. The data also show that mobile telephony is increasingly being used to make financial transactions in El Salvador, thereby helping to overcome the problem of distance to physical branches in rural areas.

In 2011, work began on a financial inclusion agenda under BCR leadership. The central bank joined the Alliance for Financial Inclusion and, with the support from the United States Department of the Treasury´s Office of Technical Assistance (OTA), set up a specialized institutional entity known as the Support Group on Financial Inclusion Issues (GATIF), comprising institutions such as the Superintendency of the Financial System (SSF) and the El Salvador Development Bank (BANDESAL), along with private and microcredit institutions.

---

[2] The 2016 BCR survey contained questions similar to those formulated by the World Bank in 2014, but there were two important statistical differences: (i) the BCR study surveyed individuals over 18 years of age, while the World Bank covered those older than 15; and (ii) BCR interviewed 5,211 people and the World Bank survey covered 1,000.

Diagnostic studies and access surveys were conducted, leading to the drafting of the Law to facilitate financial inclusion, which was passed by the Legislative Assembly on 13 August 2015 and entered into force on 11 September of that year. This Law specifies the procedure for authorizing and regulating the operations of firms issuing electronic money and providing mobile payment services; and it creates a simplified savings account mechanism. This initiative led BCR and SSF to set up specialized financial inclusion units; and firms that supply electronic money have been showing increasing interest in starting operations in El Salvador; and a variety of financial entities have created and are proposing new programmes to promote financial inclusion.

Despite the progress made, GATIF ceased to function as an interagency coordinating body. As of the end of 2016, BCR was conducting a number of surveys on financial inclusion among individuals and firms, which could serve as an input for a second phase of a broader and better articulated agenda of financial inclusion in El Salvador.

The present study systemizes, as broadly as possible, the various initiatives that have been implemented in the country in the last few years; and it will form the basis for designing a comprehensive financial inclusion strategy with actions to address three challenges:

(i) Coordination between public and private financial institutions through the creation and institutionalization of a National Commission for Financial Inclusion in the spirit of GATIF.

(ii) Transmission of information between suppliers and users of financial services, since nearly all institutions are undertaking actions which the users are generally unaware of, and of improving the approach of financial education towards inclusion.

(iii) Network regulation and interoperability. The challenge here is to consolidate reliability between financial and mobile networks, facilitate the entry of new operators leading to greater competition generally, and maintain system security.

Section A of this chapter analyses the recent evolution in access to financial services and the use made of them in El Salvador, focusing particularly on the situation prevailing in rural areas. Section B then describes the development of the financial inclusion strategy in El Salvador, and section C reviews the institutional architecture in place to implement it. Section D discusses the public-policy instruments that are available to support rural development, highlighting the role of BANDESAL, the programmes of the Ministry of Agriculture and Livestock (MAG) and the financial inclusion innovations promoted by Tigo Money, Banco Agrícola, BCR and SSF, among others. Lastly, section E concludes by considering the main challenges to increasing financial inclusion, and it proposes a strategy in three key areas.

A. Recent evolution and current situation on access to and use of financial services

This section analyses access to, and use of, financial services using the broad definition of financial inclusion, which encompasses a wide range of financial services, financial service providers and distribution channels. The statistical information comes from financial inclusion surveys conducted by the World Bank (2016a) and BCR (2016). While the results show that financial inclusion has been on the rise, the rate remains below the average for Latin America as a whole and for countries of comparable income levels elsewhere. Survey data are supplemented by BCR and SSF records. To the extent allowed by the data, the analysis highlights the situation in the rural sector.

1. Access to and use of financial services

Financial services in El Salvador remain sparsely used. According to figures from the World Bank (2016a), in 2014 just 36.7% of Salvadorans over the age of 15 held an account at a formal financial institution or operated an account through their mobile phone. Over 63% are subject to some type of exclusion (see table IV.1). Notwithstanding the challenge that persists, there has been a significant increase in the use of these services, since the rate was just 13.8%. in 2011. As discussed below, one of the determinants of this growth has been the increasing use of mobile phones for financial transactions.

As shown in table IV.1, El Salvador is well below the average both in Latin America, where 51.4% of individuals aged over 15 years had an account in 2014, and also in lower middle-income countries, where the proportion was 42.7%. The comparison with countries of similar income levels shows that part of the observed exclusion is involuntary, associated with factors that include information constraints and inability to enforce contracts.

According to BCR (2016) figures, 47% of adults had access to an account in 2016, compared to the 36.7% reported in the World Bank survey of two years earlier. The main gateway consists of services supplied through accounts with traditional financial services providers (34.6%), and a growing proportion of accounts operated through mobile phones (4.6%). The latter highlights the innovative role being played by a telephone operator, through its electronic money product Tigo Money.

In contrast, just 14% had a savings account in 2014, slightly above the 12.9% registered in 2011. These figures are similar to the averages for Latin America (13.5%) and for lower middle-income countries (14.8%).

Table IV.1
El Salvador: financial inclusion, total and rural, 2011, 2014 and 2016
(Percentages)

	Global Findex				Central Reserve Bank of El Salvador
	El Salvador		Latin America	Lower middle-income countries	
	2011	2014	2014	2014	2016
Financial and mobile phone account (*Percentages of individuals aged over 15 years*)					
Total					
All	13.8	36.7	51.4	42.7	47.0
Women	10.1	31.9	48.6	36.3	41.0
Rural		31.5			n.a.
Financial institutions	13.8	34.6	51.1	41.9	39.0
Financial institutions, rural	12.1	28.1			n.a.
Mobile phone account (Tigo Money)	n.a.	4.6	1.7	2.5	16.0
Mobile phone account (Tigo Money), rural		5.5			
Access to financial accounts					
Has a debit card	10.9	21.8	40.4	21.2	
Has a debit card, rural	8.8	15.4			
Has a credit card	5.3	8.3			
Has a credit card, rural	5.1	5.8			
Use of financial account					
Use of account to receive wage		15.1	18.0	5.6	10.0
Use of account to receive government transfer		4.4	9.0	3.3	
Saving in the past year					
Saving in a financial institution	12.9	14.0	13.5	14.8	23.0
Credit in the past year					
Loan from financial firms	3.9	17.2	11.3	7.5	12.0
Loan from financial firms, rural	3.8	16.9			
Loan from informal sources	2.0	6.2			
Loan from informal sources, rural	1.9	5.1			
Remittances in the past year					
Received remittances	n.a.	17.3	11.3	17.8	25.0
Received remittances, rural	n.a.	14.0			

Source: Prepared by the author, on the basis of World Bank, Global Findex Database, 2014 and Central Reserve Bank of El Salvador, "Demanda nacional de servicios financieros", San Salvador, July 2016.
Note: Owing to methodological differences, Global Findex data are not strictly comparable with the BCR figures.

In the case of financial services, as measured by access to credit from a financial institution, BCR reports a rate of 12%. Projecting this last figure on the total population of El Salvador aged over 15 years, which in 2014 amounted to 4.7 million (DIGESTYC, 2015), indicates that some

793,000 people have some type of credit. Considering the levels of formalization of the labour force, measured by workers who pay contributions into the Salvadoran Social Security Institute (ISSS) (794,000 affiliates in 2014), the figures show that most formal workers are likely to have some kind of credit. The proportion of people accessing formal credit in El Salvador (17.2%) is above the average both in Latin America (11.3%) and in low-income countries (7.5%) (see table IV.1).

With regard to means of payment, El Salvador is again below the average for Latin America: 21.8% of individuals aged over 15 had a debit card in 2014, well below the 40.4% recorded in Latin America as a whole, but similar to the average for lower middle-income countries (21.2%). Nonetheless, actual use of a debit card was lower, at 12.9%, again well below the 27.7% average for Latin America. This may reflect a shortage of payment infrastructure or lack of trust in making such payments. Access to credit cards was 8.3% in 2014 and usage barely reached 6.6%. The prevalence of online payments made over the Internet remains extremely low and well below the Latin American average, at 4%, although growing in importance.

In the case of firms, the evolution of access to, and use of, financial services are analysed using credit data recorded by BCR, since a survey on enterprise financial inclusion is not yet available. The information is complemented by a survey on access to financing by firms from a competitive capacity perspective.

The credit extended to the productive sector comes from domestic and external sources, which totalled US$ 9.283 billion in 2015, representing 59% of all credit supplied and equivalent to 35.9% of gross domestic product (GDP). Between 2003 and 2015, financing for the productive sector recorded a marginal increase of US$ 2.845 billion, equivalent to an average annual increase of US$ 237 million, or about 1% of GDP per year.

Domestic sources that financed the production sector, including regulated institutions such as banks, non-bank financial institutions and saving and loan associations, lent US$ 5.26 billion (56.7% of the total).[3] External financing, including offshore banking, business loans in the form of foreign direct investment (FDI) and commercial credit, amounted to US$ 4.023 billion in 2015. Funding from external sources has outpaced domestic financing, growing its share from 39.3% of the total in 2003 to 43.3% in 2015.

As a sectoral classification is not available for external sources, information from regulated institutions (banks, non-bank financial institutions, and saving and loan association) is used to analyse lending by sector. Four economic activities absorbed 75% of total credit (see figure IV.1), in order of importance: (i) consumption, for which credit surged from

[3] Non-bank financial institutions are cooperatives and their federations.

US$ 711 million in 2002 to US$ 3.121 billion in 2015; (ii) residential mortgages, for which lending totalled US$ 2.522 billion in 2015, recording the second largest increase, up from US$ 1.099 billion in 2002; (iii) services, which received US$ 1.84 billion in credit in 2015, with the largest increase in the business sector (US$ 573 million more than in 2002); and (iv) commerce, in which credit rose marginally by US$ 493 million. Agriculture was the sector in which credit grew the least during the 13-year period from US$ 264 million in 2002 to just US$ 383 million in 2015, reflecting its limited participation in the economy.

Figure IV.1
El Salvador: lending to production sectors from domestic sources (banks, non-bank financial institutions and savings and loan associations), 2002-2015
(Billions of dollars)

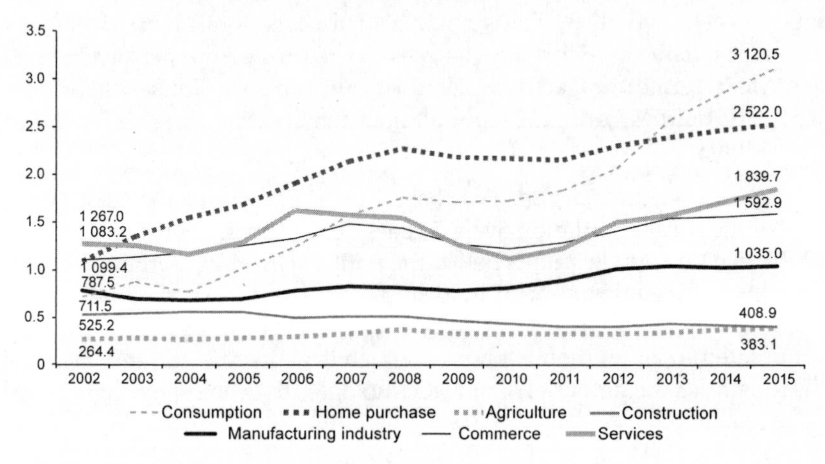

Source: Central Reserve Bank of El Salvador.

According to the results of the business competitiveness survey carried out by the Salvadoran Foundation for Economic and Social Development (FUSADES, 2015), which includes a module on enterprise access to financing, 38.4% of the firms surveyed had applied for credit in 2014.[4] The main sources were commercial banks (92%), suppliers (15%), offshore banks (4%) and nonbank financial institutions (2%). Just 7% of the firms turned to relatives and informal lenders. It is important to note that 5.3% of the firms surveyed were denied credit. The main reasons for refusal were: the economic situation of the country (52%); the risk posed by the enterprise (16%); and changes in the financial institutions' credit policies (8%).

4 The survey is applied to more than 430 micro, small, medium-sized and large enterprises, covering the whole country (FUSADES, 2015).

2. Performance of the rural sector

According to the Department of Statistics and Censuses (DIGESTYC), the rural population represented 37.7% of a total of 6.4 million inhabitants in 2014, down sharply from the 52.2% recorded in 1992 (Angel, 2011). This urbanization phenomenon is driven by poverty and opportunity gaps between the urban and rural environments. In 1992 the rural poverty rate was 65.1%, compared to an urban rate of 52.9%, thereby creating incentives to migrate from the countryside to the cities. This phenomenon still persisted in 2014, when the rural poverty rate was 37.9% and the urban rate was 28.5% (DIGESTYC, 2015). At the same time, the agriculture sector's GDP share fell from 16.5% in 1992 to 12.2% in 2014.

One of the challenges when analysing the rural environment is the vagueness of its definition. This is aggravated by the sectoral approach of many economic statistics, which makes it necessary to proxy rural performance by reference to agricultural activities. In the Multi-purpose Household Survey, DIGESTYC defines "urban" by population-density criteria, with "rural" as the residual.[5]

As shown in diagram IV.1, based on World Bank (2016a) figures, 31.5% of the rural population over 15 years of age had some type of account in 2014, five percentage points below the national average. Although access to accounts through financial institutions in rural areas was below the country average (28.1% compared to 34.6%), 5.5% of accounts in the rural area are operated through mobile phones, which is above the national average. This illustrates the potential of new technologies to overcome geographical coverage challenges.

In contrast, while rural credit use (16.9%) is very similar to the national average (17.2%), savings among rural dwellers are almost 4 percentage points lower than the national figure (14%). As a reflection of this, although the rate of debit card use in rural areas grew from 8.8% in 2011 to 15.4% in 2014, this remains below the national rate of 21.8%.

The relatively large proportion of remittance recipients located in rural areas (14%) reflects the rural origin of much of the migration to the United States. Moreover, the monthly flow of remittances has encouraged the development of complementary financial services.

---

[5] The population density criterion used by the DIGESTYC defines "urban" as the census segments that meet any of the following requirements: (i) the municipal mayoralty is located in the census segment; (ii) conglomerates of census segments with a population of more than 1,000 inhabitants per km^2; (iii) census segments larger than 0.6 km2 in area; (iv) houses grouped in segments with an area of less than 20,000 m^2.

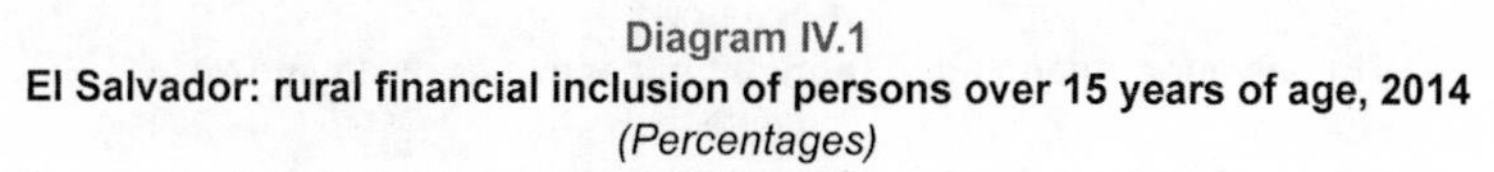

Diagram IV.1
El Salvador: rural financial inclusion of persons over 15 years of age, 2014
(Percentages)

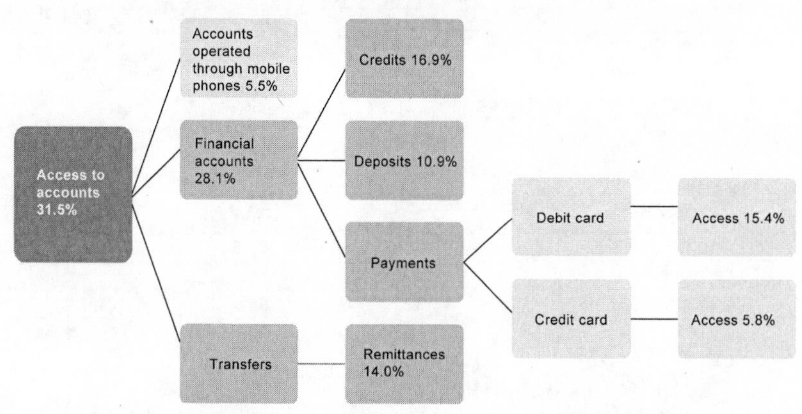

Source: Prepared by the author, on the basis of World Bank, *Doing Business 2016: Measuring Regulatory Quality and Efficiency*, Washington, D.C., 2016.

According to BCR, lending to the agricultural sector amounted to US$ 365 million in 2016, equivalent to 3.1% of the total credit extended by banks, non-bank financial institutions and saving and loan associations. Banks contribute the most to agricultural credit, accounting for 95% of total lending. An analysis of performance since 2002 shows that agricultural credit grew at a slower pace than all credit granted to the economy, accounting for 4.1% of the total in 2002 and falling to 3.1%.

The findings of the agricultural activities module of the Multi-purpose Household Survey show that crop farming was the main activity in 2014, accounting for 76.8% of the total, followed by crop and livestock farming in combination with 17.7%, and exclusively livestock activities 5% (see table IV.2).

In terms of financial inclusion among producers, 12.1% of producers applied for credit in 2014. Of the total number of applications, 98% were successful, which suggests a high degree of financial self-exclusion. Nonetheless, an analysis of credit sources shows that a quarter of all credit comes from family or friends, while the Agricultural Development Bank (BFA) was the leading source with 28.6% in 2014, up sharply from 17.1% in 2010. This increase seems to have compensated for the reduction in lending by private banks, which dropped from 25.4% of the total in 2010 to 16.5% in 2014. During the same period, cooperatives and rural credit funds reduced their share of agricultural funding from 20% to 8.3%.

Table IV.2

El Salvador: financing for agricultural activities, 2010 and 2014

(Percentages)

	2010	2014
1. What agricultural activity?		
Crop farming	66.8	76.8
Agriculture and livestock	25.6	17.7
Livestock	7.4	5.0
Others	0.2	0.5
2. Applied for credit?		
Yes	10.1	12.1
No	89.9	87.9
3. Obtained the credit requested?		
Yes	98.0	97.9
No	2.0	2.1
4. Financed by?		
Agricultural Development Bank (BFA)	17.1	28.6
Family or friends	25.4	25.4
Private bank	25.4	16.5
Others	1.6	13.0
Cooperative	9.7	5.0
Rural credit fund	10.3	3.3
Non-governmental organization	3.8	3.2
Agricultural service centre	2.0	2.5
Lender	1.9	1.7
Crop buyers	0.9	0.7
Mortgage bank	1.0	0.1
Intermediary	0.7	0.1

Source: Prepared by the author, on the basis of Department of Statistics and Censuses, Multi-purpose Household Surveys, 2011 and 2015, San Salvador.

In short, despite the progress made since 2011, there are still deficits in financial inclusion relative to the region as a whole and to other countries with a similar income levels. In 2016 there was a large increase in financial transactions channelled through phone services, exceeding traditional sources of banking institutions, and also above the averages for the region or for lower middle-income countries. Financial services are also used intensively for family remittance transfers, which is associated with the huge number of Salvadoran expatriates living mainly in the United States.

Official statistics on the rural sector are scarce or non-existent, and most are reported in terms of what is encompassed by agricultural activities. This provides a very limited representation of the concept of "rural", which hinders analysis of the performance of financial services, since commercial and tourism activities take place in rural areas without being recorded separately from those in urban zones. The available data indicate that disparities in financial inclusion are greater in rural areas.

B. The Financial Inclusion Strategy

Development of the financial inclusion strategy has been led by BCR since its inception, with support from both the United States Department of the Treasury and the Alliance for Financial Inclusion. The first phase of the process culminated in August 2015 with the passing of the Law to facilitate financial inclusion. The milestones of the process are summarized in diagram IV.2 and discussed in greater detail below.

Diagram IV.2
El Salvador: financial inclusion strategy, 2008-2015

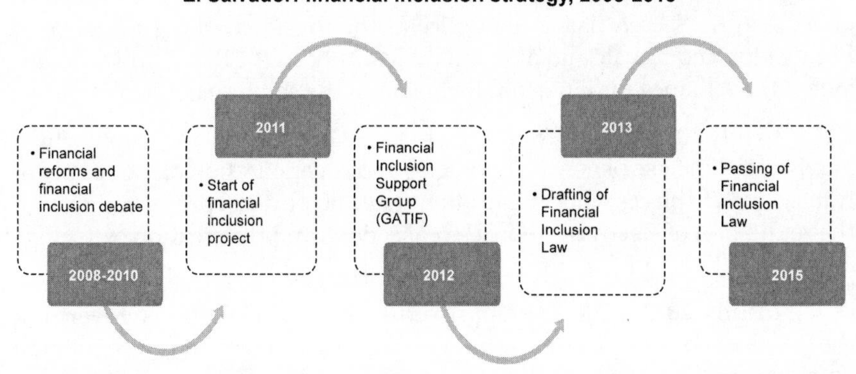

Source: Prepared by the author.

In 2008-2010, El Salvador's financial public policies were geared towards creating the Financial Education Programme (BCR, 2009), with the aim of strengthening the population's capacities to use financial services. The Quinquennial Development Plan 2010-2014 (Government of El Salvador, 2010) proposed a reform of the financial system, in which BCR would be responsible for regulating the system, while supervision responsibility was assigned to SSF. In addition, the Multisectoral Investment Bank (BMI) was restructured to create BANDESAL. In 2009 BCR received a World Bank consultancy report containing a diagnostic assessment of the legal and regulatory framework governing branchless banking in El Salvador, which recommended creating non-bank correspondents (BCR, 2010). Work also began on setting up a new guarantee fund (BCR, 2010), for which technical assistance was received from the Inter-American Development Bank (IDB) in 2010, for the design and implementation of a Salvadoran Guarantee Fund for micro, small and medium-sized enterprises (MSMEs) (BCR, 2011a).

In 2011, the Office of the Governor of the Central Bank and officials from the BCR Financial Development Division participated in international forums on financial inclusion. In this connection, the "OTA-BCR Financial Inclusion Programme" (BCR, 2011b) was designed with support from the

Technical Assistance Office (OTA) of the United States Department of the Treasury, which included a diagnosis of the status of financial inclusion in El Salvador, the implementation of financial education programmes, institutional strengthening of unregulated entities, development of regulations for mobile payment operations, adaptation of regulations to the risk of low-value operations, reinforcement of the securities guarantee regime, establishment of regulations needed for microinsurance and micropayment operations, and the leveraging of microcredit for the production sector.

With OTA support, in 2012 BCR created GATIF, with participation from SSF, BANDESAL, the Ministry of Economic Affairs, the Technical and Planning Secretariat of the Office of the President of the Republic of El Salvador, and private and microcredit institutions (BCR, 2013). El Salvador joined the Alliance for Financial Inclusion in the same year.

In July 2013, BCR drafted a bill to facilitate financial inclusion, which emphasized the use of new technologies and diversification of the supply of transactions to places where institutions have no physical presence, through the regulation of electronic money transactions and the creation of savings accounts with simplified requirements (BCR, 2014).

In July 2013, BCR also approved technical regulations governing the provision of services through financial correspondents. The regulation empowers regulated institutions (banks, non-bank financial institutions, and saving and loan associations) to provide services through a contract with non-bank correspondents, such as shops, small businesses and natural persons. This mechanism makes it easier to access financial services in remote areas, with extended opening hours. The services that can be provided in this way are loan payments, making and receiving deposits, and the receipt and payment of remittances (BCR, 2014).

In May 2014, BCR sent the draft law for discussion and debate among regulated financial institutions and telecommunications companies that conduct monetary transactions over the mobile phone network. The law was passed in August 2015 (Legislative Assembly, 2015), and BCR approved the corresponding technical standards at the end of August 2016.

The Support Group on Financial Inclusion Issues (GATIF) served as an institutional vehicle enabling entities with very different functions to adopt a common conceptual agenda and launch actions to promote financial inclusion within their jurisdictions. GATIF proposed conducting a survey, from which the findings would be used to propose an agenda for drafting a financial inclusion law that would lower the cost of using financial services, giving easier access to very-low-income families, and exploiting new technologies using electronic money via mobile phone.

C. Features of the institutional architecture

This section analyses the institutional architecture available to promote financial inclusion. First, it describes the legal framework that underpins the institutional structure of the financial system, and then it identifies the regulated financial institutions that support the rural sector. Next, it analyses the evolution of means of payment, in particular the rapid growth of electronic media. It identifies the financial services and channels offered by the main institutions supporting the rural area; and it describes recent innovations that foster financial inclusion. It then reviews user protection mechanisms, highlighting the role of the Consumer Advocacy Agency in terms of its legal powers to protect financial system users and ensure funds are reimbursed following a favourable resolution of complaints. Lastly, it makes an analysis of legal conditions for enforcing contracts.

1. Regulatory and supervisory policy

The structure of the formal financial system is defined in the Financial System Supervision and Regulation Law (Legislative Assembly, 2011b).[6] This legislation makes BCR responsible for approving the framework of technical standards that regulate the system, while SSF is required to enforce the rules governing the system.

Regulated entities are commercial banks, non-bank financial institutions, pension funds, insurance and bonding firms, stock brokerages and public credit institutions. There are other financial entities which are not regulated, such as the Federation of Credit Banks and Banks of Workers (FEDECRÉDITO), which are supervised by the Salvadoran Institute for Cooperative Development (INSAFOCOP).[7]

The Financial System Superintendency issues the rules for authorizing operating permits for banks, non-bank financial institutions and saving and loan associations. In the case of banks, the procedures are set out in the Banking Law (Legislative Assembly, 2011c), while those governing non-bank financial institutions and saving and loan associations are contained in the Law on Cooperative Banks and Firms Savings and Loan Associations (SSF, 2008). The key requirements are: presentation to SSF of a project to create the financial entity, constitution of minimum capital (depending on the type of institution) and compliance with certain conditions pertaining to the number and type of shareholders. In addition, SSF also specified the prudential rules that regulated institutions must obey in order to guarantee the liquidity, soundness and stability of the financial system.

---

6 This Law consolidated regulation and supervision. Previously, the rules were issued by SSF and supervision was segmented in specialized entities.

7 In September 2016, BCR and SSF presented an initiative to reform the Law on Cooperative Banks and Saving and Loan Associations, which seeks to expand the regulatory universe to encompass credit unions (*cajas de crédito*).

Users of the regulated financial system have their deposits protected through the Deposit Guarantee Institute (IGD), which is funded by contributions from regulated financial entities. It currently provides coverage of up to US$ 10,171 for savings held in current or saving accounts, or time deposits.

2. Financial intermediaries

As table IV.3 shows, 92% of the total credit granted by formal financial entities in 2015 was originated by 14 banks, followed by seven non-bank financial institutions that granted 6.7% of the credit and four saving and loan associations that provided 1.4%. Lending to agricultural activities amounted to US$ 383.1 million and represented just 3.2% of all funding granted in 2015.[8]

Table IV.3
El Salvador: credit granted by formal financial intermediaries, 2015

	Thousands of dollars	Percentage of total	Percentage of agricultural portfolio
Agricultural Development Bank (BFA)[a]	125 092	32.7	56.1
Banco Hipotecario[a]	102 223	26.7	16.1
Banco Agrícola[a]	56 558	14.8	1.9
Banco Davivienda[a]	29 847	7.8	1.9
Banco ProCredit[a]	21 408	5.6	9.4
Banco Promerica[a]	12 981	3.4	1.8
Integral[b]	11 388	3.0	14.6
Banco G&T Continental[a]	10 013	2.6	2.8
BAC Credomatic[a]	4 861	1.3	0.4
Banco Citibank[a]	2 903	0.8	0.3
Federación de Cajas de Crédito y de Bancos de los Trabajadores (FEDECRÉDITO)[c]	1 599	0.4	0.6
Asociación Cooperativa de Ahorro y Crédito Vicentina (ACCOVI)[c]	1 371	0.4	1.2
Banco Scotiabank[a]	1 190	0.3	0.1
Primer Banco de los Trabajadores[c]	482	0.1	0.6
Banco Azul[a]	448	0.1	0.6
Constelación[b]	350	0.1	5.1
Corporación Multi Inversiones (CMI)[c]	137	0.0	0.2
Credicomer[b]	91	0.0	0.2
Banco de los Trabajadores Salvadoreños (BTS)[c]	77	0.0	0.2
Banco Industrial[a]	66	0.0	0.0
Banco Izalqueño de los Trabajadores[c]	1	0.0	0.0
Banco Azteca[a]	-	0.0	0.0
COMEDICA[c]	-	0.0	0.0
Multivalores[b]	-	0.0	0.0

Source: Superintendency of the Financial System (SSF).
[a] Banks.
[b] Saving and loan associations.
[c] Non-bank financial institutions (cooperatives).

[8] The results of the Multi-purpose Household Survey show that between 10% and 20% of the funding for agricultural activities comes from informal financial institutions, for which no systematized information is available.

An analysis of agricultural credit by source shows that banks contributed 96%, followed by savings and loan associations (3%) and cooperative banks (1%). The two State banks (BFA and Banco Hipotecario) provided 60% of agricultural funding in 2015. BFA provided US$ 125 million (32.7% of the total) and Banco Hipotecario lent US$ 102 million (26.7%). The private banks tend to specialize in lending to medium-sized and large-scale firms and farmers, except for Banco ProCredit, which has served microenterprises and small businesses from its inception.

The small share of commercial and cooperative banks in lending for agricultural activities may be due to three risk- and cost-related factors:

(i) The vast majority of crop farmers or livestock producers carry on their activity in low-productivity micro-plots for self-consumption, which entails higher administrative costs and greater risk.

(ii) In recent years, severe droughts have caused crop losses valued in the millions of dollars. This increases the risk of non-payment, since the activities of small producers are based on the rainfall regime, and very few use irrigation techniques. Moreover, farmers' organizations have obtained decrees promoting the non-payment of debts, which discourages lenders from channelling funds into the sector.

(iii) The prevalence of crime also discourages the provision of financial services in certain areas of the country.

These three factors combine to generate perverse incentives and cause private financial institutions to reduce their exposure to risk in farming activities.

3. Payment systems

The central bank is responsible for the operation of the payment systems, whose instruments, procedures and standards are used to transfer financial resources among its participants. El Salvador has four payment systems. The real-time gross settlement system is used for high-value transactions, such as interbank transfers. The other three systems are the Electronic Cheque Clearing House (CCECH), mass payment systems and securities systems, which are considered to be of low value and are used to process operations such as cheque clearing, credit and debit card payments, and credit and debit transactions. The media used to access low-value systems include automatic teller machines (ATMs), points of sale, the Internet and mobile phones.

A study of competition conditions in the credit card market conducted by the Superintendency of Competition reported that the number of credit and debit cards grew significantly between 2004 and 2009 owing to the availability of electronic devices at points of sale. By 2012, there were five networks providing electronic payment services with broad coverage; and the number of credit card devices reached 735,919 in June 2012 (latest data available from BCR), an increase of 15,221 units since December 2011. This growth reflects the vibrancy of consumer credit (see figure IV.2).

Figure IV.2
El Salvador: electronic devices at credit and debit card points of sale, 2003-June 2012
(Thousands of devices)

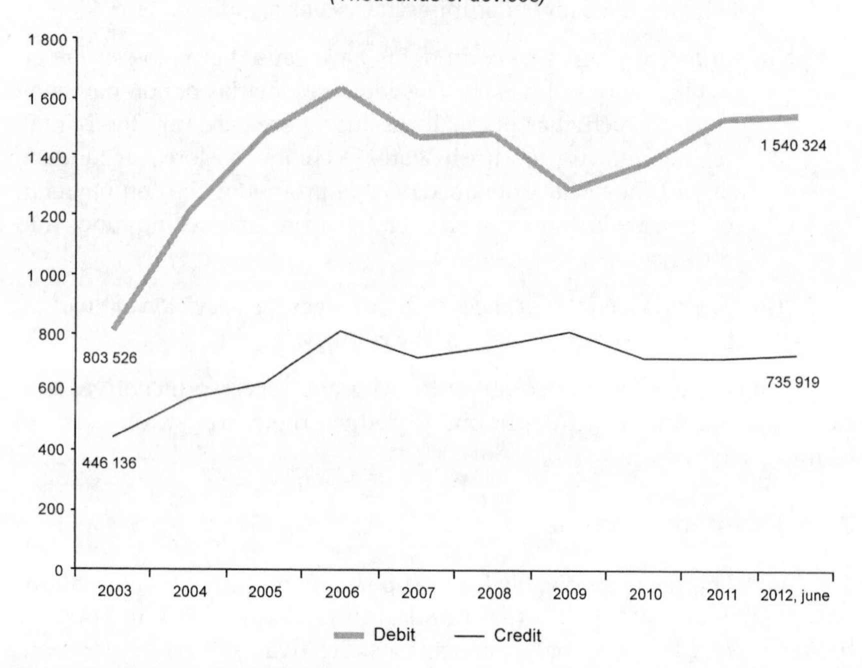

Source: Central Reserve Bank of El Salvador.

In addition to the ATM network of the main banks, Puntoxpress and Multiservice Network AKI also provide electronic payment services in El Salvador with wide geographic coverage, the details of which are reported in table IV.4.

Table IV.4
El Salvador: agencies and payment points

Firm	No. of payment points	Type of transaction
Puntoxpress	91 "Súper Selectos" stores, national coverage 28 "Biggest" restaurants 71 "Farmacias Económicas" pharmacies 2 Walmart stores 2 "Despensa Familiar" stores 6 "El Gallo más gallo" stores 49 "Almacenes Prado" stores 29 "La Buena pharmacies" (east) 5 "Tiendas Galo" shops (east) 1 "Puma" gas station (American Park) 1 Sears Multiplaza store **Total: 285**	Loan payments: Integral Sociedad de Ahorro y Crédito, Credi Q, FINCA, Presta Fácil, Lotificaciones Diversas S.A. (LOTIVERSA), Óptima Servicios Financieros, Fundación para el Autodesarrollo de la Micro y Pequeña Empresa (FADEMYPE) Utilities payment: electricity, fixed and cellular telephony, cable, insurance Credit card payment: Agricultural Bank, Citibank, Almacenes Simán, Prisma Moda, First Bank of the Workers Collection of remittances from various firms Collection of gas subsidy University fees Newspaper subscriptions Payment of catalogue sales
AKÍ multi-service network (sister firm of Servicio Salvadoreño de Protección S.A. (SERSAPROSA))	20 "Virgen de Guadalupe" pharmacies 16 "El Centro" pharmacy 4 Own agencies in the metropolitan area of San Salvador 6 "El Baratillo" stores 25 Local "Súper tiendas" stores in other cities 2 Texaco gas stations 12 Local pharmacies in other cities 20 Commercial outlets such as bookshops/stationers, mobile phone kiosks, local stores Total: 105	Utilities payment: electricity, fixed telephony, mobile, Internet, cable (all firms) Payment of colleges and university fees Payment of insurance premiums Payment of catalogue sales To be available shortly: credit card payments, loan payments and remittances from affiliate institutions

Source: Prepared by the author.

4. Financial channels and distribution services

Owing to the wide variety of institutions that provide financial services to the rural sector in El Salvador, and given the unsystemized nature of the data in question, this section identifies the three main institutions that provide support to the sector, and then analyses the financial services they provide, along with their respective distribution channels.

According to SSF figures, in 2015, the Agricultural Development Bank (BFA) had a loan portfolio of US$ 222.8 million, of which 34% were supplied to women. The main credit segments are concentrated in the agricultural sector, mainly basic grains, and the activities of micro and small-scale producers. The composition of the credit portfolio involves a higher risk profile than that of a commercial bank, so management and market knowledge have been the key to maintaining a sound portfolio.

In 2015 BFA had customer deposits totalling US$ 236 million, with 88.5% of depositors holding a balance of less than US$ 1,000. Half of the accounts are fixed-term savings, 38.8% are savings accounts and the rest are demand deposits. Microinsurance services are also provided, totalling US$ 1.1 million.

The bank has 28 branches, four service points (*serviagencias*) and nine express facilities (*cajas exprés*) located at strategic points, such as the *Ciudad Mujer* multi-service centres.[9] In 2015, it launched a pilot plan involving the installation of three ATMs. It also supplies some of its services over the Internet and by phone.

Banco Hipotecario is a publicly-owned bank dedicated to supporting micro and small enterprises and ranks second in funding the agricultural sector, with a loan portfolio of US$ 102.2 million. Unlike BFA, its portfolio is concentrated (75.3%) in meeting demand from agricultural exporters. In particular, it is funding the renewal of country's coffee plantations, which in recent years suffered a severe attack of leaf rust and other diseases that caused serious damage to the coffee trees. It also provides major support to sugarcane growers in El Salvador, whether individual producers, cooperatives or mills.

Banco Hipotecario has 28 branches in 12 departments of the country, along with 59 ATMs; and it operates telephone and internet banking services.

The FEDECRÉDITO system consolidates the operations of a wide-ranging network of cooperative banks distributed throughout the country. In 2015, its total credit portfolio amounted to US$ 266.8 million, having grown substantially in recent years from a level of US$ 141.8 million in 2010. Lending to the agriculture sector accounted for just 0.6% of the total, equivalent to US$ 1.7 million. Of this, about US$ 900,000 corresponds to an agreement with MAG to extend microcredits to small-scale producers (162 loans) from the north-east of the country, channelled through the Rural Development and Modernization Project for the Eastern Region (PRODEMORO) (FEDECRÉDITO, 2016). FEDECRÉDITO has established itself as a second-tier operator for its member entities, lending nearly US$ 201.4 million in 2014.

FEDECRÉDITO has pursued an aggressive strategy to consolidate its presence in the 14 departments of El Salvador and in most of the 260 municipalities. It is currently promoting the programme *"a la vuelta de tus sueños"* [make your dreams come true], which aims to install financial service access points in more remote areas of the country. The FEDECRÉDITO System has 57 partner institutions: seven workers' banks and 50 credit unions located in the municipalities. In addition to the branches of its partners, it provides services through a network of 160 ATMs (*FEDE red 365*), along with 229 non-bank financial correspondents (*FEDE punto vecino*), mobile banking (*FEDE Móvil*) and telephone banking.

---

[9] The *Ciudad Mujer* programme is a government initiative under which an Office for Women's Affairs consolidates various State services, such as health care, training, access to finance, legal advice, security and others.

5. Innovations

Several entities of the financial system are implementing innovative initiatives, and some are adapting their organizational structure to align more closely with their financial inclusion programmes. Given its recent implementation and innovative nature, documentary information is very limited, so much of the data on these actions were obtained through direct interviews with key system players. Some initiatives are described below, but more may exist and better systematization is needed.

The mobile phone coverage rate in El Salvador is estimated at 148%. According to the financial inclusion survey (BCR, 2016), 27% of the population claim to have used the transfer and payment service via mobile phones despite reservations about its trustworthiness. The main product used to carry out such transactions is Tigo Money, supplied by the Tigo telecommunications firm. The company has made it possible to carry out a series of transactions through its network, such as the purchase of subsidized gas, electricity bill payments, payroll via cell-phone, payments in the Older Adults programme and digitization of the payments of various firms.

At the time of the study, there were four other firms interested in obtaining authorization to provide electronic money services. One of the main obstacles to mobile financial services is the weak interoperability between telecommunications service providers and financial institutions.

Banco Agrícola ranks first in terms of both loans and assets in El Salvador. In 2016, it created a financial inclusion division to adapt the various existing products to the needs of the population that lacks access to formal financial services.

Among the innovative programmes it promotes, it has decided to take advantage of its status as the country's largest remittance payer, which enables it to access people who do not have formal bank accounts. By applying a risk-based methodology, it determines the frequency of remittance flows per month and provides users with a stable flow of financial resources that enables them to access a wide range of services, such as remittance payments, education and housing loans, microinsurance and training in financial education.

Banco Agrícola has its own network of more than 1,000 financial service access points located throughout the country; and, to continue supporting financial inclusion, it recently advocated for and promoted the regulations on the subject. It managed to expand its coverage in this modality and added over 100 correspondents.

Some mature institutions with a long tradition of financial services are investing to define their financial inclusion strategy, which includes basic tasks such as the definition and scope of financial inclusion and the definition of the actions they will take to close the exclusion gap. In this connection, the Salvadoran Banking Association (ABANSA) could play a leading role in supporting different financial institutions, along with the Government, in designing actions that promote viable, feasible and best practices that have an impact on financial inclusion.

Following the entry into force of the Law to facilitate financial inclusion, in 2016 SSF created the Superintendency of Financial Inclusion, to oversee the new entities authorized by the Law. The entity is also responsible for the supervision of other regulated activities, such as credit bureaus, reciprocal guarantee societies, remittance receivers and foreign-exchange dealers.

With support from the Alliance for Financial Inclusion, BCR is implementing the "El Salvador Financial Inclusion Project", which includes holding roundtables with industry representatives to discuss credit access for microenterprises and small businesses, and training for trainers on the Financial Education Programme. It is also holding outreach events and conducting three surveys: the National survey of access to financial services in El Salvador; the National survey of financial capabilities; and the National Survey on Access to Credit for Micro and Small Enterprises.

6. User protection mechanisms

The Consumer Advocacy Agency is the institution tasked with defending consumers' rights. In particular, pursuant to the Consumer Protection Law (Legislative Assembly, 2005) and its respective regulations, in the domain of financial transactions it establishes the mechanism for calculating interest, along with conditions governing the collection of commissions and surcharges, and a prohibition on making access to financial services conditional.

The Consumer Advocacy Agency may receive complaints in respect of interest rates being charged above the maximum specified in the Law against usury, in which case it will impose the respective sanction and notify BCR, SSF and the corresponding courts of the regulatory violation by the entity in question.

7. Rule of law and administration of justice

In 2016, El Salvador ranked 86th out of 189 countries evaluated by the World Bank's *Doing Business* indicator (World Bank, 2016a). This indicator is formed from a combination of 10 components, of which El Salvador's fifth worst is "Enforcing contracts", where it is placed 109th. As enforcing a contract takes an average of 786 days, financial institutions tend to be very cautious, particularly in small-scale loan operations.

Since 2002, El Salvador has had the Law on Mediation, Conciliation and Arbitration as an alternative conflict resolution mechanism. Under this

Law, the Chamber of Commerce and Industry of El Salvador is the only entity authorized by the Government to conduct arbitration procedures, through the Mediation and Arbitration Centre.

In contrast, "Getting credit" is the component in which El Salvador is ranked highest; in 2016 it attained 15th place, 56 positions higher than in 2015. This significant improvement reflects the passing of the Non-real Estate Collateral Act (Legislative Assembly, 2013a) and its regulations.

The Moveable Collateral Act (Legislative Assembly, 2013a) replaced several regulations that were dispersed in civil and commercial legislation. The Law extends the range of assets eligible as collateral, including tangible and intangible assets, claims over future assets that the secured debtor acquires after the collateral has been constituted, fungible assets, intellectual property rights, specific elements of a commercial company, shares and other equity participations, as well as any good, claim, contract or action to which the parties attach economic value.

It also provides for the creation of a collateral register administered by the National Registry Centre (CNR) and inaugurated in October 2014. Registration is done through an online platform, which provides an expeditious way for users to register goods or confirm them; and makes it easier for financial institutions to obtain key information on the status of the loan applicant's collateral. It also allows users to recover the collateral more easily once their commitments have been fulfilled.

Although firms that provide credit reference services have existed in El Salvador for many years, they have been increasingly subject to complaints lodged with the Consumer Advocacy Agency, relating either to inappropriate credit ratings or to the sale of the respective databases. In response, a law regulating credit bureau services was passed in 2011 (Legislative Assembly, 2011b), which made SSF responsible for approval and revocation of the operating permits of credit reference agencies. The legislation also empowered the Consumer Advocacy Agency to receive users' complaints and to set penalties for violations committed by firms that handle credit history data.

The law further requires such firms to provide any information that consumers request, to update credit status on a monthly basis, and to provide information to customers free of charge. They must also accept information technology audits performed by SSF and operate a regional service centre to facilitate access in more remote parts of the country. Moreover, any negative credit data held on customers must be eliminated three years after the rating that gave rise to it; and any negative historical data must be deleted from the record within one year after the corresponding debt has been paid. Under the Law, credit bureaus may not use basic social service contribution records without the affiliate's consent; nor may they publish the names of credit defaulters (whether natural or legal persons) in any medium, or market the respective databases.[10]

D. Identification and analysis of public policy instruments

Public policy to support financing for productive development is mainly implemented through BANDESAL, although other funds to support productivity and innovation are provided through the Productive Development Fund (FONDEPRO), which is attached to the Ministry of Economy. For its part, MAG has an extensive seed delivery programme for basic grains, provides technical assistance to small producers, and implements programmes to compensate for the effects of droughts.

There is also a national initiative to support financial education; and BCR surveys report that banks are widely recognized among users as the main source of financial education. There are also programmes in public institutions and cooperative banks.

1. Development Banking

In 2011, following approval of the Financial System Law for Development Promotion (Legislative Assembly, 2011a), the old BMI was restructured to create BANDESAL. The legislation empowers BANDESAL to engage in second-tier banking activities, make direct loans and administer trusts. It is also tasked with managing the Economic Development Fund (FDE) and the Salvadoran Guarantees Fund (FSG). These institutions target the micro, small and medium-sized enterprise (MSME) segment, coordinating actions with BFA, Banco Hipotecario, the Social Housing Fund (FSV) and the National Fund for Popular Housing (FONAVIPO).

Indirect financing through second-tier operations continues to be the main productive development support mechanism. Funding is provided through 42 financial institutions to the following activities: (i) intensive farming; (ii) agricultural development; (iii) investment in coffee plantations; (iv) promotion of family farming; (v) rehabilitation of agriculture; (vi) working capital for food security; (vii) working capital for traditional crops; and (viii) control of coffee diseases (BANDESAL, 2016). BANDESAL is also

[10] In 2013, the Constitutional Court declared Article 30 of the law regulating services that supply information on the credit history of individuals to be unconstitutional, so that in July 2016 new reforms to the Law were approved. These aimed to comply with the Constitutional Court ruling reforming Article 30. In addition, in late 2015 the Legislature approved 32 reforms to the law, including a reduction in the time for which a negative record for natural person or legal entity remains in the register; and if the arrears in question are worth less than half the minimum wage, the negative record is deleted automatically.

authorized to grant direct financing up to 50% of the value of productive projects, provided that the amount requested is less than 10% of the applicant's capital net of reserves.

BANDESAL uses FDE resources to increase production and exports, support production chains, promote enterprise competitiveness and support microenterprises and small businesses. The Fund can lend directly to natural or legal persons and provide funding to eligible financial institutions to support certain lines of production. It cannot be can be used to finance the State and institutions or firms without an SSF risk rating, or to buy shares or finance consumer loans.

BANDESAL administers several trusts, including the Special Agricultural Development Trust, the Coffee Production Support Trust, the Investment Support Trust in the Northern Zone and the Environmental Trust for the Conservation of the Coffee Forest (FICAFE).

Since 2015, it has been running a programme to promote financial inclusion among women, through credit, guarantees and training. Another inclusion support programme is *Banca Emprendes,* which supports MSME entrepreneurial initiatives.

2. Productive development policy

Acting through FONDEPRO, the Ministry of Economy provides non-reimbursable co-financing for MSMEs to strengthen their competitiveness and generate an economic impact in terms of employment, sales, new products or markets. Co-financing covers 60% of the project for MSMEs within the Metropolitan Area of San Salvador (AMSS), 75% for firms located outside AMSS and 50% for the acquisition of machinery, equipment, specialized software and infrastructure to comply with quality standards.

The Ministry of Agriculture (MAG) is implementing the Family Farming and Rural Entrepreneurship Plan for Nutritional Security, which includes the Agricultural Package Delivery Programme (seeds and fertilizers) for maize and beans. Data on the accountability of these programmes or projects are very scarce, which makes it hard to gauge the impact of the development programmes.

3. Credit Guarantee

BANDESAL manages the different guarantee funds, including FSG, which was created in 2011 (Legislative Assembly, 2011a) and the Agricultural Guarantee Programme (PROGARA). The Salvadoran Guarantees Fund focuses on supporting MSMEs in different sectors of production, for which it has 13 credit lines, while PROGARA lends mainly to small-scale farmers producing food security crops, and provides working capital for the coffee harvest.

4. Capacity building

The BANDESAL Training Centre, created in 2012, provided specialized training to 343 coffee-producing MSMEs in 2015 under an agreement with the Salvadoran Coffee Council and the "Enrique Álvarez Córdova" National Centre for Agricultural and Forestry Technology. It is also implementing strategic programmes that include human resource training as a key activity for producer development.

The central bank's 2016 financial inclusion survey found that only 4% of respondents had received financial education, which shows that much remains to be done in this domain to enhance understanding of the use of financial services. When asked what type of institution had provided the education, the most frequent reply was banks (28%), followed by non-governmental organizations (17%), cooperatives (14%) and, lastly, with very low rates, BCR (6%), and SSF (2%). These results pose two major tasks: to increase education generally, and to coordinate the different actors more effectively to disseminate financial innovations.

E. Key challenges for the financial inclusion of small rural producers

Financial inclusion in El Salvador is a relatively new topic, and the results of the latest survey on the subject show that only 12% of respondents have formal credit; 16% carry out financial transactions by mobile phone; only 20% save in the pension system and 23% have savings accounts in a formal financial institution. These results highlight the rapid growth of financial operations through mobile phones.

The high level of informality among the economically active population poses a challenge to create inclusive public policies which, in the financial sector, involve designing lower-cost instruments, promoting financial innovations that are easier for the lower-income segments to access, and designing programmes that suit their development-support needs. Simultaneously, an inclusive national policy is needed to support the increased coverage of access to education, health care, security, basic social services and productive development. Combined, these areas generate inclusive opportunities for all to develop their potential and obtain support to achieve their well-being.

A study by Villasenor, West and Lewis (2016) finds that El Salvador is a laggard in various areas of financial inclusion, such as the lack of public-private institutional coordination to define, promote and implement a coordinated strategy with all the national players. This situation is exacerbated at the rural level.

In this context, BFA and MAG have an opportunity to lead a rural inclusion initiative drawing on experience from other countries. Colombia is an interesting case in this regard, since the Intersectoral Commission for Financial Inclusion (2016) includes the rural sector among its four priorities and has proposed specific lines of action for the rural area: (i) facilitate the use of rediscount facilities offered by institutions that finance the agriculture sector; (ii) strengthen the rural guarantee scheme; (iii) design products and channels for the sector; and (iv) strengthen the rural risk management policy.

Given the high rate of informality prevailing in the economy and both national and rural problems, it is proposed to create a public-private institutional vehicle that will lead and coordinate the national financial inclusion process and make the rural sector one of its priorities. To this end, a National Council for Financial Inclusion (CNIF) will be created, to address three strategic challenges: (i) coordination failures between public and private entities; (ii) information failures between the suppliers and users of financial services; and (iii) regulatory/competition weaknesses in terms of the interoperability of traditional banking networks and mobile service networks for financial operations.

1. The challenge of coordination between public and private financial institutions

The research undertaken for this chapter revealed the existence of various financial inclusion initiatives, dispersed among different public and private institutions. Based on the experiences of countries in the region such as Colombia, Mexico and Peru, which have benefited from an entity that coordinates the financial inclusion initiative, defines national policy, identifies priorities, establishes programmes, allocates resources and promotes joint actions, it is considered justified to create a CNIF, which, under BCR leadership, engages SSF, the Technical and Planning Secretariat of the Presidency of the Republic of El Salvador, the Ministry of Economy, MAG, BANDESAL, BFA and representatives of the private sector.

In principle, the functions of the CNIF would be as follows:

- Propose a National Policy on Financial Inclusion (PNIF) to the Government, making recommendations on legislative norms or initiatives, proposing PNIF activities for the entities to implement and execute.
- Coordinate guidelines for the actions of public and private institutions, to increase financial inclusion.
- Recommend the implementation of measures to manage funding for PNIF implementation, between the public and private sectors.
- Set up a technical group specialized in rural issues to design a rural financial inclusion strategy, including both regulated and unregulated entities, and considering the dispersion of its actors, infrastructure constraints, high levels of informality and poverty.

2. The challenge of financial information between suppliers and demanders

Users of financial products face the difficulty of gaining easy access to the variety of financial services available in the different institutions. The rural sector suffers from a substantial lack of information, since dissemination is structured in the framework of agricultural activities, which excludes other activities that are important in rural areas. It is recommended that the CNIF fulfil the following tasks:

- Coordinate activities, publicity programmes or training events on financial inclusion in El Salvador. The Government and ABANSA should coordinate a "financial education week" as an anchor event, to publicize all the programmes being promoted in the country, with one day dedicated to the rural sector to disseminate what the (regulated and unregulated) public and private entities are doing.
- Design programmes to increase the financial infrastructure, targeting the rural area, since several municipalities do not have coverage; and increase the supply of financial services in municipalities with high rates of financial exclusion. The coverage of BCR surveys can provide an information base for this purpose.
- Continue to expand rural support programmes to address the negative effects of climate change, assess microinsurance coverage and efficiency, and review international experience (such as the case of Colombia).
- Design a portal on banking and mobile financial services to make it easy for the user to have all services available and get to know them.
- Produce and publish half-yearly reports on the provision of financial services in the formal and informal financial system, with an area dedicated to rural services and financial innovations (both mobile and online). These reports will assess the progress of the financial inclusion strategy.

3. The challenge of regulating the new technologies and ensuring their interoperability

The 2015 Law to facilitate financial inclusion increases opportunities to expand financial services through mobile phones, and it gives access to additional segments at a lower cost. One challenge will be to achieve interoperability between the mobile phone networks and the banking industry, thus making it possible to create a transactions ecosystem that fosters greater inclusion.

El Salvador can draw on the progress that Peru has made through the creation of the "Peru Model", under which a digital channel has been formed through mobile phones. Through this channel, 34 financial issuers and 3 of the 4 telephone firms participate in an interoperable network to carry out transactions. This has been made possible by the establishment of common rules between the banking regulator and supervisor and the telecommunications regulator. In this process, the willingness of financial and telecommunications entities to sign up to a national goal to achieve greater financial inclusion has been key (BBVA Research, 2016).

Interoperability is essential to reduce costs and increase coverage, fostering more competition among stakeholders. Financial interoperability poses technical, safety and reliability problems in the system. Traditional banks, which have invested many years in consolidating their credibility, may be more apprehensive of participating because of the risks involved, while new operators have no reputation to lose, but instead face the challenge of winning through quality and efficiency. To address these two realities and act as catalysts that generate confidence will be key tasks for the regulators (SSF, BCR and the General Superintendency of Electricity and Telecommunications).

The rural population, farmers and rural MSMEs will receive much of the benefits of interoperability, as they are widely dispersed throughout the country and face higher transaction costs to reach a financial institution, correspondent or ATM. The digital channel through mobile phones can have a greater impact in affording connectivity and inclusion to these segments of the country.

The recent Law to facilitate financial inclusion generates the conditions to authorize and regulate participation by mobile operators that provide electronic transaction services. An initial regulatory challenge will be to create conditions facilitating the entry of new operators. Although Tigo Money has an advantage in its market positioning and leadership, other firms, such as Mobile Money (MoMo), are also providing services in the country. This firm has signed an agreement with BFA to support the bank's mobile financial inclusion strategy (BFA, 2015), in what has become the first initiative to take advantage of the new Law.

Nonetheless, there are a number of risks in terms of barriers to competition. The Superintendency of Competition must also ensure that established operators do not place barriers in the path of new entrants, but instead promote and support greater competition through network interoperability that satisfies the security and reliability needs of the financial and mobile system.

It is recommended that BCR, SSF, ABANSA and the Inter-American Association of Telecommunication Firms (ASIET) make technical visits to get to know the "Peru Model" and set up interagency cooperation arrangements to enable the experts who ran the project in Peru to share the model and the strategy pursued.

Bibliography

Alliance for Financial Inclusion (2012), "Informe acerca del Foro mundial sobre Políticas de Inclusión Financiera 2012 de la AFI. Haciendo que la inclusión financiera sea una realidad", Bangkok, December.

Angel, A. (2011), "Panorama productivo e infraestructura para el desarrollo rural en El Salvador", paper prepared for the project "Determinantes de la Pobreza Rural en Centroamérica: desafíos y oportunidades para la acción", State of the Region, March.

BANDESAL (El Salvador Development Bank) (2016), "Memoria de Labores 2015", San Salvador.

BBVA Research (2016), "BIM: the Peruvian mobile wallet for the unbanked", *Digital Economy Outlook*, March.

BCR (Central Reserve Bank of El Salvador) (2016), "Demanda nacional de servicios financieros", San Salvador, July.

___(2015), "Memoria de Labores 2014", San Salvador, May.

___(2014), "Memoria de Labores 2013", San Salvador, April.

___(2013), "Memoria de Labores 2012", San Salvador, April.

___(2012), "Memoria de Labores 2011", San Salvador, May.

___(2011a), "Programa de Inclusión Financiera OTA-BCR" [online] http://www.bcr.gob.sv/bcrsite/uploaded/content/category/694410629.pdf.

___(2011b), "Memoria de Labores 2010", San Salvador, April.

___(2010), "Memoria de Labores 2009", San Salvador, April.

___(2009), "Memoria de Labores 2008", San Salvador, April.

BFA (Agricultural Development Bank) (2015), "Alianza estratégica entre BFA y Mobile Money", December.

Demirgüç-Kunt, A. and others (2015), "The Global Findex Database 2014: measuring financial inclusion around the world", *Policy Research Working Paper*, No. 7255, Washington, D.C., World Bank.

DIGESTYC (Department of Statistics and Censuses) (2015), *Encuesta de Hogares de Propósitos Múltiples 2014*, San Salvador.

___(2011), *Encuesta de Hogares de Propósitos Múltiples 2010*, San Salvador.

EIU/IDB (Economist Intelligence Unit/Inter-American Development Bank) (2016), *Global Microscope 2016. The Enabling Environment for Financial Inclusion*, New York.

FEDECRÉDITO (Federation of Credit Banks and Banks of Workers) (2016), "Memoria de Labores 2016", San Salvador.

FUSADES (Salvadoran Foundation for Economic and Social Development) (2015), "Encuesta de Competitividad Empresarial. Inversión, Competitividad e Incertidumbre", San Salvador.

Government of El Salvador (2010), *Plan Quinquenal de Desarrollo 2010-2014*, San Salvador.

Intersectoral Commission for Financial Inclusion (2016), "Estrategia Nacional de Inclusión Financiera en Colombia", May.

Legislative Assembly (2015), "Ley para facilitar la inclusión financiera", *Diario Oficial de la República de El Salvador*, vol. 408, No. 160, San Salvador, September.

___(2013a), "Ley de garantías mobiliarias", *Diario Oficial de la República de El Salvador*, vol. 401, No. 190, San Salvador, September.

___(2013b), "Ley especial transitoria para la suspensión de embargos por créditos otorgados al sector productor de café", *Diario Oficial de la República de El Salvador*, vol. 401, No. 182, San Salvador, October.

___(2013c), "Ley contra la usura", *Diario Oficial de la República de El Salvador*, vol. 398, No. 16, San Salvador, January.

___(2011a), "Ley del sistema financiero para fomento al desarrollo", *Diario Oficial de la República de El Salvador*, vol. 393, No. 197, San Salvador, October.

___(2011b), "Ley de regulación de los servicios de información sobre el historial de crédito de las personas", *Diario Oficial de la República de El Salvador*, vol. 392, No. 141, San Salvador, July.

___(2011c), "Decreto Nº 595. Reformas a la Ley orgánica del Banco Central de Reserva de El Salvador", *Diario Oficial de la República de El Salvador*, vol. 390, No. 28, San Salvador, February.

___(2011d), "Decreto Nº 596. Reformas a la Ley de bancos", *Diario Oficial de la República de El Salvador*, vol. 390, No. 28, San Salvador, February.

___(2005), "Ley de protección al consumidor", *Diario Oficial de la República de El Salvador*, vol. 368, No. 166, San Salvador, September.

SSF (Superintendency of the Financial System) (2008), *Ley de Bancos Cooperativos y Sociedades de Ahorro y Crédito*, San Salvador.

Superintendence of Competition (2011), *Sector tarjetas de crédito y débito. Estudio sobre condiciones de competencia en el sector de tarjetas de crédito y débito en El Salvador*, San Salvador, August.

Villasenor, J., D. West and R. Lewis (2016), *The 2016 Brookings Financial and Digital Inclusion Project Report: Advancing Equitable Financial Ecosystems*, Washington, D.C., Brookings Institution, August.

World Bank (2016a), *Doing Business 2016: Measuring Regulatory Quality and Efficiency*, Washington, D. C.

___(2016b), Global Findex Database [online] http://datatopics.worldbank.org/financialinclusion.

Chapter V

The financial inclusion of small-scale rural producers in Honduras[1]

Daniela Cruz[2]
Jesús López[3]
César Valenzuela[4]

Introduction

Small-scale rural producers in Honduras, and in Latin America and the Caribbean generally, face multiple obstacles in carrying out their productive activities and selling their surplus produce in the market. These include: high transaction costs, scant investment in productive assets and infrastructure, insufficient resources and lack of access to, and use of, financial services attuned to their needs (Sievers and Saarelainen, 2011).

In principle, financial inclusion increases rural producers' resilience to contingencies such as adverse weather conditions, which frequently affect their production process. It also helps to mitigate the negative impact of such adversities by making it unnecessary for producers to liquidate productive assets, thereby reducing their chances of falling into poverty traps

---

1 This chapter is based on a case study by Valenzuela and Cruz (2017).
2 Senior Researcher at Espirálica Research and Consulting.
3 Economist of the Economic Development Unit of the ECLAC subregional headquarters in Mexico.
4 Director of Espirálica Research and Consulting.

and enhancing their ability to recover economically on their own (Carter and others, 2007). In addition, financial inclusion enhances the capacity of small-scale rural producers to generate savings (Karlan, Ratan and Zinman, 2014, Efobi, Beecroft and Osabuohien, 2014).

This chapter identifies the elements of the financial sector, institutional architecture and public-policy instruments that foster the financial inclusion of small-scale rural producers, along with the characteristics of demand that limit inclusion in Honduras.

Section A presents an overview of the current status of financial inclusion and the financial sector in Honduras. The data show varying levels of financial inclusion between the country's different geographic areas, as well as a gap with respect to other countries. They also reveal that the vast majority of financial-system assets are held by banks (90.1%), followed by cooperatives (4.1%) and insurers (2.8%). The main financial products and services provided to the Honduran population by the financial system are traditional saving and credit products, followed by insurance products, remittances and pensions. Nationwide, the financial sector has a presence in all 18 departments of Honduras and in 67.1% of its municipalities. One of the determinants of the poor coverage of financial intermediaries in the other municipalities is the small resident population, since 93% of these municipalities have less than 20,000 inhabitants.

The results of the diagnostic study made as part of the National Financial Inclusion Strategy (ENIF) in Honduras show that micro- and small-scale farmers are the group that suffers the greatest financial exclusion owing to their location in rural areas of low population density. Moreover, the unstable and precarious nature of their income flows diminish their chances of gaining access to the system.

In recognition of the substantial financial inclusion gap prevailing in the country,[5] in 2015 the Honduran Government launched ENIF, the details of which are discussed in section B. The main challenges identified on the supply side are: scarcity of sector-targeted financing, regulatory constraints in terms of access requirements and reserve calculations, insufficient capacity to expand coverage and heightened citizen insecurity. On the demand side, the main constraints stem from a lack of financial and fiscal information in the sector, low levels of property titling and consequent lack of collateral, low and unstable incomes, highly dispersed rural population, weak linkage to production chains, poor articulation of actions that drive the sector, and a lack of technical assistance services.

---

[5] According to Global Findex data (Demirgüç-Kunt and others, 2015), 30.0% of the Honduran population held an account in a formal financial institution in 2014, compared to an average of 51.1% in Latin America and the Caribbean as a whole.

Section C describes the institutional architecture that underpins the financial intermediaries' supply of products. This architecture provides the conditions that foster or restrict the financial inclusion of small-scale rural producers. The institutional architecture in Honduras consists of prudential and supervisory policies, payment systems, mechanisms to protect the users of financial products and services, and complementary infrastructure and regulations that contribute to financial inclusion. Section D identifies the public policy instruments which, while reaching beyond the financial domain, affect the financial inclusion of small-scale rural producers by promoting their productive engagement. Lastly, section E discusses the main challenges.

This study shows that the financial sector supplies a broad range of products to serve the Honduran population, with regulation and supervision by government entities established some time ago. Financial institutions also have ample economic capacity to meet the demand for financial products and services.

Nonetheless, there are profound disparities in access to financial products and services, and in the use made of them; and the gaps are wider in rural areas. Although telecommunications provide a way to increase financial inclusion in rural areas, other elements of the institutional architecture could also help towards this end. The institutional architecture provides an effective mechanism for fostering greater financial inclusion among small-scale rural producers in Honduras. Having a complementary infrastructure that reduces the risks faced by rural producers, with slightly more flexible prudential regulations that are aligned with national conditions, with timely supervision and the technological improvements needed to optimize payment systems, would be an incentive to the financial intermediaries. Strengthening consumer protection institutions in financial services, financial education and the supervision of financial intermediaries will create incentives to increase the demand for financial products and services.

A. Current situation of the financial sector and financial inclusion in Honduras

This section analyses the status of financial inclusion in Honduras in the global context based on international comparator data from Global Findex (Demirgüç-Kunt and others, 2015) and the report on global financial inclusion published by The Economist Intelligence Unit and the Inter-American Development Bank (EIU/IDB, 2016). To begin with, the status of financial inclusion in Honduras is contrasted with the situation in Latin America and the Caribbean as a whole, and then the characteristics of the financial system in Honduras are reviewed, highlighting the financial inclusion deficits that persist in rural areas.

1. Status of financial inclusion in Honduras in the international context

Compared to other countries and regions of the world, Honduras displays a substantial inclusion deficit both nationally and in the rural area. Data from Global Findex (Demirgüç-Kunt and others, 2015) show that 30% of all adults aged over 15 years held an account in the formal financial system in 2014; but the figure was only 24.9% in rural areas (see figure V.1). In terms of other basic products supplied by the financial institutions, only 14.5% of Honduran adults over 15 saved in financial institutions, compared to 11.3% of their rural peers. Moreover, just 9.7% of all adults over the age of 15, and 7.8% of those in the rural area, had obtained credit of some kind from financial institutions.

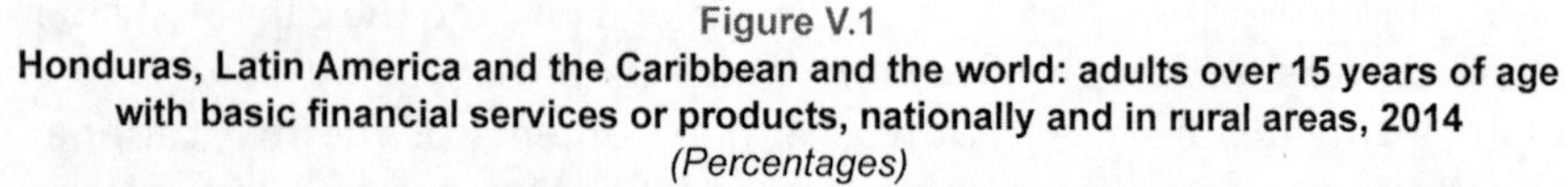

Figure V.1
Honduras, Latin America and the Caribbean and the world: adults over 15 years of age with basic financial services or products, nationally and in rural areas, 2014
(Percentages)

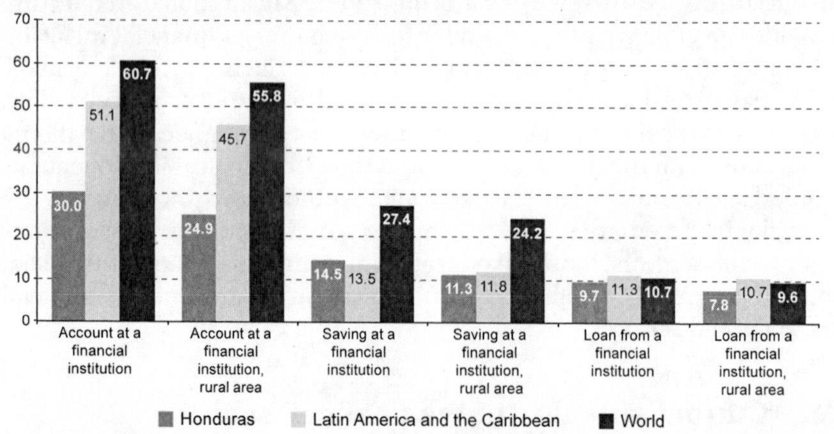

Source: Prepared by the authors, on the basis of A. Demirgüç-Kunt and others, "The Global Findex Database 2014: measuring financial inclusion around the world", *Policy Research Working Paper*, No. 7255, Washington, D.C., World Bank, 2015.

When comparing the data on the aforementioned products and services with the averages in Latin America and the Caribbean and worldwide, Honduras is a laggard in most of the traditional products supplied by the financial system, except in the proportion of the over-15 population that has savings in a financial institution. The savings and credit differentials between Honduras and the average for Latin America and the Caribbean range from +1% (saving in a financial institution, where Honduras is above the regional average) to -2.9% (loan from an institution in rural areas, Honduras below average). Relative to the world, however, Honduras lags behind in all products.

Honduras is also a laggard among the Central American countries and the Dominican Republic. Figure V.2 reports an evaluation of the three traditional variables of financial products and services in the Central American countries and the Dominican Republic, both nationally and for rural areas. A simple index of financial inclusion is calculated from these variables: the larger the polygon the higher the inclusion index. The largest polygon clearly pertains to Costa Rica, followed by the Dominican Republic, Panama, Guatemala, El Salvador, Honduras and, lastly, Nicaragua. It is also clear that most countries display a lower percentage in terms of credit than in current-account and saving products and services. This can be interpreted as both posing challenges and offering opportunities for improvement in the Honduran financial system.

Figure V.2

Central America and the Dominican Republic: adults over 15 years old using basic financial services or products, nationally and in rural areas, 2014

(Percentages)

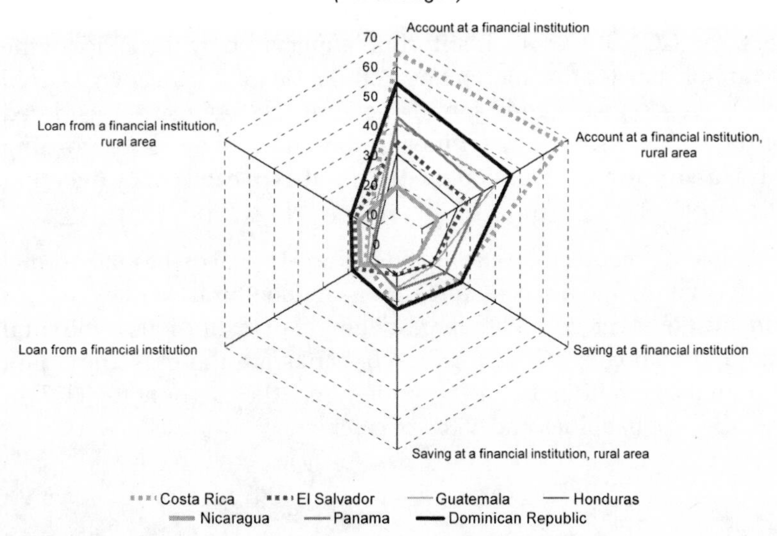

Source: Prepared by the authors, on the basis of A. Demirgüç-Kunt and others, "The Global Findex Database 2014: measuring financial inclusion around the world", *Policy Research Working Paper*, No. 7255, Washington, D.C., World Bank, 2015.

In the most recent EIU/IDB financial inclusion report (EIU/IDB, 2016), Honduras ranks in the third group of countries, scoring in the range of 30-55 points out of a maximum of 100, having risen six places to overtake countries such China and Argentina. The report attributes this progress to the commitment of its institutions to financial inclusion and the launch of ENIF in 2015.

2. Current situation of the financial system in Honduras

This section makes a detailed review of the current status of the financial system in Honduras. The following paragraphs describe the financial system from the supply side, using a general map of the suppliers of financial products and services, indicating the size and institutions that make up the country's supply of financial products. The level of access to traditional services and products provided by the financial system is also reviewed.

The Honduran financial system consists of 6,872 formal and informal suppliers of financial services and products (CNBS, 2014a and 2015a, REDMICROH, 2015a, CONSUCOOP, 2015, SAG, 2015). Formal suppliers are defined as financial intermediaries that are regulated and supervised by the Central Bank of Honduras (BCH), the National Banking and Insurance Commission (CNBS) or the National Cooperatives Supervisor (CONSUCOOP). Institutions supervised by the Office of the Secretary of State for the Interior and Population (SEIP), through its Civil Cooperatives Registry and Monitoring Unit (URSAC), are considered informal. Table V.1 lists the entities of the financial system according to this classification, indicating the legal status of each entity (whether public or private).

Table V.2 reports the assets, liabilities and capital of the main formal and informal private financial institutions in Honduras. While the legal and institutional category with largest number of institutions is the rural saving and loan cooperative (*caja rural*), banks are the most important entities in the Honduran financial system, since they account for 90.1% of assets, 95.4% of liabilities and 66.1% of capital.

Table V.1
Honduras: financial system institutions, by type of regulation and origin of capital
(Number of institutions)

	Private institutions	Number	Public institutions	Number	Total
Regulated institutions	Banks	15	Central Bank of Honduras (BCH)	1	2 782 institutions
			National Bank for Agricultural Development (BANADESA)	1	
	Financial companies	10	Public pensions funds: Public Employee Retirement and Pension Institute (INJUMPEMP), National Teachers' Pension Institute (INPREMA), (INPREMA), Social Security Institute of Employees of the National Autonomous University of Honduras (INPREUNAH), Military Pension Institute (IPM), Honduran Social Security Institute (IHSS)	5	
	Private Financial Development Organizations (OPDF)	5			
	Saving and loan cooperatives	241	Second-tier bank: Honduran Bank for Production and Housing (BANHPROVI)	1	
	Mixed services cooperatives	2 453	Second-tier financing funds: National Fund for Sustainable Rural Development (FONADERS), National Commission of Housing and Human Settlements (CONVIVIENDA) and Crédito Solidario	3	
	Second tier bank (Private contributions regime)	1			
	Insurance companies	11			
	Private pension funds	3			
	Mutual guarantee fund manager	1			
	Credit bureaus	2			
	Representation offices	2			
	Credit cards processors	4			
	Stock brokerages	1			
	Stock exchanges	8			
	General deposit warehouses	5			
	Exchange bureaus	4			
	Money remittance firms	5			
Unregulated institutions	Private Development Organizations (DPOs)	14			4 090 institutions
	Rural saving and loan cooperatives	4 062			
	Second-tier institutions	14			
Total number of institutions		6 861		11	6 872 institutions

Source: Prepared by the authors, on the basis of National Banking and Insurance Commission (CNBS), 2015 [online] http://www.cnbs.gob.hn/ and "Información financiera", Tegucigalpa [online] http://www.cnbs.gob.hn/blog/category/informacion-financiera/; Microfinance Network of Honduras (REDMICROH), *Mapeo institucional de la oferta financiera para la MIPYME en Honduras 2015*, Tegucigalpa, 2015; National Cooperatives Supervisory Council CONSUCOOP), "Registro de cooperativas", Tegucigalpa, 2015 [online] http://transparencia.consucoop.hn/estructura/servicios/requisitos/registro; and Secretariat of Agriculture and Livestock, National Sustainable Rural and Urban Development Programme, Tegucigalpa, 2015.

Table V.2
Honduras: assets, liabilities and capital of the main financial institutions, December 2015
(Millions of dollars and percentages)

Type	No.	Assets	Percentages	Liabilities	Percentages	Capital	Percentages
Banks[a]	16	19 449.5	90.1	17 819.8	95.4	1 629.7	66.1
Finance companies	10	426.4	2.0	334.0	1.8	92.3	3.7
Private financial development organizations (OPDFs)	5	80.1	0.4	54.8	0.3	25.3	1.0
Cooperatives[b]	90	881.1	4.1	438.6	2.3	442.5	17.9
Private development organizations (OPDs)[c]	12	150.9	0.7	24.1	0.1	126.7	5.1
Insurers	11	596.9	2.8	n.a.	0.0	149.4	6.1
Total	144	21 584.9	100	18 671.4	100	2 465.9	100

Source: Prepared by the authors, on the basis of National Banking and Insurance Commission (CNBS), "Memoria 2015", Tegucigalpa, 2015 [online] http://www.cnbs.gob.hn/files/memoria/MEMORIA%20 2015.pdf; Federation of Savings and Loan Cooperatives of Honduras (FACACH), "Mapeo del Sistema Federado de Ahorro y Crédito de Honduras 2008-2009. Actualizado a 2014", Tegucigalpa, 2014; MIX Market, "Honduras Market Overview", Washington, D.C., undated [online] https://www.themix.org/mixmarket/countries-regions/honduras; and Microfinance Network of Honduras (REDMICROH), 2015.

[a] Figures include information from 15 commercial banks and one public bank (BANADESA).

[b] Only includes figures available from cooperatives affiliated to FACACH.

[c] Only includes figures available from the affiliated OPDs of the Honduras Microfinance Network (REDMICROH).

The institutions described below are classified according to the functions they perform in the financial system, grouped as follows: regulatory and supervisory institutions of the financial system; financial institutions; and other institutions related to the financial system.

The regulators and supervisors of the formal financial system of Honduras are BCH, CNBS and the National Cooperatives Supervisory Council (CONSUCOOP).

The central bank is responsible for formulating, developing and implementing the country's monetary, credit and exchange-rate policy, and for ensuring the proper functioning and stability of the country's financial and payment systems. It is thus the highest prudential regulatory authority in the Honduran financial and economic system, while CNBS is specifically responsible for the control, oversight and supervision of the regulated financial system and other supervised entities that perform similar functions.[6] Lastly, CONSUCOOP supervises and regulates cooperatives.[7]

The historical evolution of non-bank intermediaries or cooperatives, coupled with the intrinsic features of their financial operation and specifics of their customers, have led to cooperatives being supervised by an institution

[6] The CNBS organizational structure includes three superintendencies, though which the Commission fulfills its responsibilities: the Superintendency of Banks and Other Financial Institutions, the Superintendency of Insurance and the Superintendency of Pensions and Securities.

[7] CONSUCOOP regulates cooperatives engaging in various activities, such as agroforestry, agriculture, savings and loans, mixed services, coffee, housing, transportation, industrial, consumer, student, fishing and agribusiness activities.

specialized in a differentiated regulatory framework that does not include prudential regulation (Arzbach, Durán and Japp, 2012).

The regulation and supervision of the informal financial system is the responsibility of SEIP, which authorizes and supervises the operation of Private Development Organizations (OPDs) through URSAC, and the Regulatory Commission for the Private System of Rural Saving and Loan Cooperatives, which, however, is not currently operating.

The Financial System Law gives banks the most flexibility to provide services and financial products to the general public, as they are authorized by law to engage in up to 26 types of transaction, including receiving demand and time deposits; granting all types of loans in national or foreign currency; issuing general, commercial, and mortgage bonds along with mortgage certificates; and accepting and administering trust funds.[8]

As detailed in Table V.1, the formal financial system in Honduras has 15 private banks, two development banks, one central bank and 10 finance companies. Of these, seven specialize in serving micro, small and medium-sized enterprises (MSMEs), or in microfinance. These specialized institutions operate through network of 164 branches throughout national territory and have a portfolio totalling roughly US$ 88.2 million.[9]

Cooperatives in Honduras can engage in production, service or consumption activities, or a mixture thereof; and they can provide both first- and second-tier financial services, as long as they comply with the cooperative principles established in the Honduran Cooperatives Law. Under this Law, financial intermediation by saving and loan cooperatives includes any act of raising money from their members to be lent on to other members or to be invested in the financial market, regardless of the document that formalizes the transaction.[10] The reforms made to the Cooperatives Law of Honduras and to its Regulations in February 2014, turned cooperatives into regulated entities with their own supervisory body (CONSUCOOP).

Of the 2,694 cooperatives distributed across all economic sectors and departments, 241 provide savings and credit services, of which 92 belong to FACACH, which manages assets of about US$ 1,862.3 million and serves over 823,000 members.

Private Development Organizations (OPDs) emerged in the mid-1980s as institutions dedicated to the promotion of local and national development, through organized civil society initiatives and development programs that mostly provided cash grants and technical assistance to set up solidarity

---

[8] The banks and other institutions regulated by CNBS can provide insurance services, but only as the financial intermediaries of insurance and reinsurance institutions as described in Resolution 1001 / 19-08-2003 issued by CNBS.

[9] At an exchange rate of 22.94 lempiras (L 22.94) per dollar (average up to November 2016, published by BCH).

[10] The Honduran Cooperatives Law was amended by Decree No. 174-2013.

groups and community banks. In 2001 the law regulating private development organizations dedicated to financial activities was issued through Decree No. 229-2000, regulating the OPDs whose main activity is the financing of micro and small enterprises (MSEs).

This legislation authorizes Private Financial Development Organizations (OPDFs) to engage in up to nine types of financial transaction, including: granting all types of loan in national or foreign currency; accepting demand and time deposits (from their borrowers only); obtaining loans from public and private institutions; and administering special funds of MSE support programmes.

The legal category of rural saving and loan cooperative (*caja rural*) was created in the Law for the Modernization and Development of the Agricultural Sector, which was passed in 1992. In the following year, specific legislation was issued through Decree No. 201-93 to create rural saving and loan cooperatives. These entities arose to promote governmental or international cooperation projects, generally channelled through non-governmental development organizations and the municipalities. The rural saving and loan cooperative system consists of a regulatory commission, the central fund (*caja central*), the rural savings banks and an advisory and promotion unit. In 2015 there were 4,062 *cajas* in Honduras, with 84,789 direct members.

Rural saving and loan cooperatives are extremely important for rural dwellers, since many financial institutions do not serve these areas (Marulanda, Paredes, and Fajury, 2011). The timely work and performance of the rural saving and loan cooperatives largely depend on the sound management and technical assistance provided to their members. The main problems faced by these cooperatives are a lack of funding under favourable credit conditions, the lack of support from technical assistance programs for their operation, and the limited national public policies to support them, beyond the granting of public funds (CNBS/IDB, 2015).

The financial system currently includes 11 insurance and reinsurance institutions, with total assets of around US$ 596.9 million at December 2015. To sell their policies, insurance companies may use direct brokerage or insurance agents or brokerage firms, either dependent or independent, that are registered in the agent and broker registry maintained by the CNBS.

Other institutions complement the supply of financial products and services, including credit bureaus, development banks, mutual guarantee fund managers, and pension fund managers.

There are two private credit bureaus (Equifax and TransUnion) and a public one (Central de Información Crediticia) that receive data both from the financial sector and from public utility providers and commerce. The information provided by the credit bureaus is available to all institutions that supply them with data. The borrower and endorser of a loan also have access to the relevant credit history and can rectify their personal information.

The credit bureaus manage information on the credit profiles of financial service users, which has allowed them to design parameterized models of credit behaviour. The situation in Honduras has been described as favourable in this regard; and the World Bank awarded the country maximum points in its depth of credit information index (World Bank, 2014).

The Honduran financial system has two institutions classified as development banks: the National Bank for Agricultural Development (BANADESA) and the Honduran Bank for Production and Housing (BANHPROVI).

The main mission pursued by BANADESA is to channel financial resources for the development of production and productivity in the areas of crop farming, livestock, fisheries, poultry, beekeeping, forestry and other activities related to the primary processing of such production (including marketing). It also carries out general banking operations of all kinds, coordinating its activities with the government's development policy for the sector.

BANHPROVI is the only second-tier publicly-owned bank in Honduras.[11] It was created in 2005 to promote the growth and development of production sectors by extending medium- and long-term credit to first-tier financial institutions. To this end, BANHPROVI was capitalized by BCH and is largely funded from its own equity.

Confianza SA-FGR is the mutual guarantee funds manager —a joint-stock corporation, created with support and impetus from the Honduran Government. It aims to facilitate MSME access to financing and support the agricultural, social housing and education sectors in the country.

The guarantee fund supplies four products that contribute to greater financial inclusion: (i) the Micro, Small and Medium-sized Enterprise Guarantee Fund (FOGMIPYME), which serves as guarantor for MSMEs in bidding processes; (ii) the Agricultural Mutual Guarantee Fund (FAGRE), which targets micro, small and medium-sized farmers and acts as credit guarantor to financial institutions; (iii) the Social Housing Guarantee Fund (FOGAVIS), which guarantees credit for social housing; and (iv) the Deposit Guarantee Fund (FOGADE), which supports educational loans for low-income students.

The pension system in Honduras consists of eight pension funds: five public and three run by private firms. The funds are under CNBS supervision and regulation. Private pension fund managers are governed by the Supplementary Optional Scheme for Private Pension Fund Management, while public pension institutions are governed by their own founding laws and the prudential regulations issued by CNBS.

Public pension institutions held cumulative assets of 102,083.5 million lempiras (L 102,083.5 million) as of end-2015. This was equivalent to 22.9% of GDP in that year, and with 81.9% of total assets concentrated in three

[11] In late 2016, BANHPROVI was authorized to engage in first-tier operations.

pension institutes. In 2015 there were also two private pension institutes with assets of L 552.2 million.

As reported in Table V.3, the traditional financial products supplied by financial institutions are current and saving accounts, along with loan and credit products. Insurance, remittance dispatch and payment and pension services are also provided.

Table V.3
Honduras: financial products and services supplied, by type of institution and level of access

Type of institution	Main products supplied				
	Current and saving accounts	Loans and credit	Insurance	Remittances	Pensions
Banks	1	1		1	
Finance companies	1	1		1	
Private financial development organizations (OPDFs)	2	1		1	
Cooperatives	3	3		1	
Private development organizations (OPDs)		1		1	
Private pension fund managers (AFPs)					1
Insurance companies			1		

Source: Prepared by the authors, on the basis of data from financial institutions and the National Banking and Insurance Commission (CNBS).
Note: 1: Available to the public at large. 2: For clients only. 3: Mixed (products either open or targeted to some sector of the population, depending on the category of the institution).

3. Geographic coverage of financial service providers

The coverage of the financial services that financial institutions provide directly to the population is formed by a network of more than 3,566 service points covering the country's 18 departments.[12] The service points used by financial institutions to supply their financial products and services are: head offices, branches, agencies, window facilities, correspondent agents, drive-in banks, ATMs and other public service outlets.

With this range of service points, financial services in Honduras cover 67% of the country's 298 municipalities. If correspondent agents are excluded, however, coverage drops to 39% of all municipalities.

Map V.1 shows the departmental distribution of service points (colour intensity denotes the degree of coverage available in each department). The departments that have improved their position since 2011 are those located in the west, such as Lempira, Intibucá and La Paz, which have graduated from the first quartile to the second, while Santa Bárbara moved up from

[12] The 3,566 service points comprise the network of banks, finance companies and OPDFs (2,303 agencies and branches), "Agente Atlántida" ATMs (870), FACACH service points (310) and REDMICROH service points (83).

the second quartile to the third; and those of the centre-east region (Colón and Olancho) dropped from the third to the last. It is important to mention that the range of financial services and products available is critical in the department of Gracias a Dios, where service points, including correspondent agents, are quite sparse at the municipal level.

Map V.1
Honduras: distribution of service points, 2011 and 2015

A. 2011

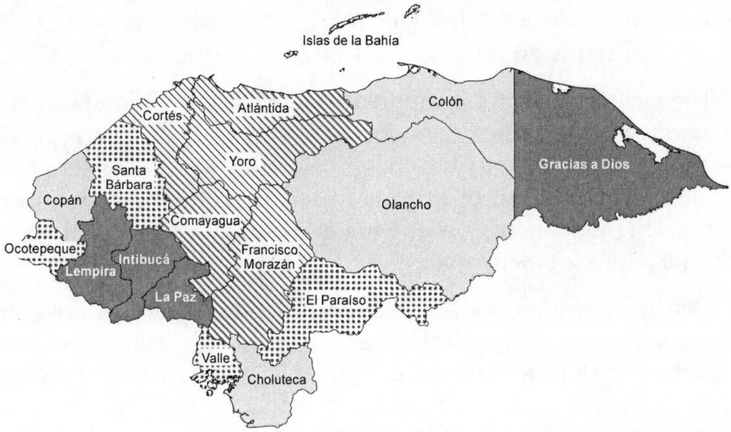

B. 2015

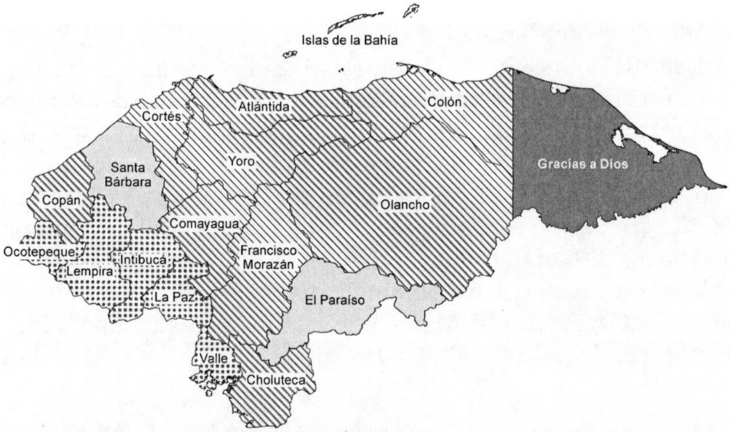

Source: Prepared by the authors, on the basis of data from the National Banking and Insurance Commission (CNBS), Tegucigalpa, 2015 [online] http://www.cnbs.gob.hn; Federation of Saving and Loan Cooperatives of Honduras (FACACH), "Mapeo del Sistema Federado de Ahorro y Crédito de Honduras 2008-2009. Actualizado a 2014", Tegucigalpa, 2014; Microfinance Network of Honduras (REDMICROH), *Mapeo institucional de la oferta financiera para la MIPYME en Honduras 2015*, Tegucigalpa, 2015.

Note: The departmental distribution represents the supply of financial services in 2011 and 2015. For both years, the departments shown with a dotted pattern were in the first quartile of the distribution, those with a dark solid shade were in the second quartile, those with a light solid shade were in the third quartile, and those shown with a line pattern were in the fourth quartile.
The boundaries and names shown on this map do not imply official endorsement or acceptance by the United Nations.

4. Financial inclusion gaps in rural areas

Despite the progress made in recent years, there are still large financial inclusion disparities. Segments that suffer the greatest exclusion include micro and small-scale farmers, microentrepreneurs and small traders, wage-earners who receive the minimum wage or less, recipients of remittances or cash transfers, either conditional or unconditional.

In the ENIF framework, a survey to ascertain why these segments suffer financial exclusion (CNBS/IDB, 2015) identified determinants stemming from both the supply and the demand side.

The factors that inhibit supply include: the lack of financial and tax information on the excluded segments (which also affects the identification and characterization of potential clients belonging to vulnerable segments), the limited coordination of actions to foster economic growth among individuals in the vulnerable segments, and the lack of technical assistance and business development services.

Demand-limiting factors include low rates of land titling (which diminishes the real collateral that can be offered), the low and unstable income of people in the vulnerable segments; territorial dispersion in the area (which increases the costs of distribution, promotion and recovery of the portfolio); crime and its impact on investment and entrepreneurship; and weak linkages to agricultural production chains.

Research undertaken in the rural sector (BID/REDMICROH/ Espirálica, 2011) found that agricultural MSEs had obtained an average of 1.5 loans from financial institutions. One of the features mentioned by the agricultural MSEs was that these loans had been paid on time or with slight delays of less than two months. The main collateral that agricultural MSEs had provided to obtain a loan had been real estate and guarantees. Just 40% of all agricultural MSEs received crop loans in 2010. In contrast, and as noted below, 49% of microenterprises and 65% of small non-agricultural enterprises, on average, have obtained credit (SIC/BID/Espirálica, 2013). In the case of agricultural MSEs, the main sources of financing were cooperatives and associations (25%), relatives or friends (18%) and private banks (15%).

Of the segments mentioned, agricultural MSEs display the largest financial inclusion gap. This is due to the intrinsic characteristics of their productive activity and the fact that the majority of this population segment lives in the rural area.

The results of the same study also indicate that 49% of non-agricultural MSEs have obtained credit, and these represented 65% of all MSEs, irrespective of the geographical area in which they are located. Non-agricultural MSEs also indicated that, on average, in the 12 months to 2012, at least three financial institutions had made them a formal offer of credit. While this shows that non-agricultural MSEs could access a dynamic supply of financing, it does not mean they find credit conditions that are appropriate to their needs.

Most MSEs that have obtained credit stated that they hold their savings in banks and only 19% of microenterprises keep their savings in other types of financial institutions (such as cooperatives, financial institutions and OPDFs).[13]

The MSEs that have obtained credit reported that they seldom use life insurance or private health insurance for employees, and only a minority use other financial products (such as factoring, leasing and pension funds). Despite the relative lack of use of these products, the trend in their use is weakly related to firm size: the larger the firm, the greater use of these products.

The financial exclusion of commercial MSEs tends to be more a partial exclusion in terms of access to other financial products, rather than loans for working capital or savings, or a supply of financial products under inappropriate conditions. The sectoral study does not identify significant differences in MSE access to financial services between rural and urban areas.

Employees earning up to one minimum wage have access to certain products and services offered by the Honduran financial system (Valenzuela, 2014).[14] These workers find it easier to open accounts, since they can demonstrate a regular income. Nonetheless, they also face restrictions when accessing and using other financial products and services, especially related to the amounts and types of credit available to them, owing to their low income level. The range of savings products available to them is also smaller (Valenzuela, 2014).

While people in this group have regular access to consumer credit, it has restricted access to housing loans because they are unable to meet all the requirements. These include: having a minimum income level, having mortgage collateral (they only have moveable assets that are not accepted as collateral), and having a home located in a non-residential area (CNBS/IDB, 2015).[15]

Moreover, according to figures from the National Statistical Institute of Honduras (INE), just 8.7% of the wage-earning population contributed to public pension systems in 2012, and only 1.2% paid into private pension schemes. These statistics show that both the formal-sector working population and informal workers in Honduras continue to have limited access to social security and pension services. It has been argued that the pension and

[13] According to the Sectoral Diagnosis of Non-agricultural MSMEs in Honduras, 81% of microenterprises and 95% of small businesses indicated that they kept most of their savings in banks (SIC/IDB/Espirálica, 2013).

[14] The minimum monthly wage in Honduras in 2014 was L 7,419 (roughly US$ 353) (La Prensa, 2013).

[15] The Law on moveable collateral of 28 January 2010, described below, was issued to support credit to MSMEs but does not include individuals such as wage earners.

insurance products associated with private funds are less attractive than those of the existing public schemes.

Remittance recipients usually interact with the financial system exclusively to receive money remittances and pay public utility bills (electricity, water and others); but they tend not to have a stable relationship with any financial institution in particular, since it is usual to receive remittances from different institutions. Similarly, according to a study by Valenzuela and Puerta (2007) and INE figures, the majority of households receiving remittances used their own or family resources (77%) to finance house purchases.

Other transfer recipients also often only interact with the financial system to pay public utilities (electricity, water, and so forth). As described above, and according to the available data, recipients of conditional transfers comprise an unbanked population group that usually keeps its savings at home.

Through the Ministry of Social Development and Inclusion (SEDIS), since 2015, the Honduran Government has been promoting the use of banking services among conditional transfer recipients by opening basic accounts for this population group. This process aims to make it possible to credit the bond in the recipients' saving accounts and thereby foster their interaction with the financial system.

B. National Financial Inclusion Strategy

As of 2015, several public and private initiatives were being implemented to promote financial inclusion in Honduras, but these were not coordinated. They included financial education activities promoted and implemented by the Honduran Microfinance Network (REDMICROH) and saving and loan cooperatives, public policy proposals and funding for the agricultural sector. Many of the initiatives were used as inputs when setting up ENIF, which was created as a Honduran Government initiative and conceived as a comprehensive strategy to include and engage various economic sectors.

The explicit aim of ENIF is to ensure that excluded persons have access to a wide range of financial services provided on favourable terms and under conditions appropriate to their characteristics and needs. This raises the need for these people to have sufficient financial education and technical skills to optimize their access to and use of financial services, for the purpose of reducing poverty.

The organizational structure that was approved by the Government of Honduras to serve as ENIF coordinating entity was that of a "Presidential commission for financial inclusion", with its respective executing agency. At the time of the study, late 2016, the coordinating entity was in the process of establishing its structure and appointing staff. Diagram V.1 summarizes the organizational structure, with the main functions and the members that were proposed in the design of the Strategy.

Diagram V.1
Honduras: organizational structure for implementation of the National Financial Inclusion Strategy (ENIF)

Organizational structure	Main functions	Members
Office of the President of the Republic or Coordinating Secretary-General of the Government	1. Make decisions on proposals for inclusion policies or strategies, regulatory reforms and others 2. Define inclusion policies or strategies 3. Supervise the work of the Special Financial Regulation Commission	Office of the President of the Republic or Coordinating Secretary-General of the Government
Presidential Commission on Financial Inclusion	1. Coordinate interagency actions 2. Integrate and represent the internal board of the executing agency 3. Supervise the work of the executing agency and request course corrections if it is diverging from its objective 4. Hire executing agency staff 5. Report on the progress of ENIF and present policies and strategies for financial inclusion to the President or General Coordinator	Presidential Commission on Financial Inclusion
Executing agency	1. Execute ENIF actions and implement and follow up its monitoring system 2. Implement programs within the framework of a financial inclusion policy and channel funds for technical assistance and financing 3. Formulate and propose policies or strategies for financial inclusion 4. Propose regulatory reforms 5. Generate and use information from surveys of the National Statistical Institute (INE) and other databases	Specific and specialized personnel responsible for promoting each strategic line of ENIF

Source: National Commission of Banks and Insurances/Inter-American Development Bank (CNBS/IDB), National Financial Inclusion Strategy (ENIF) 2015-2020, Tegucigalpa, 2015.

To fulfil its brief, ENIF will coordinate different public and private actors, whose roles are interrelated and necessary to foster financial inclusion in Honduras. To this end, it classifies the different actors according to the intervention mechanisms and components in which they play an active role, which, in turn, are classified in terms of supply and demand. ENIF specifies the role that each actor must play according to its component and intervention mechanisms, and identifies the key constraints it faces in achieving it.

Table V.4 summarizes the public and private sector actors needed to articulate ENIF, grouped by components to address the causes of financial exclusion. The components show that supply (financial institutions) and demand (excluded population) require the intervention of different actors in a given order or at a given moment, which is flexible.

Table V.4
Honduras: components and key public- and private-sector actors in the National Financial Inclusion Strategy (ENIF)

	Mechanism component	Component actors
Supply	Regulatory component	• National Banking and Insurance Commission (CNBS) • National Cooperatives Supervisory Council (CONSUCOOP)
	Governmental component	• Ministry of Finance (SEFIN) • Ministry for Development and Social Inclusion (SEDIS) • Ministry of Industry and Commerce (SIC) • Ministry of Agriculture and Livestock (SAG) • Executive Direction of Income (DEI) • Ministry of Foreign Affairs of Honduras (SRE) • Security Ministry • National Statistics Institute (INE) • National Program for Rural and Sustainable Urban Development (PRONADER)
	Technical assistance component	• Non-governmental organizations (NGOs) • Technology companies • Credit bureaus • International cooperation • Private firms providing technical assistance or business development services
	Financial component	• Second-tier institutions • International cooperation to promote financial inclusion • Mutual guarantee funds • Public pension funds
	Component of distribution of services and financial products	• Mobile telephony (Tigo) • Correspondents • Commerce
	Mechanism of internal intervention of the institutions	• Banks • Saving and loan cooperatives • Insurance companies • Private pension funds
		• Microfinance institutions and finance companies (including OPDFs) and OPDs)
Demand	Financial education component and financial user protection	• National Banking and Insurance Commission (CNBS) • National Cooperatives Supervisory Council (CONSUCOOP) • Consumer Protection Directorate • Consumer Protection Office • Courts • Education Secretariat • Higher Education Council • Financial institutions • Capital Foundation
	Technical Support Component	• Business Development Centre • Non-governmental organizations (NGOs) • Public or private entities related to technical assistance • International cooperation • Financial institutions

Source: National Commission of Banks and Insurances/Inter-American Development Bank (CNBS/IDB), National Financial Inclusion Strategy (ENIF) 2015-2020, Tegucigalpa, 2015.

In this context, the different components have different responsibilities: (i) the regulator component is responsible for adjusting the rules and regulating financial actions; (ii) the governmental component facilitates rapprochement between the financial institutions and the excluded groups; (iii) the technical assistance component strengthens the financial institutions' capacity to serve excluded population segments (iv) the financial component facilitates the channelling of funds to excluded populations; (v) the distribution component makes it possible to forge partnerships and generate investment in infrastructure to channel the new products; and (vi) the financial education and user protection component provides both excluded and non-excluded segments with appropriate knowledge on financial issues and their protection as users

The National Financial Inclusion Strategy proposes a general implementation chart and a matrix of responsibilities for the different participants, organized around four strategy lines: reducing risk, increasing profitability; increasing financial education and protecting the financial user; and improving economic and investment capacities. The design of ENIF has a system that allows for orderly and comprehensive monitoring of the status of its actions through the 57 indicators and 15 impact goals, according to the frequency of evaluation specified in the evaluation matrix.

The instruments or means of verification proposed by ENIF include the INE household surveys, which should include specific questions to measure certain indicators of financial inclusion; information provided by financial institutions and by the Government itself; progress reports from the institutions tasked with implementing the technical assistance, for both the supply of financial services and the demand for them; data provided by the mobile phone companies and the strategy's general monitoring and tracking instrument.

Lastly, ENIF also sets goals to be attained over a five-year horizon that will be used for a medium-term evaluation. The baseline values associated with the medium-term targets were calculated from a combination of indicators that took the average values of financial inclusion in Latin America and the Caribbean published by the World Bank and the Latin American Banking Federation (FELABAN), together with the figures and projections related to the Honduran context. Table V.5 reports the goals of the ENIF impact indicators. Over the five years, more than 50% of adults aged over 15 years are expected to have opened accounts in financial institutions. The volume of credit is also expected to grow as the proportion of adults over 15 who obtain financing from formal institutions rises from 7.1% to 12.0%.

Table V.5
Honduras: targets as medium-term impact indicators of the National Financial Inclusion Strategy (ENIF)

Proposed impact indicators		Year 0	Progress targets				
			Year 1	Year 2	Year 3	Year 4	Year 5
Access	Adults over 15 years old with accounts (*percentages*)[a]	31.5	33.0	36.0	40.0	45.0	51.4
	Adults over 15 years of age with accounts in financial institutions (*percentages*)[a]	30.0	31.0	33.0	39.0	45.0	51.1
	Adults over 15 who have a debit card (*percentages*)[a]	14.2	16.2	18.2	22.0	31.0	40.4
	Adults over 15 years old who are funded by formal institutions (*percentages*)[a]	7.1	8.0	9.0	10.0	11.0	12.0
	Number of credits disbursed with reciprocal guarantee funds[b]	0	25 013	29 214	33 009	36 802	40 597[c]
	Number of customers included through technical assistance to bank, cooperatives, finance companies and others[b]	0	50 000	100 000	170 000	240 000	314 366[d]
	Population receiving financial education (percentages)[e]	30.0	31.0	33.0	39.0	45.0	51.1
	ENIF-participating financial institutions receiving technical assistance (percentages)[b]	0	10	20	50	75	100
	Number of correspondent agents per 100 000 inhabitants[f]	7.6	9.6 (800 agents)	12.0 (1 000 agents)	15.6 (1 300 agents)	18.1 (1 600 agents)	25.0 (2 000 agents)

Table V.5 (concluded)

Proposed impact indicators		Year 0	Progress targets				
			Year 1	Year 2	Year 3	Year 4	Year 5
Use	Savings accounts used to receive wages (*percentages*)[a]	5.8	6.8	8.0	11.0	14.5	18.0
	Savings accounts used to receive government transfers (*percentages*)[a]	1.6	2.0	3.0	5.0	7.0	9.0
	Savings accounts used to receive remittances (*percentages*)[g]	4.1	4.2	4.4	4.6	4.8	5.2
	Number of basic savings accounts	0	50 000	100 000	170 000	240 000	314 366[d]
	Use of debit card to make payments (*percentages*)[a]	8.9	10.0	12.0	15.0	21.0	27.7
	Number of e-wallet users[h]	1 000 000	1 050 000	1 100 000	1 170 000	1 240 000	1 314 000

Source: National Commission of Banks and Insurances/Inter-American Development Bank (CNBS/IDB), National Financial Inclusion Strategy (ENIF) 2015-2020, Tegucigalpa, 2015; World Bank, *The Little Data Book on Financial Inclusion*, Washington, D.C., 2015; Latin American Banking Federation, "Indicadores financieros homologados para Latinoamérica", Bogotá, 2014.

[a] Figures to 2014.

[b] Figures according to the present study to 2015.

[c] Target based on projections made by the mutual guarantee fund manager, Confianza Sociedad Administradora de Fondos de Garantía Recíproca (Confianza SA-FGR) in its strategic plan.

[d] Target based on the estimated number of recipients of the "*Vida Mejor*" [Better Life"] conditional transfer programme, from the study conducted by the Social Forum on External Debt and Development of Honduras (FOSDEH, 2013).

[e] Indicator values calculated as the percentage of the population holding an account in a formal financial institution, since it is estimated that this is the only group that can obtain financial education from financial institutions.

[f] Figures updated to 2014.

[g] Figures for 2011. The target for this indicator was based on the percentage reported by Mexico for the use of savings accounts to receive remittances.

[h] Figures according to the present study to 2015. The target values are estimated from the "Number of basic savings accounts" indicator.

C. Institutional architecture

This section describes the institutional architecture available in Honduras to attain the ENIF objectives.

1. Regulatory and supervisory policy

The regulatory and supervisory policy for the financial system in Honduras governs the entry and operation of suppliers of financial products and services, according to the scheme outlined in diagram V.2. The requirements for admission into the formal financial system are defined by CNBS and CONSUCOOP, while those governing entry into the informal financial system are defined by URSAC/SEIP and the Regulatory Commission of the Private Rural Saving and Loan Cooperative System.

Diagram V.2
Honduras: regulatory environment and supervision of suppliers of financial products and services

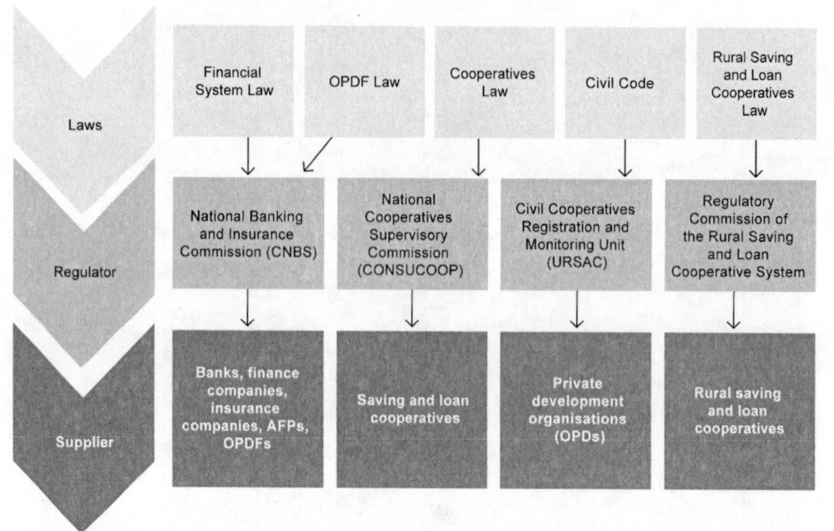

Source: Prepared by the authors, on the basis of information from Decree No. 129-2004, Decree No. 174-2013, Decree No. 229-2000, Executive Agreement No. 65-2013, Decree No. 110-2004 and Decree No. 201-93.

The National Program for Rural and Sustainable Urban Development (PRONADERS) manages the organization of rural saving and loan cooperatives at the national level, covered by the National Rural Saving and Loan Cooperatives Plan run by the Government.[16] However, the purpose

[16] See National Program for Sustainable Rural and Urban Development (PRONADERS), 2016 [online] http://www.pronaders.hn/.

of PRONADERS is to channel financial resources to the communities and thereby contribute to poverty reduction in Honduras. So, in order to achieve its mission and provide services, it sets conditions that rural saving and loan cooperatives must satisfy for registration in its directory.

The regulations on the information required of customers of financial products and services do not distinguish between type of intermediary or product. On some occasions, however, CNBS has issued specific rules for certain financial products.

As a way to complement the supply of financial products and services as described, some suppliers act on behalf of a regulated or non-regulated financial institution. These include correspondent agents and non-bank institutions that provide payment services using electronic money (known as INDELs). Correspondent agents are natural or legal persons legally set up to engage in acts of commerce, with which a supervised financial institution enters into a contract so that they can offer specific financial products or services to the customers of the institution in question.[17]

Correspondents must be authorized by the BCH to operate pursuant to the respective regulations (Minutes of Session No. 1054 of 2016). These institutions had been operating in Honduras since 2011, albeit without regulation. To promote financial inclusion in the country, BCH, along with CNBS, issued timely regulation and supervision for these entities. INDELs provide services such as the activation of electronic wallets, conversion of physical money into electronic money and vice versa, the consultation of balances, sending and receiving electronic money, transfers and payments.

2. Payment systems

The payment system is the set of rules, agreements, instruments and procedures that exist to execute fund transfer orders accepted between participating entities (Law on Payment Systems and Securities Settlement, Decree No. 46-2015). To operate a payment system requires prior authorization by the Board of BCH and, once authorized, is subject to CNBS and BCH supervision.

Payment systems in Honduras are regulated by the Law on Payment Systems and Securities Settlement. They are classified into high value and low value systems: the first are those used to make transfers between financial institutions, and with government entities, while the latter are generally used to make transfers between users through the financial system.

It is important to note that electronic money and electronic wallets are recently regulated products that are supplied by firms that provide telecommunication services.

[17] See National Banking and Insurance Commission (CNBS), "CNBS Circular No. 251/2013", Tegucigalpa, 2013.

3. Mechanisms for protecting the users of financial products and services

CNBS issued regulations titled "Rules for the Strengthening of Transparency, Financial Culture and Assistance to Financial Users in Supervised Institutions" (Circular CNBS No. 140/2012). These regulations detail the general guidelines which supervised financial system institutions must follow in order to establish policies and procedures for financial transparency, promotion of a financial culture, and efficient and effective response to claims, complaints or queries made by financial users. For this reason, CNBS is the institution that protects the rights and duties of financial users, acting through its Financial User Protection Directorate (DPUF).

CNBS requires each supervised institution to maintain areas or staff to attend to the financial user, duly identified, in order to attend their complaints or queries.[18] The regulations and circulars issued by CNBS require supervised institutions to inform financial users of all aspects of their financial products, such as the conditions, interest rates and commissions. Similarly, CNBS also collects information on the financial products supplied by the financial system and publishes it on its website.

4. Infrastructure to support financial inclusion among rural producers

In principle, the supporting infrastructure strengthens profitability and reduces the vulnerability of incomes obtained from rural production activities. Basic grain warehouses, for example, make it possible to store surplus production and to use inventories as collateral. Thus, basic grain warehouses serve as auxiliary credit organizations.

The Honduran Institute of Agricultural Marketing (IHMA), a technical institution that oversees government policies on the marketing of agricultural products by small-scale farmers, is in charge of the public storage infrastructure in Honduras. The institute has a storage capacity of 1,231,200 hundredweight (quintals) and also contributes to food security.

The private storage infrastructure in Honduras is run by private institutions known as "general deposit warehouses". Currently five of these are registered and authorized to operate by CNBS. General deposit warehouses have the function of storing, handling, guarding, conserving, transporting and delivering goods or merchandise. They also issue certificates of deposit and warrants to be used as credit guarantees.

---

[18] Saving and loan cooperatives are included under CONSUCOOP Circular No. 03-2014.

D. Public policy instruments

1. Productive development policy

Instruments whose goals include increasing the financial inclusion of small-scale rural producers in Honduras include the programmes of the Ministry of Agriculture and Livestock (SAG) and PRONADERS.

The Ministry aims to ensure that national agricultural production is competitive and sustainable, and that it has the capacity to engage in the international economy.[19] It also has to respond to the needs of the domestic market and integrate into a human, social, environmental and self-management-based development framework, with community participation, gender mainstreaming and sustainable management of natural resources.

The Ministry is responsible for the 2004-2021 State Policy for the Agri-Food Sector and the Rural Environment of Honduras, which includes rural finance.[20] The agricultural financing policy focuses on expanding and technically upgrading access to credit to support the productive modernization of the sector by diversifying financing sources and improving access conditions. The policy seeks to strengthen mechanisms such as agricultural insurance and guarantee funds to reduce risks to the financial system and producers.

The National Program for Rural and Sustainable Urban Development, which began operating in 2000, implements policies specific to the rural sector.[21] In 2014, it merged with the Honduran Social Investment Fund and the National Water and Wastewater Service to create the Institute for Community Development, Water and Sanitation (IDECOAS), which still maintains the objectives of the three original institutions.

Within PRONADERS, there is the National Fund for Sustainable Rural Development (FONADERS), an agency that responds to the demands of rural communities through sustainable rural development projects (social, productive, environmental, educational and institutional, among others). The Fund also implements rural development policies targeting the agricultural sector in conjunction with other institutions, although its links with other rural sectors is not always constant. It also implements rural development programmes financed by international cooperation.

---

19 See [online] http://www.sag.gob.hn/.

20 Information extracted and adapted from SAG "Política de Estado para el Sector Agroalimentario y el Medio Rural de Honduras 2004-2021", Tegucigalpa, 2004.

21 See [online] http://www.pronaders.hn/.

2. Moveable and mutual guarantees to increase access to credit

The Law on Moveable Collateral is designed to increase the financial inclusion of MSEs by expanding the range of assets, claims or shares that can be posted in guarantee, simplifying their constitution, advertising and execution (Decree No. 182-2009). The Law stipulates that moveable collateral may include tangible or intangible assets, merchandise, claims or shares, or obligations of another nature on movable property or merchandise.

In a complementary way, the Law on Moveable Collateral also creates a special registry for such collateral. The operation is designed to be simpler and more efficient than real estate registrations, and operates through forms and electronic access. Registration allows enforcement as agreed upon between individuals and, hence, is expeditious since it avoids recourse to the courts. The moveable collateral register is administered by the Francisco Morazán Business Registry, which, in turn, is operated by the Chamber of Commerce and Industry of Tegucigalpa which has links to the Property Institute.[22]

The Law on the System of Mutual Guarantee Funds for the Promotion of MSMEs, Social Housing and Technical-Vocational Education aims to create the business category of mutual guarantee fund managers and regulate their operation (Decree No. 205-2011). This Law regulates the constitution, organization, management and activities of mutual guarantee firms, which provide financial support to other institutions, guaranteeing or endorsing their financial obligations to enable them to finance themselves under better terms and conditions. These entities benefit MSMEs, since they provide financial backing to firms with little capital or financial support, to enable them to obtain better financing or investment conditions.

3. Capacity development among micro- and small-scale entrepreneurs

The National Vocational Training Institute (INFOP) works with government funds through an open and free service that has a specialized business development services unit. INFOP's varied range of business development services is currently focused on training, including the development of business administration and financial management capabilities.

Private institutions that provide business development services to the small and medium-sized enterprise (SME) sector in Honduras are currently entirely dependent on the availability of donor finance (grants). Similarly, the decision to serve the SME sector, or not, depends strictly on which categories of enterprise the funding donor wants to support.

---

[22] See [online] http://www.garantiasmobiliarias.hn/.

The Centre for the Development of Human Resources in Honduras (CADERH) is one of the few private entities with a nationwide infrastructure, with resources and 25 centres affiliated to its supplier network. It channels international donor funds for youth and adult development, which it executes through its network of centres identified by level of execution capacity and the areas to be improved. Private institutions mainly serve entrepreneurs, wage earners and large firms.

There are also trade association networks linked to MSMEs which supply financial products and services and provide business development services. The leaders include REDMICROH, Red Katalysis, FACACH and the Federation of Saving and Loan Cooperatives (FEHCACREL).

REDMICROH and the Katalysis Network are networks of trade associations supporting the microfinance sector, including both regulated and unregulated financial institutions; while FACACH and FEHCACREL are trade association networks supporting the cooperative sector. REDMICROH and FACACH have the largest number of affiliates and offer specialized services.

The trade association that has targeted the rural area most strongly is REDMICROH. Under its strategic framework and other auspices, it has conducted studies for financial product development and characterization of the rural area. These studies, which have received funding from international donors, aim to provide the association's members with the inputs needed to channel timely financing to those sectors. The Katalysis Network fulfils a similar function, although on a smaller scale, carrying out studies related to mobilizing savings, the network of correspondent agents and the development of financial products for rural producers.

The above shows that Honduras has entities that can provide support services to strengthen the design and management of financial products for rural producers, or to conduct sector-specific studies.

E. Conclusions

Honduran public institutions have for long shown interest in fostering financial inclusion by issuing laws and regulations, targeting public policies and implementing government projects or programs. This study also reveals that the financial sector has a wide range of products and services to serve the Honduran population, with regulation and supervision by government entities established some time ago. The study also finds that financial institutions have ample economic capacity among to meet the demand for financial products and services.

Despite the interest of the public sector, the range of products and services supplied by the financial sector and the capacity of both, there are still major disparities in access to financial products and services and the use made of them, which the institutions and available instruments have been unable to overcome. As noted above, in 2014, only 30% of Honduran adults over the age of 15 had an account, compared to an average of 51.1% in Latin America and the Caribbean as a whole. The gap between urban and rural areas is even wider.

The National Financial Inclusion Strategy seeks to solve this problem holistically. Nonetheless, small-scale rural producers are not specifically targeted in the challenges and solutions for fostering financial inclusion identified in ENIF, but instead form part of the overall strategy. Moreover, at the time of writing of the study, late 2016, the executing agency for implementing the Strategy had not yet been created.

Earlier studies and the ENIF diagnostic assessment mention a number of challenges in promoting financial inclusion among small-scale rural producers. These can be divided into two categories: (i) challenges that affect the supply of financial products and services; and (ii) those that affect demand. On the supply side, there is a shortage of financing for small-scale rural producers, compounded by regulatory constraints on access and reserve requirements, poor access to specialized technologies to serve the rural sector, lack of specialized human resources, limited tools for mitigating the risks associated with the sector, poor evaluation of the sector owing to inexperience or lack of knowledge, and increased citizen insecurity. Accordingly, differentiated and flexible regulation among the different financial intermediaries could help to enhance the financial inclusion of small-scale rural producers.

Demand-side challenges include a lack of financial and fiscal information in the sector, low rates of land titling and lack of real collateral, small and unstable incomes, high dispersion of populations in the rural area, poor linkage of small-scale producers to production chains, weak coordination of actions that drive the sector and the lack of technical assistance services to strengthen the sector. Thus, public policies to promote or modernize property registries, foster the development of production chains, achieve effective and efficient coordination of intersectoral policies, and support agricultural extension services could help to foster financial inclusion among small-scale rural producers.

Although telecommunications offer a way to increase financial inclusion in rural areas, the institutional architecture contains other lower-cost elements that could also contribute to this end. The institutional architecture offers an effective mechanism to foster the growth of financial inclusion among small-scale rural producers in Honduras. There is no doubt that a complementary infrastructure that reduces the risks faced by rural producers, together with prudential regulation aligned with national reality, timely supervision and availability of the best technologies to optimize payment systems, will provide incentives to financial intermediaries. Thus, the promotion of shared risk schemes, such as the mutual guarantee funds, and moveable collateral schemes could significantly increase the supply of credit to the sector.

Lastly, the strengthening of institutions that protect users of financial services, together with financial education and timely supervision of financial intermediaries, will strengthen trust and enhance incentives to increase the demand for formal financial products and services.

Bibliography

Arzbach, M., Á. Durán and C. Japp (2012), "Regulación y supervisión de cooperativas de ahorro y crédito en América Latina y el Caribe", *Documentos de la DGRV*, No. 3, San José, German Cooperative Confederation (DGRV).

BANHPROVI (Honduran Bank for Production and Housing) (2016), "Bienes inmuebles fondos propios", Tegucigalpa [online] http://www.banhprovi.org/DOCUMENTOS/VIVIENDA/BIENES%20INMUEBLES/BIENES%20INMUEBLES/Proyecto%20Bienes%20Inmuebles/CONDICIONES%20DE%20BIENES%20INMUEBLES%20FONDOS%20PROPIOS%20PARA%20COMITE%20DE%20CREDITO%20.htm.

___(2014), "Informe de gestión anual 2014", Tegucigalpa [online] http://www.banhprovi.org/transparencia/sitio/finanzas/PRESUPUESTO/inf-anuales/informes-gestion/informe_Anual_2014/INF_GES_2014%20web.pdf.

Carter, M. and others (2007), "Poverty traps and natural disasters in Ethiopia and Honduras", *World Development*, vol. 35, No. 5, Amsterdam, Elsevier, May.

CNBS (National Commission of Banks and Insurances) (2015a) [online] http://www.cnbs.gob.hn/.

___(2015b), "Memoria 2015", Tegucigalpa [online] http://www.cnbs.gob.hn/files/memoria/MEMORIA%202015.pdf.

___(2014a), "Información financiera", Tegucigalpa [online] http://www.cnbs.gob.hn/blog/category/informacion-financiera/.

___(2014b), "Manual reporte de datos de crédito", Tegucigalpa, May [online] http://www.cnbs.gob.hn/files/capturadores/Datoscredito/MRDC%20Capturador%20SL_Version%20public%2030May2014.pdf.

___(2014c), "Memoria 2014", Tegucigalpa [online] http://www.cnbs.gob.hn/files/memoria/Memoria_2014.pdf.

___(2013), "Normas para la gestión de información crediticia", Tegucigalpa, June [online] http://www.cnbs.gob.hn/files/GE/Compendio/2013/155-2013.pdf.

CNBS/IDB (National Commission of Banks and Insurances/Inter-American Development Bank) (2015), National Financial Inclusion Strategy (ENIF) 2015-2020, Tegucigalpa.

Confianza SA-FGR (Confianza Sociedad Administradora de Fondos de Garantía Recíproca) (2015), *Memoria Anual 2015*, Tegucigalpa [online] http://www.confianza.hn/wp-content/uploads/2016/04/Memoria.pdf.

CONSUCOOP (Consejo Nacional Supervisor de Cooperativas) (2015), "Registro de cooperativas", Tegucigalpa [online] http://transparencia.consucoop.hn/estructura/servicios/requisitos/registro.

Demirgüç-Kunt, A. and others (2015), "The Global Findex Database 2014: measuring financial inclusion around the world", *Policy Research Working Paper*, No. 7255, Washington, D.C., World Bank.

Efobi, U., I. Beecroft and E. Osabuohien (2014), "Access to and use of bank services in Nigeria: micro-econometric evidence", *Review of Development Finance*, vol. 4, No. 2, Cape Town, Africagrowth Institute, December.

EIU/IDB (Economist Intelligence Unit/Inter-American Development Bank) (2016), *Global Microscope 2016: The Enabling Environment for Financial Inclusion*, New York.

FACACH (Federation of Savings and Loan Cooperatives of Honduras) (2014), "Mapeo del Sistema Federado de Ahorro y Crédito de Honduras 2008-2009. Actualizado a 2014", Tegucigalpa.

FOSDEH (Social Forum of External Debt and Development of Honduras) (2013), "Análisis de la pobreza en Honduras: caracterización y análisis de determinantes, 2013-2014", R. Perdomo and M. Díaz (coords.), Tegucigalpa.

IDB/REDMICROH/Espirálica (Inter-American Development Bank/Microfinance Network of Honduras/Espirálica Research & Consulting) (2011), "Investigación de mercados para el diseño de nuevos productos en el sector rural de Honduras. Proyecto Mejoramiento de la calidad de los servicios financieros para la microempresa rural de Honduras", Tegucigalpa, May.

Karlan, D., A. L. Ratan and J. Zinman (2014), "Savings by and for the poor: a research review and agenda", *Review of Income and Wealth*, vol. 60, No. 1, Ottawa, International Cooperative for Research in Income and Wealth (IARIW), March.

La Prensa (2013), "Honduras: pactan aumento del 7.5% al salario mínimo para 2014", Tegucigalpa, 20 December.

Marulanda, B., M. Paredes and L. Fajury (2011), "Diagnóstico sobre el acceso a servicios financieros en Honduras", Banco Interamericano de Desarrollo (BID).

Ministry of Agriculture and Livestock (2015), Programa Nacional de Desarrollo Rural y Urbano Sostenible, Tegucigalpa.

MIX Market (n/d), "Honduras market overview", Washington, D.C. [online] https://www.themix.org/mixmarket/countries-regions/honduras.

REDMICROH (Microfinance Network of Honduras) (2015a), "Estadísticas", Tegucigalpa [online] http://www.redmicroh.org/estadisticas/.

___(2015b), *Mapeo institucional de la oferta financiera para la MIPYME en Honduras 2015*, Tegucigalpa.

SIC/IDB/Espirálica (Ministry of Industry and Commerce/Inter-American Development Bank/Espirálica Research & Consulting) (2013), "Diagnóstico sectorial de la MIPYME no agrícola en Honduras", Tegucigalpa, January.

Sievers, M. and E. Saarelainen (2011), "Value chains for rural development", Geneva, International Labour Organization (ILO) [online] http://www.ilo.org/wcmsp5/groups/public/---ed_emp/---emp_ent/---ifp_seed/documents/publication/wcms_161156.pdf.

Valenzuela, C. (2014), "Investigación sobre las estrategias preferidas por los hogares hondureños para enfrentar fluctuaciones negativas en el ingreso del hogar", Inter-American Development Bank (IDB).

Valenzuela, C. and D. Cruz (2017), "Estudio de caso sobre estrategias para promover la inclusión financiera de pequeños productores rurales en Honduras" (LC/MEX/W.22), *Project Documents*, Mexico City, ECLAC subregional headquarters in Mexico.

Valenzuela, C. and R. Puerta (2007), "Remesas, economía y estrategia para la reducción de la pobreza", Tegucigalpa, National Forum for Migration in Honduras/Human Mobility Pastoral, January.

World Bank (2014), *Doing Business 2015: Going Beyond Efficiency*, Washington, D.C.

Chapter VI

Overview and prospects for financial inclusion in the Dominican Republic

Rolando Reyes[1]
Cameron Daneshvar[2]

Introduction

Despite having rules and regulations aimed at facilitating access to financial products and services, the Dominican Republic has never had an explicit financial-inclusion strategy to systematically provide access to credit or savings products and to electronic means of payment for poor and rural populations.

The use of financial services in the Dominican Republic grew by about seven percentage points of GDP between 2007 and 2015; and the rate has accelerated since 2009, when the Dominican Republic's Payment and Settlement System (SIPARD) started operating. According to the results of the first Survey of Economic and Financial Culture implemented by the Central Bank of the Dominican Republic (BCRD, 2014a), 61.2% of the national population were "banked" in early 2014.[3] In terms of credit products, 40% of the total population receives some type of financing from the financial system or from other financial intermediaries. These figures place the Dominican Republic above the regional average.

---

1 Founding partner of Rolando Reyes y Asociados.

2 Associate Economic Affairs Officer in the Economic Development Unit of the subregional headquarters of ECLAC in Mexico.

3 The term "banked" is used in the survey to refer to individuals who have some type of banking instrument, such as accounts, loans or investment instruments.

Nonetheless, deep gaps persist in the country; and nearly all types of financial products and services are used significantly more by the urban population than by rural dwellers.

In response to these disparities, several steps have been taken in recent years to upgrade the legal and regulatory framework governing the financial system, which have facilitated and promoted access to financial services and their use. The approval and implementation of the Microcredit Regulation in 2014, followed by the Regulation for the Protection of Users of Financial Services and Products in the following year, together with its amendments, led to a deepening of financial inclusion. Likewise, measures adopted since 2005 to make the Asset Valuation Regulation (REA) more flexible also encouraged broader coverage of credit products.

In this connection, modernization of the payment system, the simplification and regulation of credit and debit card issuance procedures, the issuance of government subsidy payment cards and the emergence of mobile payment user accounts have fuelled financial inclusion both directly and indirectly. Moreover, as part of efforts to promote the use of financial services, the first National Survey of Financial Education and Culture (BCRD, 2014a) was conducted in 2014. This made the first-ever national measurement of the degree of financial inclusion and provided a comprehensive overview of the population's access to financial services and the extent to which it makes use of them.

This chapter argues that, to close the gaps in access to financial services for payment, saving, credit and insurance, and narrow the disparities in their use, both among the population groups of urban and rural environments and among high-, middle- and low-income groups, requires a comprehensive and explicit financial-inclusion strategy to be formulated and implemented, with the following specific objectives:

- Strengthen the capacities of users who are traditionally excluded from access to, and use of, financial services, as well as those of financial service providers, in particular cooperatives, in product design.
- Consolidate the leadership of development banks in the country's rural development by channelling funds through second-tier operations.
- Adjust the current regulation to strike an appropriate balance between inclusion and stability of the financial system.
- Promote access by financial service providers, in particular those serving rural users, to key financial infrastructure such as the payment system.
- Strengthen user protection and dispute resolution mechanisms, and expand their coverage.

In addition to this introduction, the chapter is divided into five sections. Section A describes the current status of financial inclusion in the Dominican Republic. Section B analyses the efforts made by the authorities thus far to increase financial inclusion. Section C describes the components of the institutional architecture currently in place in the country; while section D identifies the public policy instruments available to promote financial inclusion. Lastly, section E sets forth conclusions and recommendations, which focus on the design and implementation of a comprehensive and coordinated financial-inclusion strategy within the framework of the current National Development Strategy (END).

A. Status of financial inclusion

1. Situation in the international context

The World Bank's Global Findex database (Demirguc-Kunt et al., 2015) compiles data on financial inclusion worldwide. For the purposes of this report, figures from this database have been processed to extract basic information on financial inclusion in the Dominican Republic and aggregate information on Latin America and the Caribbean.

Although there are no other historical comparison data, table VI.1 shows that, in just three years, the proportion of the general population with an account at a formal financial institution grew by more than 15 percentage points. This vigorous growth may be largely explained by the result of the expansion of the payments system, especially in terms of debit card instruments for the payroll and mobile payments through cellphones.

Table VI.1

Dominican Republic and Latin America and the Caribbean: population with accounts in financial institutions, 2011 and 2014

(Percentages)

	Dominican Republic		Latin America and the Caribbean	
	2011	2014	2011	2014
General population	38.2	54.0	39.3	51.1
Female population	37.4	55.8	34.8	48.5
Poorest 40% of the population	22.8	41.8	24.1	40.9
Richest 60% of the population	48.6	62.6	49.5	58.1
Population with elementary education or less	25.3	41.1	30.0	42.9
Rural population	29.6	46.5	35.0	45.7

Source: Prepared by the author, on the basis of World Bank, Global Findex Database, 2016 [online] http://datatopics.worldbank.org/financialinclusion/.

The strongest growth occurred among the poorest 40% population group, followed very closely by the female population. To some extent, this reflects a relatively low starting point. The proportion of the rural population with accounts in financial institutions grew by nearly 17 percentage points, which may also be due to the growth of the means of payment.

A comparison of the results for the Dominican Republic and Latin America and the Caribbean firstly shows that, while the Dominican Republic was close to or below the regional average in 2011, three years later the only variable in which the country was lagging the regional average is the proportion of individuals with no more than elementary education who have an account in a financial institution.

One of the most significant differences occurs among the rural population, which in the Dominican case surpassed the regional average by 6.1 percentage points. Among the general population with accounts in financial institutions, the Dominican Republic exceeded the regional average by 3.4 percentage points. As noted above, the country's greater progress relative to the rest of the region is probably explained by the fact that the modernization of the payments system was also faster than in other countries, which is reflected in the declining use of cash, together with growth in the number of accounts and the higher degree of transactionality.

2. Situation at the national level

Table VI.2 reports the evolution of the GDP share of savings held in financial institutions and loans made by those institutions over the last ten years, and shows that financial intermediation grew by around seven points of GDP.

Table VI.2
Dominican Republic: GDP, loans and deposits, 2007-2015
(Millions of Dominican pesos)

Years	GDP	Total loans	Total deposits and securities (excluding shares)	Loans/GDP	Deposits/ GDP
Dec. 2007	1 455 253.30	314 243.00	452 468.80	0.22	0.31
Dec. 2008	1 656 961.70	370 043.30	497 243.70	0.22	0.30
Dec. 2009	1 729 468.40	411 726.90	575 598.80	0.24	0.33
Dec. 2010	1 978 851.90	469 018.20	657 021.10	0.24	0.33
Dec. 2011	2 218 428.80	517 806.30	744 942.50	0.23	0.34
Dec. 2012	2 377 503.70	578 096.20	808 673.70	0.24	0.34
Dec. 2013	2 558 585.60	677 212.20	906 585.60	0.26	0.35
Dec. 2014	2 786 229.70	751 852.80	992 686.50	0.27	0.36
Dec. 2015	3 023 116.10	872 426.20	1 109 688.20	0.29	0.37

Source: Prepared by the author, on the basis of figures from the Central Bank of the Dominican Republic.

The level of intermediation has been gathering speed since 2009, when the Dominican Republic's Payment and Settlement System (SIPARD), which is managed by the Central Bank of the Dominican Republic, began operations. At end-2015, the ratio of loans to GDP reached 29%, significantly above the historical average in Latin America and the Caribbean.[4]

Although it is not attempted to demonstrate statistically, the deepening of financial intermediation since 2007 must be positively related to financial inclusion measures, represented by the regulations put in place before the approval of the Regulation of the Banking Subagent (see later sections). In this context, it should be expected that the measures adopted to ease the Asset Valuation Regulations approved since 2005, and actions to expand microcredit, will have a positive effect on the ratio of loans to GDP. Thus, modernization of the payment system —with the adoption of electronic payment methods using cards and other media— together with the simplification and regulation of credit and debit card issuance procedures, should also have a positive effect on the share of savings in GDP, since opening an account or making a prior deposit is a prerequisite for receiving or making electronic payments.

Nonetheless, given the existing disparities, an increase in the number of transactions by users with accounts is not an indicator of a higher degree of inclusion, because this necessitates an increase in the number of users, as will be analysed in later sections.

According to the first Survey of Economic and Financial Culture (BCRD, 2014a) conducted by the Central Bank of the Dominican Republic in 2014, 61.2% of the Dominican population was banked at the start of that year, which means they used at least one financial product, including life and health insurance. If the definition is restricted to the number of people who own a savings or credit product, the proportion drops to 43%.

3. Gaps in the rural sector

Although financial inclusion in the Dominican Republic is well ahead of Latin America and the Caribbean nationally, there are pronounced disparities within the country, especially between rural and urban areas.

Table VI.3 shows the percentage of the population, classified as urban or rural, that uses the different types of financial services and products supplied by regulated financial intermediaries and other unregulated institutions and services related to the general financial system.

[4] Author's calculation on the basis of official figures from the Central Bank of the Dominican Republic.

Table VI.3
Dominican Republic: type of financial product or service used, by geographical area, 2014
(Percentages)

Type of financial product or service	Rural zone	Urban zone
Payroll account	18.5	28.8
Savings account	31.6	44.2
Current/checking account	2.8	5.0
Savings account in cooperative	9.8	12.5
Term deposit or financial certificate	2.2	3.0
Savings account or time deposit in foreign currency	0.6	1.5
Credit card	13.2	23.4
Prepaid card	5.7	7.5
Payroll loan	3.5	4.8
Vehicle loan/credit	1.2	2.7
Loan or deferred credit line	2.1	2.7
Loan for the purchase of appliances, equipment or fixed assets	2.0	3.9
Another personal or consumer loan	11.1	11.8
Cooperative loan	7.5	7.1
Loan or mortgage loan for acquisition/remodelling	1.2	2.5
SME loan from Banca Solidaria or PROMIPYME	1.2	2.8
SME loan from NGO or microfinance	1.0	0.8
SME loan from private banks	1.9	2.0
Pension fund managed by private institution (AFP)	16.4	25.7
Pension fund managed by employer	7.2	7.7
Health insurance	61.7	62.0
Life insurance	9.2	13.5
Personal accident insurance	4.8	6.3
Vehicle insurance law	14.6	14.1
Online banking service	2.6	5.0

Source: Prepared by the author, on the basis of figures from Central Bank of the Dominican Republic, first Survey of Economic and Financial Culture of the Dominican Republic 2014, Santo Domingo, 2014.

The payroll account —a product that is not always subject to the user's free choice— is used ten percentage points more frequently by the urban population than by the rural sector, which probably reflects the greater informality prevailing in the rural domain. In the case of credit cards, which are freely chosen and fundamental for good financial management, the difference between urban and rural use is the same as in the payroll account. The fact that the difference between the use of the payroll account and credit cards is the same between the urban and rural population reflects the structural aspects of the system and the financial architecture that limits financial inclusion, regardless of the specific type of financial product.

The difference is greater with savings accounts, but much smaller in the case of credit products or loans, particularly personal or consumer loans, where the gap is negligible. This is probably because the conditions and reasons leading people to take out personal and consumer loans are not influenced by the zone in which they live. The result could be related to the supply of this type of product by microfinance institutions that serve rural users.

As expected, the urban population use nearly all of the different types of products and services significantly more than their rural peers. Nonetheless, loans extended by cooperatives display the reverse situation, reflecting the rural focus of cooperative lending.

B. Financial inclusion initiatives

As noted above, despite the existence of rules and regulations to facilitate access to financial products and services, the Dominican Republic has never had an explicit and coordinated financial-inclusion strategy to systematically promote access to credit and savings products or electronic payment media, among poor and rural populations.

Nonetheless, improving access to bank credit for urban small and medium-sized enterprises (SMEs) and small-scale rural producers has been an ongoing concern of public policy. The first public policy action to improve access to credit was the creation of Banco Agrícola in 1947, which had the mission of financing agricultural activity in general.[5]

Many initiatives or programmes have emerged in the form of actions by governments and public institutions without an explicit institutional framework to promote financial inclusion. In fact, until the start of the financial reform that led to the adoption of the Monetary and Financial Law in 2001, and its subsequent regulations, small loans and microenterprise financing were not separate from larger-scale financing, and there was no difference in credit risk assessment criteria. The amendments made to the Asset Valuation Regulations (BCRD, 2004) represented a major step forward in facilitating access to credit for microenterprises and SMEs; as the division between small and large borrowers made a substantial difference in terms of credit history and ability-to-pay criteria, and their preponderant role in assessing credit risk among borrowers in the regulated banking system.

A turning point in financial inclusion occurred in 2013 with the entry into force of the Regulation on Banking Correspondents (RSB) (BCRD, 2013), which allows basic financial services to be provided by different types of commercial establishment. In addition, financial inclusion was further boosted by the approval and entry into force of the Microcredit Regulation on August 14, 2014 (BCRD, 2014b) and subsequently by the Regulation on the

---

[5] For a history of the operations and transformations undergone by this institution from its creation until 2015 see Banco Agrícola (2015).

Protection of Users of Financial Services and Products, of 30 September 2015, and its amendments (BCRD, 2015).

Although the country has no comprehensive financial-inclusion strategy, the Dominican authorities have made headway in formulating a financial education programme as a key element of a potential broader strategy. In 2014, a working group was set up to prepare the National Economic and Financial Education Strategy, which was coordinated by the Central Bank of the Dominican Republic and had collaboration from the Superintendency of Banks, Pensions and Securities; the Commercial Banks Association; the Association of Savings and Credit Banks; the League of Savings and Loan Associations; as well as collaboration from the Ministry of the Office of the President; the Ministry of Economy, Planning and Development; the Ministry of Industry, Commerce and Micro, Small and Medium-sized Enterprises (MSMEs); the Ministry of Education; and the Ministry of Finance.

With a view to strengthening the design of the financial education strategy, the first Survey of Economic and Financial Culture (BCRD, 2014a) was conducted in 2014, generating the first-ever comprehensive overview of access to financial services and their use nationwide. In addition, as part of the financial education effort, the authorities launched a programme to train 1,800 teachers (600 in 2014 and 1,200 in the following year) from across the Dominican Republic, to disseminate knowledge on financial services more widely throughout the country.

C. Institutional architecture

1. Regulation and supervision of the financial system

The Constitution of the Dominican Republic and the Monetary and Financial Law empower the Monetary Board and the Central Bank of the Dominican Republic to issue regulations for proper governance of the monetary and financial system, and to introduce the changes and innovations needed to improve the efficiency of financial services. The Monetary and Financial Law applies to all banking and foreign-exchange intermediaries, except for cooperatives, whose regulations are discussed below.

The legal framework governing the monetary and financial system establishes guidelines on minimum capital, regulatory solvency, liquidity and management, in order to guarantee the stability of the system in a competitive environment. In addition to this, an efficient structure of corporate governance and risk management is required, adapted to the nature, size and risk profile of the entities in question.

In the case of banking services, the entities responsible for regulation and supervision of financial service providers are the Monetary Board and the Superintendency of Banks, respectively. Stock market and fiduciary services are regulated by the National Securities Council and supervised by the Superintendency of Securities. In the case of pensions, oversight is provided by the National Council for Social Security (regulator) and Superintendency of Pensions (supervisor); while insurance activities are governed by the Ministry of Finance (regulator) and the Superintendency of Insurance (supervisor). Lastly, although saving and loan cooperatives are not subject to prudential regulation and supervision as financial intermediaries, they are generally regulated by the Cooperative Development and Credit Institute (IDECOOP).

The changes that have affected the financial sector in recent years, and hence the needs in terms of regulation and supervision, include the entry of foreign banks into the banking market; the development of the payment system; the geographical expansion of financial services and distribution channels; the increasing use of electronic payment services; technological innovations in payment services made available to the public; the emergence of new (non-financial) payment service providers; the adoption of new payment instruments and the establishment of banking correspondents.

The latter change was a regulatory initiative that led to the emergence of banking correspondents as a new distribution channel for financial services. At its meeting on February 14, 2013, the Monetary Board approved the Regulation on Banking Correspondents (RSB) to increase financial inclusion, facilitating access to financial services for the most impoverished population groups that do not participate in the formal financial system. The stated objectives clearly indicate that RSB is considered to have the status of a regulatory reform with a potential for high impact on financial inclusion. It is an innovation in financial service distribution channels, which significantly facilitates access to basic financial services without lowering their quality and without increasing the financial institutions' operational risk.

2. Financial intermediaries

At the national level, the main providers of financial services include commercial banks, saving and loan associations, saving and credit banks, credit corporations, Banco Agrícola, saving and loan cooperatives, and microfinance entities. Saving and loan cooperatives play a dominant role in providing financial services to the rural segment of the population; but informal financial service providers are also important, especially in rural areas. In this connection, the constraints on access to the savings and credit services of the formal financial system prevail, as shown by the Survey of

Economic and Financial Culture (BCRD, 2014a), which revealed that 13.5% of the population obtains credit through informal lenders.

Given the eminently rural focus of savings and credit cooperatives, one would expect their offices to be concentrated in municipal districts, sections and rural areas. It is therefore striking that the proportion of the population with savings accounts in cooperatives is significantly higher in urban than in rural zones. Nonetheless, the percentage of the rural population with loans from cooperatives is very similar to that of the urban population. This suggests that some of the factors constraining access to these financial service providers stem from low income levels among the rural population, compounded by rural users' mistrust of formal providers of financial services, and a product range that is unsuited to the rural environment.

Despite the key role played by saving and loan cooperatives in expanding financial services, these entities are currently not subject to prudential regulation or supervision, as are other financial intermediaries operating in the country. Because of this situation, cooperatives are excluded from the payment system and electronic payment instruments involving cards and mobile devices, which in practice restricts access by rural populations that are geographically dependent on such devices to obtain financial services.

The fact that there is no regulator of saving and loan cooperatives that perform financial intermediation means there are no consolidated statistics on entities of this type. In 2014, the total assets and loan portfolio of the Association of Rural Savings and Credit Institutions (AIRAC), which encompasses the main saving and loan cooperatives, totalled 33,465.1 million pesos and 23,850.3 million pesos, respectively. At the end of the year, the consolidated financial system loan portfolio amounted to 725,586.3 million pesos; so the loan portfolio of AIRAC member cooperatives represented 3.3% of the total portfolio of the entire financial system. If all saving and loan cooperatives are considered, their overall loan portfolio is likely to be close to 5% of the financial system total —sufficient to warrant greater oversight and regulation by the authorities of this important segment of the system and of financial intermediation itself.

The fact that Banco Agrícola disbursed loans totalling 14,765.3 million pesos in 2014, when its loan portfolio stood at 11,561.4 million pesos, means that AIRAC cooperatives provided 2.1 pesos for every peso supplied by Banco Agrícola; and the amount would rise to 3 pesos if the cooperatives outside AIRAC are included. The fact that unregulated and supervised cooperatives manage a credit portfolio three times larger than that of the main public institution for agricultural and rural development financing highlights the importance and urgency of supervision and regulation of these institutions.

Microfinance institutions also play a leading role in bringing credit products and services to the rural population. These include the Association for the Development of Microenterprises (ADEMI) and the Women's Bank, known as Banco ADOPEM.

3. Main products and distribution channels

Table VI.4 reports the proportion of the population that uses the different types of financial services and products supplied by regulated financial intermediaries and other unregulated institutions, and services related to the general financial system.

Table VI.4
Dominican Republic: population that currently owns different types of financial products, 2014
(Percentages)

Type of product or service	Percentage of population
Health insurance	61.9
Savings account	43.0
Payroll account	27.8
Pension fund managed by private institution (AFP)	24.8
Credit card	22.5
Legally required vehicle insurance	14.1
Life insurance	13.1
Savings account in cooperative	12.2
Other personal or consumer loan	11.7
Pension fund managed by employer	7.7
Prepaid card	7.4
Cooperative loan	7.1
Personal accident insurance	6.1
Checking/current account	4.8
Online banking service	4.7
Payroll loan	4.6
Loan for the purchase of appliances, equipment or fixed assets	3.8
Time deposit or financial certificate	2.9
SME loan from Banca Solidaria or PROMIPYME	2.6
Loan or deferred credit line	2.6
Vehicle loan or credit	2.5
Loan or mortgage loan for acquisition/remodelling	2.3
SME loan from private banks	2.0
Savings account or time deposit in foreign currency	1.4
SME loan from NGO or microfinance	0.8

Source: Prepared by the author, on the basis of figures from Central Bank of the Dominican Republic, first Survey of Economic and Financial Culture of the Dominican Republic 2014, Santo Domingo, 2014.

Savings products include savings accounts (43% of households use this product), payroll accounts (27.8%), savings accounts in cooperatives (12.2%), certificates of deposit and time deposits (2.9%) and stock market investments (0.4%). Credit products include mortgage loans (1.0%) and consumer loans (11.7%), and loans from cooperatives (4.0%). Payment services include electronic banking services (1.0%), credit cards (22.5%), and government subsidy services, electronic channels and devices. Lastly, insurance products include health insurance (61.9%), life insurance (13.1%) and legally mandated vehicle insurance (14.1%).

If all the credit products are combined, 40% of the population receives some type of financing from financial intermediary institutions. This figure is much higher than the percentage of the population that has a credit card (22.5%), but very similar to the proportion with a savings account (43%).

Lastly, two very significant findings: firstly, many more people hold savings accounts in cooperatives than borrow from them. Since the savings account can serve as the entry point and hub for other more sophisticated financial products, these data suggest an opportunity to increase the use of various products that are currently being ignored. Secondly, the proportion of the population with loans from the public microcredit bank, Banca Solidaria, or from non-profit institutions, or microcredit from private banks, is very similar to the percentage with consumer loans from formal private banks. This illustrates the degree of penetration or use of this type of financing.

Table VI.5 reports disaggregated information on the use of financial services according to the users' income level. As would be expected, use of the main financial products and services rises with income.

Payroll, checking and savings accounts are the most widely used; while credit cards and loans of all kinds are used much less by middle-, lower-middle, and low-income populations than by high- and upper-middle income groups. Apart from health insurance, the product most widely used in the low and lower-middle income strata is the savings account, which highlights potential for leveraging the use of this instrument as a gateway to other financial products. The relatively high level of use of payroll accounts by low and lower-middle income groups suggests a close relationship between formal employment and financial inclusion.

The main channels through which financial services are supplied in urban areas are main offices, branches, electronic channels, banking correspondents and payment points. In rural areas, distribution channels include branches, electronic channels and banking correspondents. There are marked differences between rural and urban areas in the way financial services are supplied.

Table VI.5

Dominican Republic: use of financial products and services by income level, 2014

(Percentages)

Type of financial product or service	High and upper-middle income	Middle income	Lower-middle and low income	Don't know or no reply
Payroll account	50.6	36.0	21.4	8.4
Savings account	73.5	61.6	30.1	34.9
Checking / current account	19.5	6.4	1.8	0.0
Savings account in cooperative	29.7	15.4	8.3	2.7
Term deposit or financial certificate	12.1	3.5	1.2	0.7
Savings account or time deposit in foreign currency	3.4	1.7	1.1	0.0
Credit card	56.5	37.4	10.8	8.4
Prepaid card	23.6	11.5	3.1	0.4
Payroll loan	12.5	6.7	2.7	0.0
Vehicle loan or credit	13.3	3.3	0.5	0.0
Loan or deferred credit line	6.4	5.7	0.6	2.7
Loan for the purchase of appliances, equipment or fixed assets	8.5	6.5	1.8	2.7
Another personal or consumer loan	22.3	17.6	7.8	3.6
Cooperative loan	14.7	8.7	5.6	0.0
Loan or mortgage loan for acquisition or remodelling, or both	7.4	3.7	0.8	2.7
SME loan from Banca Solidaria or PROMIPYME	5.3	3.5	1.6	5.4
SME loan from NGO or microfinance	0.2	2.1	0.5	0.0
SME loan from private banks	2.3	3.1	1.5	0.5
Pension fund managed by private institution (AFP)	54.3	31.2	18.1	4.8
Pension fund managed by employer	15.2	10.5	5.6	0.9
Health insurance	81.1	70.2	56.0	46.3
Life insurance	32.0	18.7	8.1	2.6
Personal accident insurance	20.1	7.4	3.4	1.2
Legally mandated vehicle insurance	45.2	21.9	5.9	4.6
Online banking service	20.9	7.0	1.2	0.0

Source: Prepared by the author, on the basis of figures from Central Bank of the Dominican Republic, Survey of Economic and Financial Culture of the Dominican Republic 2014, Santo Domingo, 2014.

As noted above, the introduction of bank correspondents represents a new and potentially very important distribution channel, especially for segments that suffer severe restrictions in accessing financial products and services because financial intermediaries are not physically present in their localities. Financial intermediaries that can supply their products through correspondents include commercial banks, savings and loan associations, and saving and credit banks. Pharmacies, hotels, telecommunication service centres, supermarkets, mini-markets, grocery stores, hardware stores and other convenience stores can all be used as correspondents.

The receipt of all types of payment, deposits, withdrawals, credit processing and applications, along with other types of products and services, is what turns the bank correspondent into a quasi- bank branch that is present among poor rural populations that are remote from large centres, enabling users who have already opened accounts to conduct all types of banking transactions. Nonetheless, the fact that account opening is not included among their services means that the effect on financial inclusion is limited to more intensive use of financial services by those who already have access to some financial product.

Piña (2016) reports that there was a total of 3,106 correspondents in January 2016, used by nine financial institutions, which in turn represented about 80% of all assets of the financial intermediation system.

4. Payment systems

Access to means of payment is a necessary condition for effective financial inclusion, since the use of any means other than cash requires a debit or deposit account or a credit product. In the Dominican Republic, the expansion of the means of payment has had a significant effect on financial inclusion. The following is a descriptive analysis of the Dominican Republic's Payment and Settlement System, and its modernization aimed at expanding access to payment services and thus increase financial inclusion.

The retail payment systems of the Dominican Republic are used by three operational entities: financial intermediaries, customers or users, and administrators of payment and settlement systems. Each of these entities accesses the retail payment systems in a different way, financial intermediaries enter into agreements with payment system administrators who operate retail payment systems. In the case of customers, they only need one of the payment instruments defined in the regulation —provided by their own financial intermediary— which can be used in any of the existing retail payment systems. To gain authorization to operate a retail payment system, administrators must comply with the requirements established in the Payment System Regulation and its application instructions.

The regulation and functioning of the Dominican Republic's Payment and Settlement System (SIPARD) is the responsibility of the Monetary Board, and all financial intermediaries have to be connected to the system. Moreover, multilateral systems for the clearing and settlement of means of payment cannot be organized outside such a system.

Table VI.6 summarizes the recent evolution of the use of means of payment. The debit card is by far the most widely used electronic payment instrument, exceeding the credit card by more than 1 million units. Nonetheless, while this means an increase in the number of banked individuals, the intensity of the use of financial services does not increase commensurately, since some of the users of payroll accounts merely receive payment through this mechanism and then withdraw the money to make payments in cash.

Table VI.6

Dominican Republic: volume and values of electronic payments executed through the payment system, 2010-2016

Type of card	December 2010	December 2011	December 2012	December 2013	December 2014	December 2015	July 2016
(Number of cards)	3 068 394	3 329 294	3 296 797	3 290 107	3 327 324	3 295 037	3 594 824
Debit							
Credit card	1 668 514	1 994 972	2 160 107	2 420 054	2 339 569	2 210 698	2 399 113
Prepaid card	177 252	220 160	254 354	91 746	76 797	83 276	139 422
Government subsidy card					924 648	975 399	950 385
(Number of transactions)							
Credit Card Transactions	1 827 198 019	19 199 038	21 371 298	25 126 974	31 451 110	15 078 655	23 996 379
Debit Card Transactions	9 918 208 435	50 806 703	56 873 846	63 707 081	73 596 061	34 352 144	57 388 397
Prepaid Card Transactions					792 734	187 180	381 230
Transfers with government subsidies card					25 731 309	10 610 169	15 330 144
(In Dominican pesos)							
Value of credit card transactions	20 919 554 540	24 449 568 702	27 979 315 644	33 044 892 032	42 119 794 501,8	202 351 849 418,0	31 126 391 391
Value of debit card transactions	114 244 533 492	137 924 900 728	156 396 328 624	175 058 112 204	18 777 092 492	86 081 680 505	139 723 384 349
Value of transactions with prepaid card					1 159 581 650	235 848 044	572 917 563
Value of transactions with government subsidies card					12 996 137 370	5 469 300 659	801 228 451
Total	146 914 408 646	162 450 019 597	184 459 600 670	208 197 640 198	75 190 845 566	294 205 471 184	172 328 101 648

Source: Prepared by the author, on the basis of figures from the Central Bank of the Dominican Republic.

When analysing the data in table VI.6, the payment of public payroll and government subsidies should also be considered. According to the Labour Survey of the Central Bank of the Dominican Republic, the labour force employed in the public sector in early 2016 consisted of 603,919 people, and government subsidy payment cards totalled 986,224 units. Therefore, if these data are considered and the number of valid debit cards on that date is subtracted from both figures, the number of debit cards obtained by individuals who are not public employees and do not receive government subsidies, but did obtain such instrument for private payments, amounts to 1,718,940 —well below the total number of credit cards in existence.

In terms of general access to means of payment —a prerequisite both for financial inclusion and for access to savings and credit products— the universalization and coverage of electronic payments and clearing between entities accelerated sharply, as explained above, following the entry into force of the Real-time Gross Settlement System in 2008. The availability of means of payment, savings and electronic credits also grew significantly, which had repercussions on financial inclusion.

5. Consumer protection mechanisms

Consumer protection is a key factor in financial inclusion. By boosting consumer confidence, regulations to strengthen the protection of users of financial products should also increase financial inclusion, as more people will join the system as regular users.

The Regulation on the Protection of Users of Financial Products and Services (RPUPSF) was approved in January 2006; but it was amended in September 2015 to include a larger number of protection mechanisms and intensify existing ones. In this regard, the amendments introduced procedures for internal complaints and requirements on adequate disclosure of the costs of financial services, consumer rights and the obligations of financial service providers. They also prohibited abusive practices and aggressive marketing, and the strengthened the National Commission for the Defence of Competition (ProCompetencia).

6. Complementary infrastructure

In the Dominican Republic, credit information systems operate through credit bureaus. These systems collect information from all financial-system debtors, and on the services they have contracted with various firms. The information is confidential and can only be accessed by its owners and the bureaus for portfolio management and file evaluation purposes.

Given the preponderance of agricultural production in rural areas and its possible use as collateral, an important issue in terms of complementary infrastructure for the rural sector is the existence of a commodity storage infrastructure. There are collection centres in sectors such as dairy and certain agricultural products —mostly private sector initiatives and, in some cases, public-private partnerships supported by a number of government entities.

In terms of connectivity, the main problems, especially for rural populations, stem from poor access to main highways owing to the state of local roads. Another problem faced by rural inhabitants concerns access to basic utilities, such as water and electricity.

There are three administrative dispute resolution mechanisms in the Dominican Republic: forced liquidation, the Subsidiary Administrative Liquidation Mechanism and the Subsidiary Voluntary Liquidation Mechanism. The criteria for prioritization of creditors are specified in the Monetary and Financial Law and give first preference to private-sector deposits.

Financial assets, real estate, capital goods, inventories, means of transport and fiduciary guarantees are all eligible as collateral. The main challenges when using goods as collateral involve their registration, monitoring, custody and valuation.

D. Public-policy instruments

1. Development banks

The main development bank targeting the Dominican rural sector is Banco Agrícola de la República Dominicana, which was created to finance agricultural activity in general; and, although it lends to medium- and large-scale producers, its market segment also includes small-scale farmers.

There are also public-sector initiatives that extend financing to micro-, small and medium-sized enterprises through Banca Solidaria, created in 2012. This institution operates a programme specialized in microfinance, which provides financing and financial education services to microentrepreneurs to support their development and foster their financial inclusion.

The Special Fund for Agricultural Development (FEDA), founded in 1972, also implements policy actions to promote sustainable rural development, including support by financing small-scale and microenterprise agriculture. The Fund has designed a credit policy that provides financing at a low interest rate (5% per annum) and without any collateral, with a fund of 125 million pesos available to finance activities that benefit affiliated small-scale producers.

2. Regulatory and supervision policy

Analysis reveals several specific areas in which public policy in the Dominican Republic has had a significant impact on financial inclusion, including the promulgation and application of a number of financial regulations. The three with the greatest direct effect are the Asset Valuation Regulations, Regulations for the Protection of Users of Financial Products and Services, and the Microcredit Regulation.

The 2004 Asset Valuation Regulations have undergone two major amendments, with profound implications for the financial inclusion of microenterprises and small-scale entrepreneurs through access to credit from financial institutions. The first amendment, in July 2009, raised the credit limit for the "small-commercial borrowers" classification to 15.0 million pesos. Following this amendment, the credit risk of all those owing up to that amount was evaluated on the basis of their payment arrears. The main consequence of this change in terms of increased financial inclusion through credit products occurred through specialized lending institutions. In 2010, the credit portfolio of the private microfinance institutions, ADEMI and ADOPEM, grew by 19.5%.

The second amendment was introduced in March 2013, when the "small-commercial borrowers" credit risk classification ceiling was raised again to 25.0 million pesos, based on their payment arrears. This amendment, for the first time, strikes the appropriate balance between SME promotion and development and the intermediaries' risk.

The amendments made to the September 2015 Regulations on the Protection of Users of Financial Products and Services introduced internal complaint procedures and requirements on adequate disclosure of financial service costs, the rights of consumers of financial services and the obligations of financial service providers, together with the prohibition of abusive practices and aggressive marketing, and strengthening of the ProCompetencia Commission.

The third regulation with a direct impact on financial inclusion is the Microcredit Regulation, which was approved in 2014. Its main effect is to afford greater flexibility by allowing microcredits to be evaluated on the basis of their arrears, and giving exemption from formal documentation to determine the corresponding credit risk.

Regulatory actions aimed at facilitating and promoting the financing of microenterprises and small businesses have had a fundamental impact on access to credit products. Greater flexibility in the Asset Valuation Regulation and the microenterprise financing activity of the Reserve Bank (through its Banca Solidaria programme) have been decisive for the doubling of microcredit between 2009 and 2015, as shown in Table VI.7.

Table VI.7
Dominican Republic: valuation of the portfolio of specialized microcredit institutions, 2009-2015
(Millions of Dominican pesos)

Specialized entities	December 2009	December 2010	December 2011	December 2012	December 2013	December 2014	December 2015
ADEMI	6 127.13	7 319.57	8 574.86	9 574.66	10 910.38	12 157.78	13 260.84
ADOPEM	1 777.84	2 131.24	2 598.37	2 994.28	3 603.69	4 335.44	5 164.05
Total private institutions	7 904.97	9 450.82	11 173.23	12 568.93	14 514.07	16 493.22	18 424.89
Total microcredits	11 422.20	10 252.20	11 842.20	11 598.40	13 075.60	16 972.80	22 701.10

Source: Prepared by the author, on the basis of data from the institutions' financial statistics.

3. Capacity building

Financial education and building the capacity to manage a financial-inclusion strategy are two transversal goals needed to ensure the strategy's success. As noted above, the Dominican authorities have already made headway in formulating a financial education strategy. The objective of this initiative is to achieve a higher level of public awareness regarding rights and opportunities when using the financial system, so that they feel included and foundations are laid for a higher level of economic development.

On the capacities needed to manage an inclusion strategy, the introduction to the report of the first Survey of Economic and Financial Culture (BCRD, 2014a) states that, regarding planning, the authorities of the Central Bank of the Dominican Republic, supported by the Inter-American Development Bank and the United States Department of the Treasury, convened other public and private entities in late 2013 to form a working group to develop a National Strategy for Economic and Financial Culture (ENCEF). The central bank's leadership in ENCEF implementation is a factor that increases its chances of success.

With regard to financial education as a necessary condition for ensuring the success of a financial-inclusion strategy, it should be noted that appropriate use (demand for financial services), and the intensity and quantity of financial products depend essentially on the knowledge and culture that the new users drawn into the system have of the products and services in question. An initial factor in this connection is the universal campaign run by the Superintendency of Banks of the Dominican Republic on the responsible use of credit cards and personal loans.

Although the campaign to educate the population on the best use of financial products is being executed by the Superintendency of Banks, formal training for the teachers who will transmit the basic knowledge of financial culture was, and continues to be, headed by the Central Bank.

Through public-private partnerships and academic alliances with six universities in the country, the Ministry of Industry, Commerce and Micro-, Small and Medium-sized Enterprises has formulated a strategy to provide business development services through the Small and Medium Enterprise (SME) Centres with the following strategic locations: three centres in the city of Santo Domingo (the Pedro Henríquez Ureña National University (UNPHU), the Ibero-American University (UNIBE) and the Autonomous University of Santo Domingo (UASD)); one in Cibao (the Higher Institute of Agriculture (ISA)); one in the east of the country (UASD-Hato Mayor); and, lastly, one in the south (the Catholic Technological University of Barahona (UCATEBA)). The SME Centres provide training, technical assistance, business consulting, and connection services. This strategy aims to encourage and promote good production practices and other necessary tools among rural entrepreneurs located in the vicinity of these universities.

E. Conclusions and recommendations

Although there is still no comprehensive financial-inclusion strategy in the Dominican Republic, as has been reiterated throughout this chapter, some elements are implicit in the specific objectives and lines of action of the National Development Strategy (END) 2030. Accordingly, the formulation of a financial-inclusion strategy should take into account of the END and make the most of the available instruments that promote such inclusion. In the author's view, the objective of the overall financial-inclusion strategy should aim, specifically, at bridging the gap between rural and urban population groups, and between the high- and middle-income groups, in terms of access to credit, savings and payment services, and the use made of them. The strategy should also aim to protect these vulnerable groups' access to such services without increasing the risk to their providers. This requires the following specific objectives to be met:

- Increase the rural population's participation in a wide range of financial services supplied by the formal financial system and reduce the gap existing in 2014 relative to the urban population.
- Increase the share of saving and loan cooperatives in total formal financial system credit, and reduce their risks through a reform that allows them to be regulated and supervised as financial intermediaries.
- Promote the Banco Agrícola share in total rural credit through a transformation and a new institutional architecture that allows it to act as a second-tier bank, and promote greater specialization in rural microcredit.

- Boost the share of microcredits in the total credit of the formal financial system by reforming existing rules and regulations, without increasing the risk to suppliers of microcredits and other financial services.
- Expand access to electronic means of payment and provide protection to those who are in a situation of vulnerability that makes it hard for them to access services.
- Improve the population's knowledge on financial services through explicit financial education actions.

Attaining the goal of increasing financial inclusion among the rural population presupposes the creation of a legal framework to regulate and supervise cooperatives, and a new architecture for Banco Agrícola and FEDA, together with the adaptation of rules and regulations on financial inclusion, including the formulation of a programme of financial literacy activities.

1. Reform to regulate and supervise saving and loan cooperatives

As discussed above, saving and loan cooperatives are too important to ignore in a national financial-inclusion strategy. Although these entities perform financial intermediation activities, they are not regulated or supervised by the Monetary and Financial Authority, although many have two and up to three times more assets than duly regulated financial intermediaries.

Considering their high level of penetration in rural populations and their large participation in the entire financial market, and assuming that due regulation and supervision increases confidence and boosts public demand for the services and products of cooperatives, reform may be needed to achieve these conditions to ensure the success of a financial-inclusion strategy. The exclusion allowed by the existing regulatory and supervisory framework limits the role they can play in promoting financial inclusion by restricting the supply of available products. Since they do not have a clearing account at the Central Bank of the Dominican Republic, they cannot participate in the Payment System, which in turn prevents them from offering electronic means of payment. Lastly, since there is no systematized information about the cooperatives' performance, their members have few ways to evaluate their institutional soundness.

Two alternatives emerge from the analysis of the national framework and international experiences. The first is to include cooperatives within the scope of the Monetary and Financial Law, to put them on the same footing as other financial intermediaries. The second is to place the cooperatives under the regulation and supervision of the Monetary and Financial Authority, but with a special law that considers the special nature of their emphasis on savings and rural credit, and which enables them to connect to the payments system with real clearing accounts and electronic products.

2. New architecture of Banco Agrícola and FEDA

Banco Agrícola and the Special Fund for Agricultural Development (FEDA) are two institutions with a high impact on the financial inclusion of the rural population. So a reform to improve these institutions' targeting on the rural poor and other groups excluded from bank credit would also be a necessary condition for successfully implementing a truly effective financial-inclusion strategy.

A first step involves formulating a FEDA financing policy through surprise visits,[6] whose objectives should be aligned with the Government's agricultural development policy and other public policies. A first necessary condition for achieving this objective is that the groups that are the targets of these visits and their fundable projects are consistent with the Banco Agrícola lending policy, since, ultimately it is this entity that maintains and manages a loan portfolio for small-scale rural producers. Once a policy of surprise visits is in place, along with the consequent FEDA lending policy, it will be necessary to turn Banco Agrícola into a second-tier bank, with a portfolio consisting exclusively of loans of profound social impact and high-risk, such as FEDA loans and surprise visits.

The reform to create a framework for the regulation and supervision of cooperatives, and the transformation of Banco Agrícola into a second-tier bank that prioritizes high-risk financing with a profound social impact, should be complemented by a review of the regulations on financial inclusion: the Asset Valuation Regulation, the Banking Correspondent Regulation, the Microcredit Regulation and the Regulation for the Protection of Users of Financial Products and Services.

---

[6] Surprise visits are visits by the President of the Republic to different regions of the country with the objective of promoting dialogue between different actors.

Bibliography

Banco Agrícola (2015), *Evolución histórica del Banco Agrícola, 1945-2015*, Santo Domingo.

___(2008), *Propuesta para la creación de un sistema que garantice el fomento y el financiamiento de la producción agropecuaria y forestal en la República Dominicana*, Reform Commission.

BCRD (Central Bank of the Dominican Republic) (2015), "Reglamento de protección a los usuarios de servicios y productos financieros", Aviso, 16 April.

___(2014a), *1ra. Encuesta de Cultura Económica y Financiera de la República Dominicana 2014*, Santo Domingo.

___(2014b), "Reglamento de microcréditos", Aviso, Santo Domingo.

___(2013), "Reglamento de subagente bancario", Aviso, Santo Domingo, 12 March.

___(2004), "Reglamento de evaluación de activos", Aviso.

Demirguc-Kunt, A. and others (2015), "The Global Findex Database 2014: measuring financial inclusion around the world", *Policy Research Working Paper*, No. 7255, Washington, D.C., World Bank.

Piña, L. (2016), "Subagentes: los colmados y pequeños negocios convertidos en brazos de la banca", *Argentarium tu portal financiero*, 1 February [online] https://www.argentarium.com/veedor/reportajes/14271-los-colmados-y-pequenos-negocios-convertidos-en-brazos-de-la-banca/.

World Bank (2016), Global Findex Database [online] http://datatopics.worldbank.org/financialinclusion/.

Chapter VII

Architecture of rural financial inclusion in Mexico

Pilar Campos[1]

Introduction

Starting in 2001, a series of institutional changes aimed at incorporating broad segments of the population into the formal financial system appeared in Mexico for the first time. Nonetheless, financial inclusion in general, and in rural areas particularly, still show clear lags despite the profound changes experienced by the financial system during the current century and the transformation of the institutional scaffolding that culminated in the financial reform of 2014. The latter includes the formalization of many financial intermediaries and the reorientation of development banks, supported by institutional strengthening for financial regulation and supervision.

In Mexico financial inclusion started to emerge as a public-policy topic in 2009 and was officially defined in 2011 as access to, and use of, financial services under an appropriate regulation that protects consumers and promotes financial education to improve the financial capacities of all segments of the population (Mexico, Presidency of the Republic, 2011). Despite this formal definition, there is still confusion over the comprehensive nature

[1] Independent researcher with degrees from the Autonomous Technological Institute of Mexico and the London School of Economics and Political Science.

of the concept of financial inclusion among some decision-makers in both the public and private spheres.

In terms of supply indicators, figures from the International Monetary Fund (IMF, 2015) show that Mexico is a clear laggard not only relative to countries of comparable development level, but also compared to other less developed countries. In 2014, Mexico was below the average for Latin America and the Caribbean in terms of the density of branches of financial institutions: 1.5 for every 10,000 adults compared to a regional average of 2.6. The same was true of automatic teller machines (ATMs), of which there were 4.9 per 10,000 adults, compared to 5.2 regionwide. In the rural area, the lag was accentuated, as in the same year the number of branches and ATMs were just 0.9 and 0.7, respectively, per 10,000 adults in municipalities with fewer than 50,000 inhabitants.

The challenges facing both the rural population and the financial institutions that seek to serve it are diverse. They include a markedly seasonal economic activity, compounded by increasing uncertainty surrounding the impact of climate change; a low population density that entails significant transaction costs for both users and institutions; growing, but still sparse, connectedness; serious problems of insecurity; land deterioration and plot fragmentation; displacements and migration; limited productive linkages, which hinders access to key markets; highly volatile input prices, which generates uncertainty about firms' payment capacity and planning. Despite these factors, the weak penetration of the financial sector, even in urban centres, means that financial institutions continue to perceive advantages in expanding their services to low- and middle-income urban sectors (Trivelli and Venero, 2007).

In Mexico, development banks are key players in this domain. Those operating in the rural sector alone include the National Financial Institute for Agricultural, Rural, Forestry and Fisheries Development (FND) and the National Bank for Savings and Financial Services (BANSEFI), which offer credit programmes, savings products, guarantees, technical assistance and financial education, among other services.[2] In addition, there are the Agricultural-related Trust Funds (FIRA), which run programmes that foster rural credit through a variety of vehicles. Other public funds, mainly from the Secretariat of Economy and the Secretariat of Agriculture, Livestock, Rural Development, Fisheries and Food (SAGARPA), use development banks as trustees and provide support in the rural sector.

---

[2] Mexico has a total of six development banks and one rural financial institution. These are the National Bank for Public Works and Services (BANOBRAS); Nacional Financiera (NAFIN); Banco Nacional de Comercio Exterior (BANCOMEXT); the National Bank of the Army, Airforce and Navy; the National Bank for National Savings and Financial Services (BANSEFI); the Federal Mortgage Company (SHF) and the National Financial Institute for Agricultural, Rural, Forestry and Fisheries Development (FND).

Recognizing the shortcomings that exist in this area, in 2013 the Government of Enrique Peña Nieto submitted a financial reform bill to the Congress of the Union, which was passed in January 2014. This sought to promote financial inclusion through five actions: broadening of the range of products and distribution channels available to popular saving and loan entities;[3] [4] strengthening of transparency and consumer protection; greater competition among financial service networks; redefinition of the development banks' mandate to strengthen their targeting on priority groups;[5] and legal amendments to enable private institutions to supply more credit, especially to micro and small and medium-sized enterprises (MSMEs).

Subsequently, in June 2016, the National Policy for Financial Inclusion (PNIF) was launched by the National Council for Financial Inclusion (CONAIF). The Policy is built on six pillars: capacity building for financial service users; use of technological innovations for financial inclusion; development of financial infrastructure in neglected areas; promotion of the provision and use of formal financial services for underserved and excluded population groups; strengthening of trust in the formal financial sector; and generation of data and measures to evaluate financial inclusion efforts.

The following sections of this chapter make a diagnostic assessment of the architecture of financial inclusion in Mexico, starting in section A with a critical description of existing laws and mechanisms, and their advantages and contradictions in terms of fostering rural financial inclusion. Section B then discusses the role of development banks in promoting rural financial inclusion; while section C addresses the challenges faced by both users and providers of financial services in rural areas. Lastly, section D concludes with a number of public-policy reflections.

A. The institutional architecture of rural financial inclusion

In Mexico the most significant changes aimed at bringing financial services to population groups that have typically been underserved by traditional suppliers —commercial and development banks— began in the early years of the twenty-first century. In 2001 and 2002, two far-reaching processes coincided with changes in both government and the political regime in

[3] The Saving and Loan Cooperatives (SOCAPs), Popular Finance Institutions (SOFIPOs) and Community Finance Institutions (SOFINCOs) constitute what are known as popular saving and loan entities.

[4] Correspondents were authorized in 2010, but for commercial banks only. Since the recent financial reform, however, popular saving and loan entities can also expand their services through this modality.

[5] Since the Felipe Calderón administration (2006-2012), priority groups have been defined as those with insufficient income to overcome their vulnerability status, and have specific characteristics and needs. These groups include indigenous peoples and communities, agricultural day laborers, women and the elderly, and also children living on the street.

Mexico. The first was the approval of the Popular Saving and Loans Law which formalized non-bank entities supplying financial services to middle- and lower-income population groups. The second involved devising a different role for development banks and turning them into second-tier lenders. Thus, the National Savings Trust (PAHNAL) was transformed into BANSEFI and the National Rural Credit Bank (BANRURAL) became Financiera Rural (later FND).

From the outset of the discussions that gave rise to the Popular Saving and Loans Law, concern for the rural area was crucial. The main goal was to protect savings and expand regulated financial services to rural and marginalized localities in Mexico in the light of the frauds and bankruptcies that had occurred in several saving and loan cooperatives in the 1990s. Saving was prioritized as a vehicle of inclusion, which would make it possible to serve the poorest population groups and accumulate and mobilize local savings for community development. Saving would also form the basis for fostering financial habits and disciplines for the prudent use of formal credit, for which it was essential to have entities authorized to accept savings from the public.

The argument for regulating and strengthening non-bank financial intermediaries was justified, among other things, by the lack of interest that commercial banks had thus far shown in serving marginalized populations, even in urban areas. In Mexico, non-bank institutions had been providing financial services for decades, such as savings banks (*cajas de ahorro*) and, more recently, organizations that disseminated microcredit innovations in those years.

By the mid-2000s, with the development banks refocusing their activities on second-tier services, the Secretariat of Finance and Public Credit (SHCP) detected the need for larger credit dissemination vehicles. For this purpose, the category of unregulated multiple-purpose financial institution (SOFOM E.N.R.) was created, which, in addition to not being restricted to a specific credit product, did not need to be associated with financial groups or regulated by the National Banking and Securities Commission (CNBV).[6]

Table VII.1 summarizes the legal categories that, in addition to commercial banking, are relevant in Mexico for financial inclusion, along with the laws governing them —when they were created or amended, whether they are regulated and whether they are under direct or auxiliary CNBV supervision.[7]

---

[6] Previously, there were limited-purpose financial institutions (SOFOLs); then, to be able to disseminate credits for different purposes, the SOFOM Regulated Financial Institution (SOFOM E.R.) was created, linked to financial groups.

[7] CNBV can subject financial institutions to both types of supervision. Indirect supervision is done through authorized auxiliary agencies, known in Mexico as federations, which supervise and inform the authority about the financial situation of the popular savings and loan institutions.

Table VII.1
Summary of the architecture of laws and financial suppliers for financial inclusion[a]

Laws or regulations	Type of entity	Launch of laws or entities	Accept deposits?	Type of CNBV supervision	Regulated?
Popular Saving and Loans Law[b]	Popular finance institutions (SOFIPOs) and community finance institutions (SOFINCOs)	2001 and amended in 2009	Yes	Auxiliary	Yes
Law regulating the activities of saving and loan cooperatives	Saving and loan cooperatives (SOCAPs)[c]	2009	Yes	Auxiliary	Yes
Law of Auxiliary Credit Organizations and Activities	Unregulated multi-purpose financial institution (SOFOM E.N.R)[b]	2006	No	n.a.	No
Credit Institutions Law[d]	Niche banks	2008 (amended)	Yes	Direct	Yes
Credit Institutions Law[d]	Bank correspondents	2009 (amended)	Yes	Direct	Yes

Source: prepared by the author.
[a] All institutions are supervised by the National Commission for the Protection and Defence of Financial Service Users (CONDUSEF).
[b] The SOFOM unregulated entity (E.N.R.) is subject to certain provisions of the General Law on Credit Institutions and Auxiliary Activities and those which the Bank of Mexico issues on the subject.
[c] Financial cooperatives are also governed by the General Law on Cooperatives.
[d] The Law on Credit Institutions, equivalent to banking laws in other countries, aims to legislate on multiple banking institutions, development banks and niche banks.

1. Popular saving and loan entities

The Popular Saving and Loans Law and the creation of BANSEFI in 2001 aimed to organize and formalize a sector comprised of different legal entities that accepted deposits —cooperatives, saving and loan associations, microfinance NGOs and solidarity funds— in order to protect the savings of these institutions' members and customers. To that end, the Law focused on eliminating the problem of regulatory arbitrage caused by the existence of different laws for non-bank financial intermediaries engaged in the same activity, thereby launching a new generation of prudential rules for popular finance.[8] Under the first version of the Popular Saving and Loans Law, CNBV was given powers to authorize, supervise, regulate and sanction non-bank intermediaries of different types.

[8] Financial cooperatives had the alternative of operating under the guidelines established in the General Law of Cooperative Societies or in the General Law of Credit Organizations and Auxiliary Activities if they became saving and loan associations. The main difference is that in the first case they were not regulated by the financial authority, whereas in the second they were.

In 2001, institutions serving small-scale rural producers basically consisted of 42 credit unions with a total of 38,000 members; 211 solidarity funds serving 200,000 customers; an unknown number of cooperatives, savings banks and NGOs, with a sparse presence in rural areas, along with several, predominantly urban, saving and loan cooperatives, which were tentatively approaching the rural sector (Campos, 2005).[9]

Prior to 2009, the Popular Saving and Loans Law recognized two legal categories: cooperatives and popular finance institutions (SOFIPOs). While the cooperatives are made up of members and are non-profit associations, SOFIPOs serve customers and are microfinance institutions constituted as variable capital corporations (*S.A. de C.V.*), so they also have to comply with the General Law of Commercial Companies. Under the first version of the Popular Saving and Loans Law, both types of entity were subject to the same regulation based on auxiliary supervision. For most of the first decade of this century, the popular saving and loan entities and their federations, with the support of consultants hired by BANSEFI, focused on building and professionalizing the institutional scaffolding provided for in the Law.

The Popular Saving and Loans Law was conceived as functional legislation that would regulate the activity of non-bank saving, irrespective of the entity. The law envisaged four levels of operation for entities with different degrees of development, whether cooperatives or SOFIPOs, ranging from level I for the simplest entities —generally rural— to level IV for the most sophisticated institutions. As the level rose, the law permitted more sophisticated operations and consequently imposed a greater regulatory burden. The Popular Saving and Loans Law was criticized for the implications of the regulatory burden imposed by the Law for institutions serving the rural population. As a result, the sector underwent a process of consolidation; and, although the number of members of solidarity-based funds is practically the same as 15 years ago, the number of entities serving them has been cut to just 10% of those existing in 2001.

In order to incorporate other rural entities that wished to be regulated and supervised but did not comply with the requirements established in the Popular Saving and Loans Law, this legislation underwent far-reaching amendments in 2009 when the Law Regulating the Activities of Saving and Loan Cooperatives was passed. This resulted in regulatory duality: a specific law for cooperatives and another one for commercial microfinance institutions that accept deposits (SOFIPOs) and a specific category for the rural sector —community finance institutions (SOFINCOs).

---

9 Only a few credit unions, such as the Mexican Association of Social Sector Credit Unions (AMUCSS), provided credit and saving products to very-low-income farmers.

SOFINCOs were incorporated into the Popular Saving and Loans Law in the 2009 reform, as a solution to serve the marginalized rural sector. The purpose of the Law is for these entities to be affiliated to Rural Financial Integration Organizations (OIFRs), which are legal entities authorized by CNBV to help SOFINCOs become operational.

Both the Popular Saving and Loans Law and the Law to Regulate the Activities of Saving and Loan Cooperatives have the four levels of operation created under the first law in 2001. The financial activities authorized in the first three tiers of operation are practically the same under both laws. In contrast, in addition to being able to carry out the operations of saving and loan cooperatives (SOCAPs), in level IV, SOFIPOs are authorized to issue securities for sale among the investing public at large and to issue subordinated bonds, among other faculties.

In terms of supervision, the Popular Saving and Loans Law maintains the auxiliary supervision scheme for SOFIPOs and SOFINCOs through the federations. The Law to Regulate the Activities of Saving and Loan Cooperatives, for its part, also exercises auxiliary supervision, but it does this through the Auxiliary Supervisory Committee of the Technical Committee of the Protection Fund, whose members are representatives of the cooperative sector. This design is criticized because the members are judges of their own cause in the operation and supervision of SOCAPs.

Both the Popular Saving and Loans Law and the Law to Regulate the Activities of Saving and Loan Cooperatives allow SOFINCOs and SOCAPs, respectively, to maintain a basic level for firms that have assets equivalent to less than UDI 2.5 million,[10] which is highly relevant to the rural sector. At this level, they do not need CNBV authorization, although they do have to register. They are allowed to conduct limited saving and loan operations, but are not covered by deposit insurance. In the case of SOFINCOs, at the basic level they can only operate with members as a small cooperative.

As of June 2016, there were 146 SOCAPs authorized and supervised by CNBV at the national level, out of the roughly 400 companies that began the transformation process in 2002. In that year, with a total of 1,747 branches, they served over 5.2 million members across the country and were managing assets worth more than 89,000 million pesos, representing approximately 85% of the total assets of the popular saving and loan sector.

In terms of the rural presence of SOCAPs, in March 2016 there were 670 branches (one third of the total) in municipalities with fewer

[10] Investment units (UDIs) are units of value indexed to inflation. They are used to settle the obligations arising from mortgage loans or any commercial contract. The Bank of Mexico publishes the national currency value of the UDI in the Official Gazette of the Federation for each day of the month. In October 2016, one UDI was equivalent to 5.47 Mexican pesos and to US$ 0.29 (the exchange rate was 19 Mexican pesos per dollar in that month).

than 50,000 inhabitants; in other words, they represented the second most important financial service suppliers after the commercial banks. Among municipalities with fewer than 15,000 inhabitants, SOCAPs are the most widespread institution, surpassing banks and any other institutional category. In the same year there were 218 branches in these municipalities. It should be noted that SOCAPs are the only regulated financial intermediary available in 111 municipalities, representing almost a quarter of the municipalities in which cooperatives are present.

In addition to the authorized SOCAPs, there are basic-level, mainly rural, cooperatives. In August 2016, there were a total of 444 such cooperatives, nine of which were solidarity funds. Of the total, 32 were classified in category D by the Trust Fund for Auxiliary Supervision of Saving and Loan Cooperatives and Protection of their Savers (FOCOOP), which is why CONDUSEF advised against saving in such funds.[11]

With respect to the legal categories envisaged in the Popular Saving and Loans Law, in 2016 there were 44 SOFIPOs authorized nationwide, serving 3,057,140 customers through 1,043 branches in 1,199 municipalities —mostly of low levels of marginalization. In the rural sector, authorized SOFIPOs or microfinance institutions play a less important role than SOCAPs. In March 2016, municipalities with fewer than 50,000 inhabitants had 143 SOFIPO branches, while those with fewer than 15,000 had only 16 branches, and those with fewer than 5,000, just two.

In the case of SOFINCOs, only one institution had been authorized as of September 2016. It has 30 branches in marginalized localities of the country and serves 60,000 customers, mainly from indigenous population groups. As of the same date, eight SOFINCOs and 12 SOFIPOs had filed applications with CNBV and were going through the authorization process. In total, SOFINCOs encompass 110,000 customers. Thus, the difficulties of serving the rural sector were not solved with the new mechanisms. Seven years after the law was reformed, no OIFRs had been authorized.

According to BANSEFI estimates, in July 2016, including popular savings and loan institutions authorized by CNBV and at the basic level, these entities were serving 10.4 million users across the country, and had 140 billion pesos in assets and 110 billion pesos in funding. The authorized popular saving and loan entities served 86% of the users and held 88% of the assets of the entire popular savings and credit sector (BANSEFI, 2016).

The 2014 financial reform included amendments to the Popular Saving and Loans Law and the Law to Regulate the Activities of Saving and Loan

[11] Popular saving and loan entities are required to maintain accounts in accordance with solvency and stability criteria indicated by general provisions. The criteria range from series A —which represents an entity with a strong financial situation— to series D, under which insolvent and higher risk institutions are rated.

Cooperatives. With respect to the expansion of access points, the reform allows SOFIPOs and SOCAPs to participate in supplying mobile banking products and services; and it offers the possibility of having correspondents and operating accounts with simplified documentation, as is the case with commercial banks.

2. Unregulated credit institutions

Unregulated SOFOMs emerged in 2006 as active credit dissemination agents. Although they are outside the regulatory perimeter, these entities are subject to the provisions of the General Law on Credit Institutions and Auxiliary Activities, as well as those issued by CNBV and SHCP under the terms of that Law. They must also comply with the Law on Protection and Defence of Financial Service Users and the Law for Transparency and Regulation of Financial Services. In 2012, the Financial Service Providers Registration System (SIPRES) comprised 2,755 SOFOMs; but a further 921 entities were known not to have registered, and were therefore in serious breach.[12]

The SOFOM legal category covers the largest number of microfinance institutions (ProDesarrollo, 2015). The vast majority are in the urban sector, where they supply microcredits to the middle- and low-income population in outlying urban neighborhoods. In 2012, CONDUSEF's Register of Adhesion Contracts (RECA) contained at least 250 SOFOMs in the primary sector and a total of 342 working capital loan products. Similarly, about 200 SOFOMs were supplying 225 construction loan products.

The 2014 Financial Reform created the Financial Entities Bureau, to report on the performance of all financial institutions in the country, including SOFOMs, which represent 85% of all financial institutions in Mexico, and thus provide users with elements for decision making.

SOFOMs must register with CONDUSEF and submit reports on the prevention of money laundering to CNBV. In addition, following the financial reform, they must consult and notify one of the credit bureaus and apply for registration with CONDUSEF before their constitution, and must also notify any changes in their statutes.

3. Commercial banks

The incursion of commercial banks into the microfinance sector is an important indicator of the expansion of financial services to the typically excluded population. Interest among commercial banks in serving

[12] Interview with the Technical Vice-Presidency of the National Commission for the Protection and Defense of Users of Financial Services (CONDUSEF), July 17 2012.

low-income sectors began in 2002 with Banco Azteca, and was strengthened in 2005 with Compartamos Banco. In the ensuing years, other entities entered the market, most of them linked to supermarket chains. Those that have targeted the microfinance sector are Compartamos Banco, Banco Azteca and Wal-Mart Bank. These banks cater to low- and lower-middle-income people in poor neighborhoods of cities and conurbations; but their presence in the rural sector is scarce. The case of Compartamos Banco is particularly important given the number of customers it serves, its business model and its rapid urban and semi-urban expansion, having been based for many years almost exclusively on group microcredit without providing saving services. Unlike its banking competitors, Compartamos Banco originates from a SOFOL.

As shown in figure VII.1, bank branches in the rural sector are sparse; and, since 2010, banks have tended to withdraw from municipalities with fewer than 15,000 inhabitants. In 2016 these municipalities had only 142 branches; and those withdrawn have not been replaced by correspondents; in fact, this access channel has also tended to retreat from rural areas.

Figure VII.1
Mexico: bank branches in rural municipalities, 2010-2016
(Number of branches)

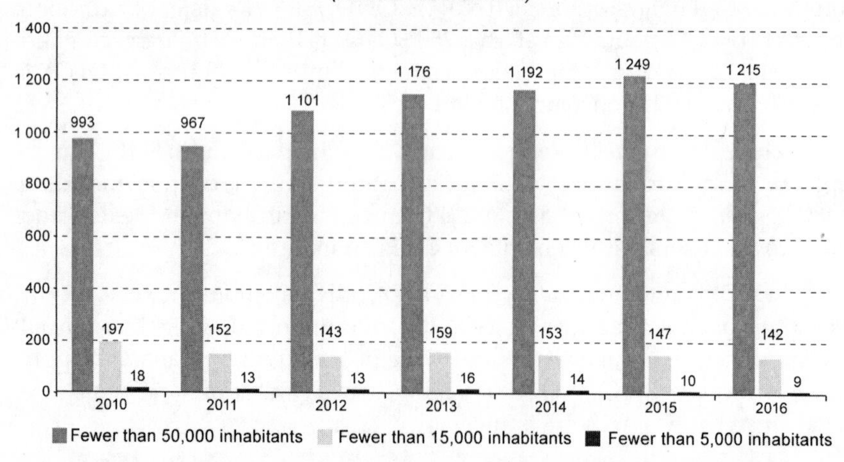

Source: Prepared by the author, on the basis of figures from the National Council for Financial Inclusion (CONAIF).

In 2008, reforms were approved to authorize niche or limited-purpose banks. The requirements for authorization are the same as for multiple-service banks. Nonetheless, as the name suggests, niche banks specialize in a specific product, region or population segment; and they are authorized to undertake basic financial transactions with lower capital requirements than those required for multiple-service banks. Between 2012 and 2016, CNBV authorized seven niche banks, but both Banco de México (Román, 2014) and Moody's Investor Service (2014) have questioned the viability of these institutions. In particular, the niche bank business model is considered to be poorly diversified and face difficulties in complying with prudential regulation.

The financial reform authorized the commercial banks, along with popular saving and loan entities, to offer accounts with simplified documentation. The innovation entailed the incorporation of four levels with specific requirements for account opening and limits on transactionality —three of low risk and the traditional account. The three low-risk levels can be contracted through alternative channels, such as bank correspondents or electronic media, while the traditional account can only be opened at a branch. The PNIF report maintains that Level 2 accounts have proven a suitable fundraising product to develop business models targeting the low-income population, unbanked clients and even population groups living in areas where the only access to the system is through correspondents.

The financial reform banned bundled-product sales, which was a relatively common practice that affected lower-income bank customers, in particular, and discouraged financial inclusion. On the other hand, the reform gives the Bank Savings Protection Institute (IPAB) intervention powers to protect depositors who meet certain requirements. This will allow more orderly and expeditious solutions that benefit creditors with guarantees.

4. Bank correspondents, automated teller machines and point-of-sale terminals

The bank correspondent scheme was launched in early 2010 as a complement to bank branches, with the aim of serving places that did not have them and providing a lower-cost point of access to the financial system. According to CNBV data, from March 2010 to May 2012 the number of authorized bank correspondents grew at a monthly average rate of 7.9%. In 2012, 15 banks had commission agents representing 21,161 service points nationwide; and in 2016, 18 banks had such agents. In 2015, the number of bank correspondents peaked nationwide; but between March 2015 and March 2016, 1,671 service points disappeared, equivalent to 6% of the total.

According to the regulations, the commission agents can be shops, gas stations, pharmacies, telegraph offices and other commercial establishments. As of 2016, only CitiBanamex and Compartamos Banco used small businesses as agents, for example, grocery stores, which could reach the rural sector; but these were few in number. In contrast, the Compartamos Banco correspondents network "Yastás" had nearly 3,000 service points in August 2016.

Correspondents perform a limited range of operations, the type and number depending on the bank and the agent. The emphasis is on collecting loans extended by the creditor bank rather than on any other financial service. Loan payments can be made at nearly all service points of virtually all commission agents, but only for the bank of which it is correspondent (Only Afirme Grupo Financiero accepts payments from other banks). In a considerably smaller number and in decreasing order, deposits, service payments and withdrawals can be made at correspondents. Very few agents offer balance consultation services.

In 2010, the network of stores supplied by Sistema de Distribuidoras Conasupo, S.A. de C.V. (DICONSA)[13] were authorized to act as BANSEFI commission agents, to provide banking services to the lower-income population living mainly in the rural sector. The shops in question are owned by the community, which organizes to request their opening, provide a space for the store and appoint a manager to operate it. In March 2016, out of a total of 20,101 DICONSA stores, BANSEFI was using 258 as active correspondents —mostly located in areas with cell-phone connectivity.

In 2016, municipalities with fewer than 50,000 inhabitants had just 2,429 service points of bank correspondents, or less than 10% of the national total. Municipalities with fewer than 15,000 inhabitants had only 571 service points; and those with fewer than 5,000 had only 91 (CONAIF, 2016b).

The number of ATMs has been growing; and in March 2016 there were 47,043 ATMs nationwide. Despite progress, they remain scarce, mainly in the rural sector. Municipalities with fewer than 50,000 inhabitants account for just 7% of ATMs, even though 22% of the country's adult population lives in these municipalities. Most ATMs belong to the commercial banks, but some SOFIPOs, SOCAPs and even BANSEFI also have them, although they are thinly distributed.

Point of sale (POS) terminals are essential for bank correspondents and are considered an essential complement to the financial ecosystem, since they enable electronic media to be used to make purchases and other payments, thereby reducing the need for cash. The PNIF report recognizes the persistently low rate of terminal-based commerce in Mexico, since only 10% of commercial entities nationwide (574,000 out of a total exceeding 5.6 million) has a POS terminal. In March 2016 there was a record of 874,419 TPVs in the country. Although the increase has occurred in all sectors, there is a persistent and pronounced lag in rural areas.

---

[13] DICONSA is the public agency responsible for the social supply programme in rural areas, which operates through a network of fixed and mobile stores.

B. Development banks in the rural financial architecture

It is impossible to understand the financial inclusion architecture in Mexico, especially in the rural sector, without analysing the development banks' heavy involvement and types of intervention, in both first- and second-tier activities. Despite their important public action, there is still no clear model of the type of relationship that should be established between different development banks and private financial institutions, users and other development agencies, to enhance rural financial inclusion.

1. Brief background

Over the past 15 years, three periods of development banking can be identified. The first, from 2001 to 2006, was one of stabilization and modernization aimed at achieving financial sustainability, and enhancing operational guidelines and corporate governance. The second period spans 2006 to 2012 and involves an expansion of credit, which was curtailed by the conditions imposed for restructuring. According to their statutes, development banks had to fulfill their mission using their own assets and, although they could receive additional resources from the public sector, these conditions restricted their actions.

The third period —which began with the promulgation of the 2013 financial reform and its implementation in 2014— gave development banking a new mandate: the promotion of the economy by serving strategic sectors that face constraints on access to financing alternatives. Financial reform made the regulatory framework governing development banks more flexible, with the aim of streamlining loan processes, and enabling them to raise and manage the necessary resources, especially human capital, to fulfill their mandate.

The following sections describe development bank programmes specifically related to rural financial inclusion.

2. Financiera Nacional de Desarrollo Agropecuario, Rural, Forestal y Pesquero

The National Financial Institute for Agricultural, Rural, Forestry and Fisheries Development (FND) undertakes operations directly with users through a network of 95 agencies, and channels resources through non-bank financial institutions. According to estimates from the former Financiera Rural, for each financial intermediary receiving credit in 2010, 700 borrowers were indirectly served (Merino, 2011). Nonetheless, on the same date, half of the institution's resources were still being channelled through first-tier operations.

The Institute channels funds to all activities related to the rural sector, prioritizing those destined for localities with fewer than 50,000 inhabitants. Its credit products are simple credit, working capital, title loans, construction loans, current account and multiple agricultural working capital. In August 2016, it had eight financing programmes for different purposes, including the Small-scale Producers Financing Programme, which the Government views as FND's key strategy for rural financial inclusion (CONAIF, 2016a).

The Small-scale Producer Financing Programme arose in 2014 as a result of a change to the FND regulations. Previously, access by small-scale producers was limited to construction loans owing to the levels of collateral required. Following the change, the natural working capital collateral, in other words the harvest, came into force, thereby opening up the possibility for a smallholder with half a hectare in the southeast of the country, for example, to borrow to purchase agricultural inputs. The programme's first-tier credits are granted through the FND agencies; and its second-tier lending is channelled through credit lines to financial institutions or credit disseminators. In 2016 the programme served 40,000 producers: 90% first tier and 10% second tier.[14]

The programme sets ceilings on loan rates, which include a margin of three percentage points for the operating expenses of fund disseminating entities. Interest rate caps aim to subsidize the producer rather than the intermediary. Nonetheless, the setting of rate caps has discouraged financial intermediaries from joining the programme. Considering that in 2016 this credit represented the first formal financing experience for 80% of the programme's beneficiary producers, the lack of participation by financial intermediaries makes it harder for them to become permanent customers of a financial institution with access to a wide range of products.

Another problem faced by the programme in terms of financial inclusion is the impossibility of verifying whether the new borrowers of the programme are relatives of the owner or tenant (*ejidatario*) of the land whose production is pledged as collateral. This may cause the credit to be concentrated in beneficiaries or co-producers who pledge the harvest from the same land. The problem is that Mexico has no land records with disaggregated data, so FND cannot identify this situation. Lastly, a large proportion of the producers invited to learn about the Small Producers Financing Programme did not want credit, despite the favourable conditions. This shows that the key element of financial inclusion is not always credit, but instead the package of complementary products and services.

Despite its shortcomings, the rural financial inclusion programme has managed to include producers who traditionally did not access development banks, thereby expanding the social base of beneficiaries of production loans under preferential conditions.

[14] Interview with FND officials from the Deputy General Directorate of Credit, October 29, 2016.

3. Banco del Ahorro Nacional y Servicios Financieros

The National Bank for Savings and Financial Services (BANSEFI), created in 2002, supplies savings, transfer and remittance services along with microinsurance products. It also distributes various government subsidies through a network of 428 branches, mainly in urban areas. According to BANSEFI data, in June 2016 the institution handled more than 13 million accounts, 6.5 million of which belonged to beneficiaries of the PROSPERA conditional cash transfer programme. No information is available on the number of customers or the transactionality of the accounts or intensity of their use, however.

BANSEFI has contributed to financial inclusion in Mexico mainly through its institutional strengthening programme. For nearly 15 years, this programme has helped most popular saving and loan entities to formalize and supply more soundly based financial services regulated by the authority to users who are traditionally excluded from commercial banking. Among its different programmes, BANSEFI has three strategies that are totally or partially linked to the rural sector: The People's Network (*L@ Red de la Gente*), the Rural Microfinance Technical Assistance Programme (PATMIR) and the Comprehensive Financial Inclusion Programme (PROIIF).

The People's Network, a commercial alliance created by BANSEFI in 2002, is made up of popular saving and loan entities and the bank's branches. It is a voluntary association of intermediaries who seek to promote savings and offer financial products and services under competitive conditions to reduce costs, share risks and scale up their operations. In August 2016, 189 popular saving and loan entities were participating in the programme, encompassing a total of 2,298 branches in 938 municipalities across the country, and serving 4 million members or customers. In addition to savings, credit, remittances, transfers between accounts and microinsurance, 58 organizations from The People's Network disseminated the support of the PROSPERA Programme to about 100,000 beneficiaries in 19 Mexican states. These benefits are made through a "closed channel", whereby the transfer is paid in cash and not deposited into an account, because the savings accounts of PROSPERA beneficiaries are held in BANSEFI and not in the source fund. As a result, few savings banks have been able to attract PROSPERA beneficiaries, which hinders their full integration into the financial system.

The Rural Microfinance Technical Assistance Programme (PATMIR) began in 2002 within SAGARPA, before being transferred to BANSEFI in 2010. It is Mexico's most important public programme on rural financial inclusion, having incorporated a large number of marginalized rural clients into the formal financial sector. Broadly speaking, in the programme's 14 years of existence, it has sought to ensure that cooperatives, and more recently

SOFIPOs also, serve the rural poor by promoting financial inclusion based on savings. In this way, it has provided funding to enable the entities to admit, as members or customers, members of the rural population in zones of very high, high and medium marginalization (as measured by the indices of the National Population Council (CONAPO)),[15] who in general have not had access to formal financial services.

The third BANSEFI financial inclusion strategy for the rural sector is PROIIF, which was created in 2015 in response to the financial reform mandate that stresses the role of development banks in promoting credit access for priority groups. PROIIF targets PROSPERA beneficiaries, offering a programmed savings account, an on-demand savings account, and two credit products. Owing to the system's operational complexities, there is a time lapse between the contract or the request and the execution of the transactions. Over time, the system will have to adjust, as one of the characteristics of a good saving and loan product is precisely its timeliness. Usually, this feature is valued above a better interest rate, mainly owing to the highly seasonal nature of rural economic activities and susceptibility to emergencies to which this population is exposed, which make the availability of savings or credits an essential resource.

4. Agricultural trust funds

The Agricultural-related Trust Funds (FIRA)[16] provide access to credit through loan and discount operations, and also by extending guarantees to projects related to agriculture, livestock, poultry, agribusiness and fishing, along with other activities related to the rural domain.

In the last decade, FIRA started working with non-bank intermediaries and unregulated financial entities. The financial entities with which it currently works, in addition to commercial banks, are SOFOM, SOFIPO, SOCAP, credit unions and general deposit warehouses. These entities can lend to natural and legal persons whose activity involves the production, storage and distribution of goods, and services related to the agricultural, forestry and fishing sectors, and other activities undertaken in the rural sector.

The FIRA trust funds also lend to non-traditional activities in the rural sector, through rural finance and microcredit schemes. The first of these seeks

---

15 The National Population Council stratifies the states, municipalities, localities and basic geostatistical areas (AGEB) by five levels of marginalization according to an index created from basic development indicators: levels of schooling, quality of housing, drainage, use of appliances, among others. Marginality is divided into high, very high, medium, low and very low.

16 The FIRA trust funds are the Guarantee and Development Fund for Agriculture, Livestock and Poultry (FONDO); the Special Fund for Financing the Farm Sector (FEFA); the Special Technical Assistance and Agricultural Credit Guarantee Fund (FEGA); and the Fishing Activities Guarantee and Development Fund (FOPESCA).

to finance any economic activity that takes place in rural areas, other than those carried out by firms in the agricultural, forestry and fishing sectors. Projects implemented in localities with fewer than 50,000 inhabitants are eligible. The second is more significant in terms of inclusion: specifically, it seeks to increase the penetration and coverage of rural financial markets to afford credit access to small-scale producers whose net annual income is less than 3,000 times the minimum daily wage in the area in which the investments will be made.

The programme authorizes credit lines to financial intermediaries in accordance with their business plan, for them to on-lend with microcredits to individuals. The amounts and terms granted to applicants must be aligned with the activity they finance, the type and recurrent nature of their income, and their ability to pay (excluding consumer credit). Microcredits are subject to an upper limit of UDI 33,000 and have terms of up to three years.

The interest that FIRA charges the intermediaries must adhere to the interest rate scheme prevailing when the funds are released. FIRA offers intermediaries variable interest rates and risk hedging schemes with fixed rates. The borrower intermediaries sign promissory notes in favor of the trustee.

The interest rate paid by producers is that charged by microfinance companies for this product. Unlike the FND Small Producers Financing Programme or BANSEFI's PROIIF, the rates have no upper limits, so producers that borrow under the FIRA microcredit scheme pay a rate that is higher than that paid by borrowers in the other two programmes. Nonetheless, the latter has considerably broader coverage: in 2014 the programme had 724,977 borrowers.

The trust fund also supports training activities among financial intermediaries and both BANSEFI and FND. In no case is there coordination between the technical assistance programmes and the three development banks.

Table VII.2 compares the three programmes of the three development banks analyzed in this study which offer credit to the unbanked rural population. As can be seen, there is a relationship between the interest rate, the distribution channel and the coverage of the programme. Unsubsidized interest rate credit programmes, distributed through the second tier, achieve greater coverage than subsidized programmes distributed through first-tier operations. PROIIF lies between the two extremes, but, unlike its counterparts, it is a very small credit and is guaranteed by conditional cash transfers. As all three cases are public financial inclusion programmes, one should ask where the balance should be struck between the interest rate, the coverage and sustainability of the programme, security for the user and the efficiency of the service.

Table VII.2

Comparison between three public credit programmes targeting the rural population to support financial inclusion, 2014-2016

Institution	Programme	Maximum amount	Maximum term	Annual interest rate	Borrower collateral	Destination of credit	Borrower characteristics	Tier	Number of borrowers	Year
FIRA	Microcredit	33 000 UDI	3 years	Total annual cost 35%-45%	As requested by the popular saving and loan entities and SOFOM[a]	Productive	PD1 and PD2[b]	2nd	724 977	2014
BANSEFI	Comprehensive Financial Inclusion Programme (PROIIF)	2 000 Mexican pesos	1.5 years	9.99%	Conditional cash transfers	Unrestricted	PROSPERA beneficiary	1st	400 013	2015
FND	Small-scale Producer Financing Programme	45 000 UDI	5 years	Women: 6.5% Men: 7.0%	The harvest	Productive	Smallholder	1st[c]	40 000	2016

Source: prepared by the author.

[a] If the microcredit is extended to a group, no collateral is required; if it is personal, a pledge or photocopy of the deeds is generally required.

[b] PD1: Developing producers whose net annual income does not exceed 1,000 times the daily minimum wage in the area in which the investments will be made; PD2: Developing producers whose net annual income is between 1,000 and 3,000 times the minimum daily wage of the area in which the investments will be made.

[c] Only 10% of the credits are issued through the second tier.

C. Challenges faced by the users and the financial institutions in rural areas

1. Evolution of access points in the rural sector

As shown in figure VII.2, despite the progress made between 2011 and 2014, the number of branches of regulated entities (banks, development banks, SOCAPs and SOFIPOs) has fallen since 2015, particularly in the rural areas, where the decline started in 2014. This accentuates the already meager presence of financial institutions in rural zones. From 2014 to 2016, the number of branches per 10,000 adults fell from 0.68 to 0.58 in municipalities with a population of less than 5,000 inhabitants; remained at 0.80 in municipalities with fewer than 15,000 inhabitants and fell from 1.20 to 1.16 in those with fewer than 50,000.

Figure VII.2
México: branches of regulated entities in municipalities with fewer than 15,000 inhabitants, 2010-2016
(Number of branches)

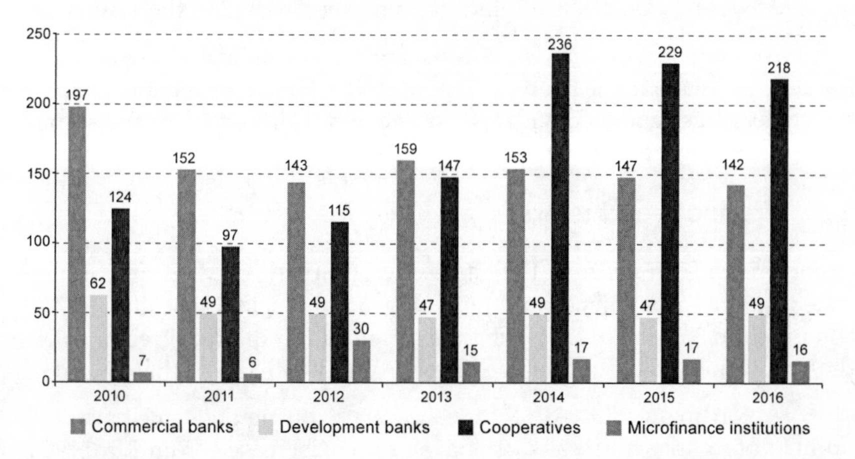

Source: Prepared by the author, on the basis of figures from the National Council for Financial Inclusion (CONAIF).

In addition to the fall in the number of branches, the number of bank correspondents in the rural sector has also been dwindling since 2012. By 2016, the number of correspondents in municipalities with fewer than 5,000 inhabitants had declined by virtually half from 179 to 91. CONAIF explains the exit of correspondents from the rural sector by the complicated authorization process, which entails a long waiting period, unlike the urban commercial networks, which allow many points to be set up simultaneously (CONAIF, 2016a).

The only access points that increased nationally between 2011 and 2016 were ATMs, although their number in the most rural areas peaked in 2010. Nonetheless, in 2011 there was a sharp fall of 60% in municipalities with fewer than 5,000 inhabitants —from 118 to 50—and a drop of 30% in municipalities with a population below 15,000 —from 687 to 479. The difficulties facing ATMs when expanding into the rural sector relate to the costs that their use implies for users and to the break-even point in terms of transactions that the financial institutions need for them to be a profitable business activity.[17] According to figures from the 2015 National Financial Inclusion Survey (ENIF) (INEGI / CNBV, 2016), only 2% of the rural population uses ATMs.

The disparity between rural and urban municipalities in terms of financial sector access points is clearly reflected among the country's regions. The results of the Seventh National Financial Inclusion Report (CONAIF, 2016b) show that in 2015 the number of branches, ATMs and correspondents for every 10,000 adults was lower in the southern states than in other regions. That year the national average was 1.9 branches per 10,000 adults, while in the south it was 1.6. In the case of correspondents, the figure was 3.1 nationally, but barely reached 2 in the south of the country. Similarly, the average coverage of ATMs was 5.1 per 10,000 adults nationally, but just 3.7 in the south.

Although net progress has been made on rural financial inclusion over the past six years, it has been very slow or else has made a good start and then faltered, as happened with correspondents, ATMs and even the number of branches, particularly in municipalities with fewer than 5,000 inhabitants.

2. Products and users

According to ENIF figures (INEGI/CNBV, 2016), 44% of Mexican nationals stated that they had an account with a formal financial institution in 2015, compared to 36% in 2012. The change originated in the rural sector, where the proportion of account holders grew from 23% to 35% in that period.

According to CONAIF figures however, during the same period the number of savings and transactional accounts decreased from 5,590,292 to 5,072,930 in municipalities with fewer than 50,000 inhabitants, and declined from 917,699 to 785,388 in those with a population of under 15,000. The discrepancy may partly reflect issues related to the wording of the questions in both years and to the recording of accounts tied to social programmes.

In the case of credit obtained from a formal institution, ENIF 2015 data indicate a low incidence in both the rural and urban sectors. The picture changes when regional patterns are considered, however, since credit and microcredit tend to be concentrated in large and medium-sized cities and

---

[17] Interview with María O'Keefe, expert on rural finance in Mexico, August 2016.

conurbations. In these zones, there are even problems of over-indebtedness due to the excess supply of expensive microcredit, while other (mainly rural) regions remain unserved (Marulanda Consultores Ltda./DAI, 2011).

In terms of the type of credit, between 2012 and 2015, personal credit accelerated (from 2.7% to 3.3%) while group credit slowed (from 3.5% to 2%) in the rural sector. This may be due to the closure of SOFOMs with group credit methodologies, but also to a tendency among all microfinance institutions to retarget their loan portfolio towards personal and individual credit. The good news may be a better product for the rural sector, since personal credit tends to be characterized by higher amounts, longer terms, less risk for the user and, at times, lower interest rates. In contrast, however, it usually requires collateral that is not always available to low-income users.

Meanwhile, credit card use has spread in rural areas. According to ENIF, in just three years the number of people using this instrument grew by a third. In semi-urban populations, cards are more convenient than microcredits, since they can be used to pay for domestic and business items in interest-free installments. However, access to cards is still extremely low. The fact that credit cards are almost the only financing instrument that has grown in recent years in rural areas suggests a promising banking potential that could benefit from digital technology and other joint actions discussed in the conclusions. What the data show is that any substitution between credit products has been towards the credit card.

3. The challenges facing non-bank financial institutions in the rural sector

As shown in figure VII.2, in municipalities with fewer than 15,000 inhabitants SOCAP branches are the most common of all regulated entities, followed by commercial banks, development banks and SOFIPOs. The main challenges faced by these institutions are discussed in the following paragraphs.

The first challenge is mistrust in the popular saving and loan sector. For popular saving and loan entities there is a "before and after" in their relationship with the authority, relative to the SOFIPO Ficrea fraud in November 2014. After this, in 2015 a reform was proposed to the Popular Saving and Loans Law, known locally as the Ficrea Law. This regulation proposed prudential measures that put the financial viability of popular saving and loan entities seriously at risk.

They also face a regressive form of regulation. Under the financial reform, CNBV certifies auditors and compliance officers and other professionals in all financial entities —whether regulated or unregulated— in the area of anti-money laundering and terrorist financing (AML/FT) operating in the country. The requirements of the compliance officer are the same for a commercial bank as for a solidarity fund. Nonetheless, in the rural sector the costs of meeting the requirements are high and it is difficult to do so. Moreover, current regulations do not allow a compliance officer to provide services to several entities, which could ease this burden. This is only possible if they are part of the same financial group, such as a bank or a regulated multiple-purpose financial institution (SOFOM E.R.); but in the popular saving and loan sector, the vast majority of entities do not belong to financial groups.

The reform also gives a more active role to CONDUSEF in terms of contract regulation. Again, institutional size is not taken into consideration, so a bank pays the same fine as a rural saving and loan cooperative. These situations can cause the demise of the few financial institutions that serve the rural sector. Of course, the aim is not for rural savings and loan cooperatives not to be fined or reprimanded in the event of default, especially since they serve vulnerable population groups; but a sanction that is more proportional to their assets could give better results.

Another issue that needs to be addressed is the relationship with commercial banks. Popular saving and loan entities and SOFOMs need the services of commercial banks to be able to carry out their operations. In addition to the services used by any legal entity —payment of payroll, rental or services—others are fundamental for serving and expanding their customer base. The latter go to the banks with cheques issued by the popular saving and loan entities to withdraw the loan proceeds, and to pay the corresponding installments through a deposit in the institution's account. The microcredits that customers receive from microfinance institutions generally require weekly or fortnightly payments, which involves frequent transactions between the microcredit institution, the bank and microfinance customers.

SOFIPOs and SOCAPs do not have a branch network infrastructure like the banks. Channelling operations through the banking network offers greater opportunities for popular saving and loan entities to serve a larger number of customers with a considerably larger number of access points and to handle a greater volume of transactions. Thus, SOFIPOs and SOFOMs need bank accounts to operate and to scale up.

Nonetheless, the relationship between popular saving and loan entities and commercial banks has been hampered in recent years. In 2011, based on the new regulations to prevent money laundering, which requires suspicious transactions to be reported to the authorities, banks started to close the basic accounts of popular saving and loan entities and SOFOMs. Yet, while the vast majority of entities are fully compliant with their prevention of money laundering obligations they still have their bank accounts closed.

An emblematic example of this situation involves the entities affiliated to ProDesarrollo Finanzas y Microempresa, A.C., the largest network of microfinance cooperatives in Mexico. These fully comply with the anti-money-laundering regulations; but, in 2015, bank account closures affected about 1 million microentrepreneur customers among these entities (out of a total of 6.4 million).[18]

Faced with this situation, some saving and loan institutions affiliated to ProDesarrollo and led by SOFIPO Solución ASEA, which operates in the rural sector of Chiapas state, are building a model to incorporate shops owned by their microenterprise customers as commission agents and adapt less expensive technology to expand their service network through these correspondents. This will bring them even closer to the people and make them less dependent on bank services. These measures cannot be adopted by SOFOMs however, since they are not authorized to have correspondents. Nor can they be customers of popular saving and loan entities since they are legal entities. So, regardless of the parallel strategies that some legal entities may pursue, the issue of banking in this situation needs to be addressed by the competent authorities.

4. Financial education

The various financial education programmes that exist in Mexico, provided by different public and private institutions, are poorly coordinated.

The National Bank for Savings and Financial Services (BANSEFI) development bank, BANSEFI, is the institution that has worked the most on financial education, through three lines of action. First, it holds workshops for the popular saving and loan sector, to train trainers to give financial education courses to users. In addition, there are mobile units, where brief workshops are held directly with current and potential users. Lastly, the bank forges partnerships with academic institutions to bring courses to marginalized communities. It also created the "Finance for All" microsite to enable people to develop financial literacy skills and complete three levels of online courses.[19]

Within the framework of the National Policy on Financial Inclusion, the main Federal Government investment for making headway in the area of financial education is being implemented by *México Digital* as part of the National Digital Strategy. This is a responsibility of the Presidency of the Republic and is still at the pilot stage. As part of this strategy, the *Prospera Digital* pilot programme is being developed for the lower-income population and specifically for PROSPERA beneficiaries. This has components including mother and child health, along with financial inclusion and education provided through communication platform with mobile tools and technologies.

---

18 Interview with Claudia Revilla, General Director of ProDesarrollo Finanzas y Microempresa, A.C., August 3, 2016.

19 See National Bank for Savings and Financial Services (BANSEFI) [online] http://www.bansefi.gob.mx/Finanzasparatodos/Pages/default.aspx.

D. Conclusions

While significant progress on financial inclusion has been made over the last 15 years, efforts have been insufficient, and rural financial inclusion has not been consolidated. Even more worrying, access to rural financial services and the use of them seem to have retreated in recent years.

In general, the justification for rural backwardness is lack of infrastructure and technology. Nonetheless, the difficulties and dilemmas of complex rural financial penetration are closely related to non-technological variables. Poverty in the rural sector, low levels of human capital, limited formality, lack of safety nets, insecurity and seasonal variation, among other factors, require interventions designed with the greatest possible knowledge and sensitivity.

In Mexico, various actions have been designed to strengthen rural financial inclusion, either through the creation of legal mechanisms, or through first- and second-tier credit programmes, guarantees, the opening of savings accounts, or technical assistance for financial intermediaries and rural producers, and also various financial education initiatives. The results have been meagre, however. Several reasons for this have been discussed in this chapter.

One reason is that development banks do not share either basic information or successful or failed experiences. Nor do they strategically target or differentiate many of their actions. As noted above, there is no clear model on the type of relationship that should be established between the different development banks and private financial institutions, users and other development agencies to enhance rural financial inclusion.

A number of measures related to the pillars of the National Financial Inclusion Policy are outlined below.

The first pillar refers to "the development of knowledge for the efficient and responsible use of the financial system by the entire population". On this point, it is important to clarify what is meant by financial education, and the materials that are relevant for the different priority groups. As a certifier of financial education BANSEFI, may have a more active role to play in this regard.

Regardless of the channel through which education is transmitted, this service must be suited to the needs and capabilities of its target audience. There are interesting and necessary pilot projects, such as Prospera Digital, which are harnessing experts in behavioral economics to develop financial education programmes with a better understanding of the economic decisions made by the target group to be included.

It is also important that financial institutions and public programme operators receive this specialized financial education, to be able to anticipate responses to situations and the doubts that may arise among the rural customers they serve.

The second and third pillars of the PNIF deal with the "use of technological innovations for financial inclusion" and the "development of financial infrastructure in neglected areas". The two pillars go hand in hand and are relevant, primarily, to remote and laggard areas.

Nonetheless, at least two aspects arising from this study need to be considered. The first is the need to invest in product development; in other words, ensure that technological innovation has content, which means distinguishing between the channel and the product. Technology can improve the access channel by reducing transaction costs; but, if the design of the product does not meet users' needs, financial inclusion will run into problems of non-use or, worse, a use of products that can generate greater problems.

Technology also needs to be affordable. In Mexico there is information showing what media can be used or where it is necessary to invest and provide support. In the case of the rural sector, ENIF 2015 showed that 38.3% of adults in towns with fewer than 15,000 inhabitants do not have a cell phone; and the figure rises to 40.8% among rural women. Accordingly, technological innovations will need to adapt to the conditions prevailing in rural areas, without neglecting the unresolved challenge of expanding and strengthening connectivity in these areas.

The fourth pillar refers to a "greater supply and use of formal financial services for the underserved and excluded population". In terms of use, development banks seem to believe that improving the product consists of reducing the interest rate on loans. Accordingly, both PROIIF and the Small-scale Producers Financing Programme offer below-market rates. Of course, low interest rates are more attractive for the user; but the interest rate is not the financial product's only attribute. Over many years, studies have revealed how ease of use of the system, accessibility, security, timely availability of funds, the payment schedule, deadlines and even treatment play a crucial role in trust and the use of products (Adams and Fitchett, 1992). The problem of viewing product improvement exclusively in terms of lowering the interest rate is that it affects the supply of credit, since the programmes' funds are limited (Yaron, Benjamin and Piprek, 1997).

Products supplied by the private rural financial sector have improved, as exemplified mainly by product substitution. In deposit services, transactional accounts with simplified records have been well received in the rural sector, especially because of the ease with which they can be opened; so they are judged to be a success of the reform. In credit services, the supply and use of group methodologies have declined. In contrast personal credit and credit cards are increasing, with financing terms and conditions that are more attractive than group credit.

Despite improvements in the products supplied, financial services and their use have declined in municipalities and localities with fewer than 50,000 inhabitants in recent years. This should give pause for thought.

As discussed in this chapter, in the rural sector popular saving and loan entities, along with unregulated institutions such as the SOFOMs, have had to deal with reputational problems caused by the Ficrea fraud, which have affected the regulatory burden and their relationship with commercial banks. Nonetheless, these entities are the main suppliers in the rural sector. The regulation on the prevention of money laundering and financing of terrorism (AML/FT) has imposed an additional cost burden. This raises the need for schemes to achieve economies of scale in compliance with regulations, alongside regulatory cost schemes that are proportional to the size of the financial institutions' assets, otherwise the smaller and rural regulated entities will be unable to bear the burden.

The closure of bank accounts held by popular saving and loan entities is what has most affected the sector. In addition to the need to solve this problem, alternatives should be sought that make non-bank intermediaries less reliant on commercial banks. The correspondents of the popular saving and loan entities are an example of this: another success of the financial reform.

Account closures affecting the operations of non-bank entities and their users, both rural and urban, are compounded by the fact that commercial banks have eliminated branches and correspondents from the rural area. Moreover, a large number of SOFOMs have been wound up and liquidated, and some rural saving and loan entities have been shut down because of their financial situation. This calls for an in-depth discussion of rural financial markets, involving development banks, authorities and private providers to reverse the shrinking of rural finance.

Another alternative to strengthen access points in the rural sector is to view the second tier as a development banking priority, since its coverage is limited. This brings benefits in terms of the number of users and institutional strengthening. Nonetheless, the equilibrium level of the lending interest rates needs to be found, to avert a situation in which the intermediary benefits from a cheap portfolio discount to the detriment of the user, who should be the development bank's ultimate target beneficiary.

The fifth and sixth pillars of PNIF seek to "increase trust in the formal financial sector through consumer protection mechanisms" and "generate data and measures to evaluate financial inclusion efforts." In the rural sector, additional efforts will need to be made to build trust in formal financial institutions. For obvious reasons, financial education has a key role to play here; but the contents will have to reinforce everything related to the rights of the user, since this topic is less well known to individuals who are in a situation of poverty and isolation. Making these rights effective requires seeking innovative, different and easy methods of consultation and reporting of abuses, using the available technology.

Lastly, there is no doubting the wealth of information that has been generated in the databases, of both institutions and users, stemming from the creation of CONAIF and the implementation of ENIF. In the space of just a few years, information of enormous value for making diagnoses and designing public policies has been generated, which did not exist in the previous decade. The databases have been growing and have been improved over time. Two suggestions arise from their use. First, in the case of financial inclusion induced by the savings accounts of social programmes, it is important to keep information obtained from the beneficiaries separate from that sourced from other users. The second suggestion is that the planning, prospective studies and evaluations conducted by professional academics and experts on financial inclusion need to be strengthened.

Bibliography

Adams, D. and D. Fitchett (eds.) (1992), *Informal Finance in Low-Income Countries*, San Francisco, Westview Press.

BANSEFI (National Bank for Savings and Financial Services) (2016), Presentation at the Seminar "Promoting financial inclusion via development banks' innovation policies", Mexico City, 4-5 July, Economic Commission for Latin America and the Caribbean (ECLAC).

Campos, P. (2012), "Estudio de *benchmarking*: trayectoria de las microfinanzas y la participación del PRONAFIM (2000-2012) como insumo para la planeación futura", National Microenterprise Financing Programme (PRONAFIM).

___(2005), *El ahorro popular en México: acumulando activos para superar la pobreza*, Mexico City, Centre of Research for Development (CIDAC)/Editorial Porrúa.

CONAIF (National Council for Financial Inclusion) (2016a), *Política nacional de inclusión financiera*, Mexico City, June.

___(2016b), *Reporte Nacional de Inclusión Financiera*, No. 7, Mexico City.

CONDUSEF (National Commission for the Protection of Users of Financial Services) (2012), "La importancia de las SOFOM ENR para la CONDUSEF", *Comunicado*, No. 47, Mexico City.

DICONSA (Sistema de Distribuidoras Conasupo, S.A. de C.V.) (2016), "Metodología de evaluación de propuestas para la prestación del servicio de plataforma de pagos en tiendas comunitarias de DICONSA", August.

Gutiérrez, J. and E. Servan (2012), "Análisis descriptivo de los cuestionarios de medios de pago para la titular beneficiaria de Oportunidades y operadores. Versión final", Cuernavaca, National Institute of Public Health, October.

IMF (International Monetary Fund) (2015), *Financial Access Survey 2015*, Washington, D.C.

INEGI/CNBV (National Institute of Statistics and Geography/National Commission of Banks and Insurances) (2016), *Encuesta Nacional de Inclusión Financiera 2015*, Mexico City.

Mansell, C. (1995), *Las finanzas populares en México: el redescubrimiento de un sistema olvidado*, Mexico City, Autonomous Technological Institute of Mexico/Editorial Milenio.

Marulanda Consultores Ltda./Development Alternatives Inc. (DAI) (2011), *Estudio: microfinanzas en México* [online] http://www.microfinancegateway.org/sites/default/files/mfg-es-documento-estudio-microfinanzas-en-mexico-3-2011.pdf.

Maxfield, S. (1993), "The politics of Mexican financial policy", *The Politics of Finance in Developing Countries*, S. Haggard, C. Lee and S. Maxfield (eds.), Ithaca, Cornell University Press.

Merino, G. (2011), "Financiamiento al sector rural", paper presented at the Chamber of Deputies, Mexico City, Financiera Rural, August.

Mexico, Presidency of the Republic (2011), "Acuerdo por el que se crea el Consejo Nacional de Inclusión Financiera", *Diario Oficial de la Federación*, Mexico City, 3 October.

Moody's Investor Service (2014), "El fracaso de Banco Bicentenario expone debilidades de la estrategia de bancos de nicho en México", 12 August.

ProDesarrollo (ProDesarrollo Finanzas y Microempresa, A.C.) (2015), *Benchmarking de las microfinanzas en México 2014-2015*, Mexico City.

Román, R. (2014), "Bancos de nicho son los más vulnerables", *El Economista*, Mexico City, 18 November.

Trivelli, C. and H. Venero (2007), "Banca de desarrollo para el agro: ¿qué podemos aprender de la experiencia latinoamericana?", *Debate Agrario: Análisis y Alternativas*, No. 42, Lima, Peruvian Social Studies Centre, November.

Yaron, J., M. Benjamin and G. Piprek (1997), "Rural finance: issues, design and best practice", *Environmentally and Socially Sustainable Development Studies and Monograph Series*, vol. 14, Washington, D.C., World Bank.

Publicaciones recientes de la CEPAL
ECLAC recent publications

www.cepal.org/publicaciones

Informes periódicos / *Annual reports*

También disponibles para años anteriores / *Issues for previous years also available*

- Estudio Económico de América Latina y el Caribe 2017, 218 p.
  Economic Survey of Latin America and the Caribbean 2017, 214 p.
- La Inversión Extranjera Directa en América Latina y el Caribe 2017, 206 p.
  Foreign Direct Investment in Latin America and the Caribbean 2016, 196 p.
- Anuario Estadístico de América Latina y el Caribe 2016 / *Statistical Yearbook for Latin America and the Caribbean 2016, 132 p.*
- Balance Preliminar de las Economías de América Latina y el Caribe 2016, 132 p.
  Preliminary Overview of the Economies of Latin America and the Caribbean 2016, 124 p.
- Panorama Social de América Latina 2016, 290 p.
  Social Panorama of Latin America 2016, 272 p.
- Perspectivas del Comercio Internacional de América Latina y el Caribe 2017. Documento informativo, 176 p.
  International Trade Outlook for Latin America and the Caribbean 2017. Briefing paper, 170 p.

Libros y documentos institucionales / *Institutional books and documents*

- Plan de acción regional para la implementación de la nueva agenda urbana en América Latina y el Caribe, 2016-2036, 2017, 64 p.
  Regional Action Plan for the implementation of the New Urban Agenda in Latin America and the Caribbean 2016-2036, 2017, 62 p.
- Brechas, ejes y desafíos en el vínculo entre lo social y lo productivo, 2017, 182 p.
  Linkages between the social and production spheres: Gaps, pillars and challenges, 2017, 170 p.
- Derechos de las personas mayores: retos para la interdependencia y autonomía, 2017, 176 p.
  Challenges to the autonomy and interdependent rights of older persons, 2017, 162 p.
- Panorama fiscal de América Latina y el Caribe 2017: la movilización de recursos para el financiamiento del desarrollo sostenible, 2017, 115 p.
  Fiscal Panorama of Latin America and the Caribbean 2017: Mobilizing resources to finance sustainable development, 2017, 108 p.
- La matriz de la desigualdad en América Latina, 2016, 96 p.
  The social inequality matrix in Latin America, 2016, 94 p.
- Autonomía de las mujeres e igualdad en la agenda de desarrollo sostenible, 2016, 184 p.
  Equality and women's autonomy in the sustainable development agenda, 2016, 168 p.
  Autonomia das mulheres e igualdade na agenda de desenvolvimento sustentável. Síntese, 2016, 106 p.
- La Unión Europea y América Latina y el Caribe ante la Agenda 2030 para el Desarrollo Sostenible: el gran impulso ambiental, 2016, 112 p.
  The European Union and Latin America and the Caribbean vis-à-vis the 2030 Agenda for Sustainable Development: The environmental big push, 2016, 112 p.

Libros de la CEPAL / *ECLAC books*

- 150 ¿Quién cuida en la ciudad?: aportes para políticas urbanas de igualdad, María Nieves Rico, Olga Segovia (eds.), 2017, 476 p.
- 149 Manufactura y cambio estructural: aportes para pensar la política industrial en la Argentina, Martín Abeles, Mario Cimoli, Pablo José Lavarello (eds.), 2017, 336 p.
- 148 Planificación para el desarrollo en América Latina y el Caribe: enfoques, experiencias y perspectivas, Jorge Máttar, Luis Mauricio Cuervo (eds.), 2017, 336 p.
- 147 Inclusión financiera de pequeños productores rurales, Francisco G. Villarreal (ed.), 2017, 218 p.
  147 Financial inclusion of small rural producers, Francisco G. Villarreal (ed.), 201, 196 p.
- 146 Institucionalidad social en América Latina y el Caribe, Jorge Martínez (ed.), 2017, 334 p.
- 145 Política industrial rural y fortalecimiento de cadenas de valor, Ramón Padilla (ed.), 2017, 242 p.
  145 Rural industrial policy and strengthening value chains, Ramón Padilla (ed.), 2017, 236 p.

Páginas Selectas de la CEPAL / *ECLAC Select Pages*

- Empleo en América Latina y el Caribe. Textos seleccionados 2006-2017, Jürgen Weller (comp.), 2017, 446 p.
- Planificación y prospectiva para la construcción de futuro en América Latina y el Caribe. Textos seleccionados 2013-2016, Jorge Máttar y Mauricio Cuervo (comps.), 2016, 222 p.
- Desarrollo inclusivo en América Latina. Textos seleccionados 2009-2016, Ricardo Infante (comp.), 2016, 294 p.
- Globalización, integración y comercio inclusivo en América Latina. Textos seleccionados 2010-2014, Osvaldo Rosales (comp.), 2015, 326 p.

Copublicaciones / *Co-publications*

- El imperativo de la igualdad, Alicia Bárcena, Antonio Prado, CEPAL/Siglo Veintiuno, Argentina, 2016, 244 p.
- Gobernanza global y desarrollo: nuevos desafíos y prioridades de la cooperación internacional, José Antonio Ocampo (ed.), CEPAL/Siglo Veintiuno, Argentina, 2015, 286 p.
- Decentralization and Reform in Latin America: Improving Intergovernmental Relations, Giorgio Brosio and Juan Pablo Jiménez (eds.), ECLAC/Edward Elgar Publishing, United Kingdom, 2012, 450 p.
- Sentido de pertenencia en sociedades fragmentadas: América Latina desde una perspectiva global, Martín Hopenhayn y Ana Sojo (comps.), CEPAL/Siglo Veintiuno, Argentina, 2011, 350 p.

Coediciones / *Co-editions*

- Perspectivas económicas de América Latina 2017: Juventud, Competencias y Emprendimiento, 2016, 338 p.
  Latin American Economic Outlook 2017: Youth, Skills and Entrepreneurship, 2016, 314 p.
- Desarrollo e integración en América Latina, 2016, 314 p.
- Hacia un desarrollo inclusivo: el caso del Uruguay, 2016, 174 p.
- Perspectivas de la agricultura y del desarrollo rural en las Américas: una mirada hacia América Latina y el Caribe 2015-2016, CEPAL/FAO/IICA, 2015, 212 p.

Documentos de Proyectos / *Project Documents*

- El gran impulso ambiental en el sector de la energía, Andrés Arroyo Peláez, 2017, 62 p.
- La transversalización del enfoque de género en las políticas públicas frente al cambio climático en América Latina, Marina Casas Varez, 2017, 101 p.
- Financiamiento para el cambio climático en América Latina y el Caribe en 2015, Joseluis Samaniego y Heloísa Schneider, 2017, 76 p.
- El cambio tecnológico y el nuevo contexto del empleo: tendencias generales y en América Latina, Sebastian Krull, 2016, 48 p.
- Cambio climático, políticas públicas y demanda de energía y gasolinas en América Latina: un meta-análisis, Luis Miguel Galindo, Joseluis Samaniego, Jimy Ferrer, José Eduardo Alatorre, Orlando Reyes, 2016, 68 p.

Cuadernos estadísticos de la CEPAL

- 44 Las cuentas de los hogares y el bienestar en América Latina. Más allá del PIB, 2016
- 43 Estadísticas económicas de América Latina y el Caribe: Aspectos metodológicos y resultados del cambio de año base de 2005 a 2010

Series de la CEPAL / *ECLAC Series*

Asuntos de Género / Comercio Internacional / Desarrollo Productivo / Desarrollo Territorial / Estudios Estadísticos / Estudios y Perspectivas (Bogotá, Brasilia, Buenos Aires, México, Montevideo) / *Studies and Perspectives* (The Caribbean, Washington) / Financiamiento del Desarrollo / Gestión Pública / Informes y Estudios Especiales / Macroeconomía del Desarrollo / Medio Ambiente y Desarrollo / Población y Desarrollo / Política Fiscal / Políticas Sociales / Recursos Naturales e Infraestructura / Seminarios y Conferencias

Manuales de la CEPAL

- 5 Estimación de las erogaciones sociales a partir del sistema de cuentas nacionales: una propuesta para las funciones de educación, salud y protección social, María Paz Colinao, Federico Dorin, Rodrigo Martínez y Varinia Tromben, 2016, 63 p.
- 4 Territorio e igualdad: planificación del desarrollo con perspectiva de género, 2016, 84 p.
- 3 Manual de formación regional para la implementación de la resolución 1325 (2000) del Consejo de Seguridad de las Naciones Unidas relativa a las mujeres, la paz y la seguridad, María Cristina Benavente R., Marcela Donadio, Pamela Villalobos, 2016, 126 p.

Revista CEPAL / *CEPAL Review*

La Revista se inició en 1976, con el propósito de contribuir al examen de los problemas del desarrollo socioeconómico de la región. La *Revista CEPAL* se publica en español e inglés tres veces por año

CEPAL Review first appeared in 1976, its aim being to make a contribution to the study of the economic and social development problems of the region. CEPAL Review is published in Spanish and English versions three times a year

Observatorio demográfico / *Demographic Observatory*

Edición bilingüe (español e inglés) que proporciona información estadística actualizada, referente a estimaciones y proyecciones de población de los países de América Latina y el Caribe. Desde 2013 el *Observatorio* aparece una vez al año

Bilingual publication (Spanish and English) proving up-to-date estimates and projections of the populations of the Latin American and Caribbean countries. Since 2013, the Observatory appears once a year

Notas de población

Revista especializada que publica artículos e informes acerca de las investigaciones más recientes sobre la dinámica demográfica en la región. También incluye información sobre actividades científicas y profesionales en el campo de población. La revista se publica desde 1973 y aparece dos veces al año, en junio y diciembre

Specialized journal which publishes articles and reports on recent studies of demographic dynamics in the region. Also includes information on scientific and professional activities in the field of population. Published since 1973, the journal appears twice a year in June and December